TOO THIN FOR A SHROUD

8 JUNE 1982, FALKLANDS:
BRITAIN'S MOST LETHAL DAY OF COMBAT
SINCE WORLD WAR II

CRISPIN BLACK

&

JAN KOOPS
HUGH BODINGTON

'An important new book… a repository of damning facts… 'idiotic Falklands commanders.'
DAILY TELEGRAPH

'Reveals how mistakes and prejudice led to an avoidable tragedy.'
THE TIMES

'A weight has fallen off my shoulders'
PHIL ROBERTS DSO, CAPTAIN OF *SIR GALAHAD*

'I implore you to read this compelling and important book. There are numerous moments when you stop aghast and re-read a paragraph. There are surprises, there are times when you have to stop reading to reflect and ponder over a passage and digest precisely what you have just read… some passages are as powerful as any great poem…'
MARK CORETH, BLUES & ROYALS TROOP LEADER FALKLANDS

'…Also a powerful case for a public inquiry…'
GENERAL JULIAN THOMPSON, ADMIRAL JEREMY LARKEN

'Forensically dissects what went wrong…. compelling and disturbing.'
GENERAL MICHAEL SCOTT DSO, SCOTS GUARDS FALKLANDS

'Gruesome detail, what a bunch of w*****s the top commanders were.'
ROBERT LAWRENCE MC, SCOTS GUARDS CAPTAIN FALKLANDS

'A very detailed and enthralling account.'
MAJOR KEITH BUTLER, DIVISIONAL SIGNALLER FALKLANDS

'As I grow older, I'm dragged back daily to the grey hulking inferno—will I ever leave that ship? The book has an easy readable style that is genius.'
MIKE HERMANIS, WELSH GUARD FALKLANDS

'Compelling, focused, incendiary. Many books have been written about the Falklands War, but none until now from the point of view of the two Guards battalions up to Tumbledown. *Too Thin for a Shroud* fills that gap and, after 40 years, at last sets the record straight.'
GENERAL SEBASTIAN ROBERTS

'I finally understand what really happened on 8th June.'
KAREN EDWARDS, SISTER OF LANCE CORPORAL JOHN NEWBURY

'I am delighted Crispin Black has written *Too Thin for a Shroud*... ensuring that those who suffered and died, fighting for the freedom of others shall not be forgotten.'
IAN DUNCAN-SMITH MP

This edition first published by Gibson Square in 2023

rights@gibsonsquare.com

www.gibsonsquare.com

The authors are grateful to the Oxford and London students who helped make this a better book.

CONTENTS

I'R GWARCHODLU CYMREIG GYDA CHARIAD
FOR THE WELSH GUARDS WITH LOVE

8th June 1982

*Those of us who were uninjured were at Fitzroy. We expected to
be taken forward after reorganising the troops and re-equipping
with the arms stored by 81 Ordnance on Fitzroy beach. We could
put together one amalgamated Welsh Guards rifle company from
the men on shore to join the other half of the battalion forward at
Bluff Cove. We were keen to get going.*

IR GWARCHODLU CYMREIG GYDA CHARIAD
FOR THE WELSH GUARDS WITH LOVE

Author's Note

As the Falklands War is part of Britain's living memory and may be of interest to readers who have no military background, explanations of standard terms (eg battalion) are provided. Expert readers will find this unnecessary, but I hope both will bear with each other. For the sake of clarity, I will refer to 3 Commando as 'Royal Marines' and to the Army brigade as '5 Infantry'. This is, of course, not strictly speaking correct as 3 Commando was expanded with Army battalions 2 and 3 Para—with 2 Para moving back to 5 Infantry's chain of command on 30th May when 5 Infantry's Brigadier Wilson landed—while 3 Para remained with 3 Commando for the duration of the Falklands War. Likewise two 40 Commando rifle companies were placed under 5 Infantry's chain of command from 10th June to replace the two Welsh Guards rifle companies lost on *Sir Galahad* on 8th June. Later, these troops moved together from 5 Infantry to 3 Commando. Finally, times and dates are Falklands local and not Zulu. In case Zulu is quoted, the local time is provided in brackets. Part of the proceeds of this book are donated to the Welsh Guards Charity.

Introduction

While going through the last proofs of this book, I decided to make a trip to Kew. An article said that the National Archives had just released the report on where the wounded and dead of 8th June 1982 were found on the RFA *Sir Galahad*. In seconds, a clear, sunny afternoon turned into the most lethal day of the entire Falklands War and accounted for more than half of all its land-phase deaths. Britain sustained 56 casualties and more than 150 wounded in an Argentine bombing raid that caused chain explosions of ammunition in a confined space, which also inflicted chronic mental scarring on some 300 troops—most of them aged between 19 and 22 years of age, almost all of them from Wales and the Welsh Guards—that decades past have not alleviated.

The historic significance of 8th June 1982 is underlined by the fact that it is still the single most devastating day in British military records after World War II. Other units who shared in the attacks' toll, and the courage and discipline shown by all during and after the Argentine bombings, were the Royal Fleet Auxiliary (5 casualties), Royal Marines (4 casualties), Army Catering Corps (4 casualties), Royal Army Medical Corps (3 casualties), Royal Electrical and Mechanical Engineers (3 casualties), Royal Engineers (2 casualties), Royal Navy (2 casualties). The 8th—and the War itself—could have been even more lethal (though thankfully by sheer luck it wasn't). In all, some 600 other troops found themselves suddenly in the firing line, too, that day. Only hours earlier, close to 250 more young men (SAS, Royal Army Medical Corps field ambulance, Royal Artillery air defence and Fleet Air Arm and their Sea King helicopter) had been on board. Some still were when the attack started. A second vessel was targeted and sunk, killing 6 wheelhouse crew, though fortunately not its tankdeck passengers (in contrast to *Galahad*). HMS *Plymouth*, a frigate with at least 200 Royal Navy crew on board, was also bombed with eight 500lbs bombs, listed by several degrees as she took water, but fortuitously suffered only a few wounded (5) despite 5 direct hits and an exploding depth charge stored on deck. Oddly, however, this book is the first to preserve this day in its dramatic detail for future generations of readers, military historians, experts and strategists.

It was going to be a difficult and gloomy time in Kew, but after laying ghosts of the last forty years to rest in my Falklands research, I wanted to make the journey to reflect privately on the men we lost that day. The very helpful Kew staff guided me through some of the confusing numbering and kindly gave me everything that had been newly declassified from 'secret' to 'publicly accessible' so that I didn't have to go backwards and forwards.

One of the dossiers immediately caught my eye as it had a stamp across saying 'Closed for 51 years'. As a former cabinet-office official, curiosity got the better of me. It was a report called 'Air Attack Narrative'. It captured in detail the minutes I recalled as roaring airplane engines followed by hellfire. It ended with a precise graph of where the bombs dropped by four swooping airplanes struck: an even three each hit *Sir Galahad* and sister ship *Sir Tristram* anchored right next to it. Five other bombs narrowly missed. The attack was over in the blink of an eye that seemed to last an eternity. The aftermath was not and still rumbles on.

To me it was deeply moving despite the clinical tone adopted by the civil servant who wrote it. More in order to delay the inevitable dread of the report I had come to see, desultorily, I started to flick through another report even though it lacked this enticing stamp. I soon stopped myself for a moment to catch my breath and carried on reading every single word, and also every single word in all the other documents.

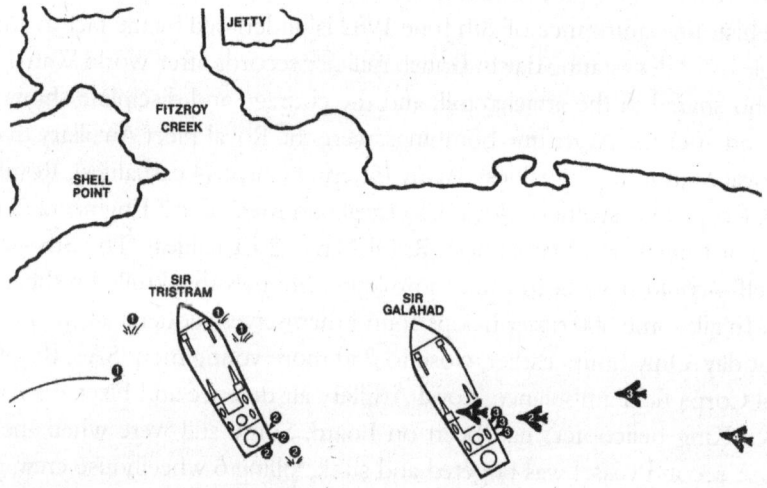

I couldn't quite believe what was said in these official records on that day's devastation.

Shortly after returning to Britain in 1982, I had stopped reading accounts of the Falklands War. It was both too depressing and too distressing to think about the many young lives that were lost or injured.

As the years grew into decades, I took part in some of the inevitable documentaries and had noticed that a theme hardened overtime. The Welsh Guards were being blamed. Though professional soldiers and a constituent part of the

Task Force—who responded in an exemplary manner under attack on 8th June—they were poorly trained, it was now repeatedly being said. Their brigade communication systems failed. Everything and the kitchen sink was thrown at us. So, when asked, I would take part in them to counter these peculiar ideas. As an officer, I had seen the hurt about the allegations in the eyes of the relatives of the deceased and injured who attended commemorations of the War.

In preparation for this memoir, many decades later, I was finally ready to read all the books on the Falklands War. But there, too, the Welsh Guards and their brigade, 5 Infantry, had become history's piñata—anyone could have a go at beating us with a stick—and did.

But as I put down the final page of the new releases at Kew, I realised that none of these stories and accusations after the Falklands War had a connection to the truth. A very different picture emerged from the musty archive pages after secrecy lasting for generations. In collusion, two senior commanders between themselves turned everything that had happened upside down. I had to retrieve the proofs and rewrite the entire book to tell the real story. The result is what you will read below.

I then went back a second time to Kew. I wanted to make doubly sure that I had copied every single document and hadn't missed anything as a result of my surprise. I had. I would have to make even more changes. I had been so focused on written documents that I had overlooked a map that had the title 'SHIPS OF FRIGATE DRAUGHT AND ABOVE CANNOT ENTER PORT PLEASANT'.

Its caption was irrelevant, but I took one look at it and all of a sudden I understood everything—location:

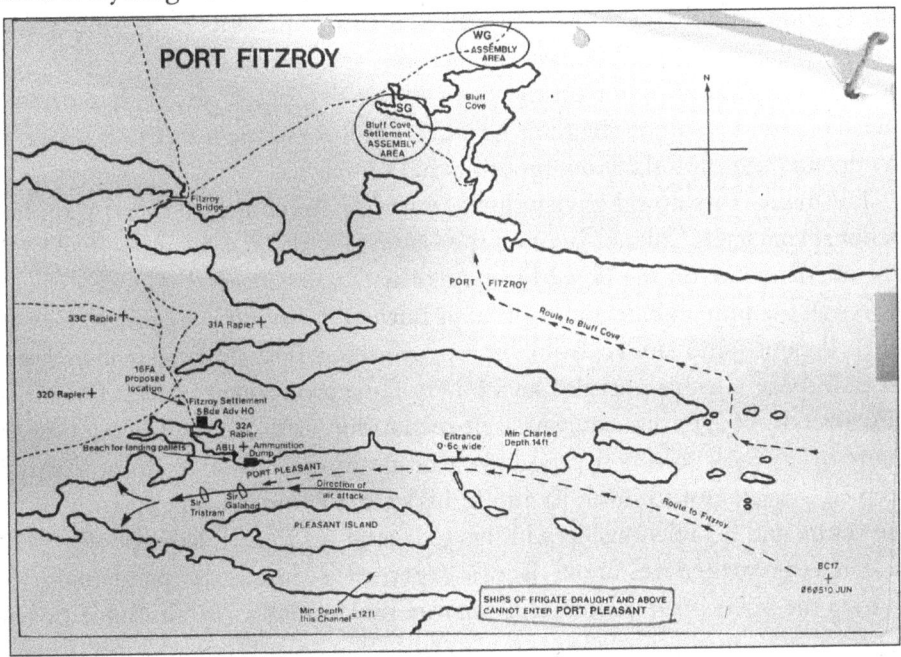

1

'What dreams may come'
Hamlet, Act 3, Scene 1

Recently, I dreamed I was back on the Royal Fleet Auxiliary *Sir Galahad*. Again. I used to dream like this often in my twenties and thirties. Then the dreams went away. I'm not sure why, but getting married and having children probably helped, and leaving the Army. That night they came back. I'm not sure why. They still come.

The dreams are always disturbing, but strangely, since they arise from the same event, often different. Themed dreams. I'm not sure diversity in dreams is a good idea—better just one bad dream that repeats itself over and over. At least I could get used to it, possibly even bored, which would be wonderful.

They run through the senses in random order. The smell-taste combi one is the worst—the smell of burning human flesh. Not an unattractive smell at all. A bit like barbecuing pork but stronger, richer, more promising. My mouth waters in the dream. Army 'compo' rations cooked on a small hexamine burner on which we subsisted down South are sustaining but flavourless. Burning flesh smells good—until you realise what it really is, and the appetising smoky top-notes are the result of damp combat jackets.

My mouth didn't water on the day—it was dry, desert dry with a peculiar metallic taste, a result of the flames and, if I'm honest, the fear. But it waters in my dreams and on waking my mouth is full of saliva.

For many years now, I have written by way of home-grown therapy about a fictional character, Colonel Jacot of the Celtic Guards (*bien cuit* in the Falklands in a missile strike on the Royal Fleet Auxiliary *Oliver Cromwell*). He wears black gloves all the time to hide and soothe his burned hands, and has rough, Gothic, smell dreams—the smoke from his own burning flesh (a twist which I was spared) rising into his nostrils like a burst of overpowering incense. They send him over the edge, his extensive self-medication with Veuve Clicquot (what many of us took to—at five pounds a bottle in the duty-free Rhine Army it seemed a waste not to drink it) and in his case cocaine, storing up trouble for the future and his relationship with his girlfriend—a French lady spook.

I haven't written yet about Jacot's experiences during the pandemic—the third in the series is set in Venice just before the dreaded virus hit. But if he had contracted Covid and lost his sense of smell he would have been grateful. If you can't smell in real-life you can't have a smell dream, I assume.

What's fact for many of us who survived 8th June is that sleep becomes unwelcome because it is difficult to control dreams—the subconscious runs riot. Shakespeare has a lot to say about sleep—Macbeth, Caliban and Henry IV all long for sleep for different reasons. Hamlet's famous musings are on death, not sleep, but make the point.

Most of us know insomniacs or people who can't sleep much but would like to. Billions of pounds, dollars and euros are spent every year on sleeping pills. Sentries, night workers, airport staff, nurses, doctors, policemen, are required to stay awake through the night—sustained by tea and coffee and if it is still permitted, cigarettes. But most of them as they come to the end of their shifts must be looking forward to a good kip even if it is in daylight hours. There are few accounts of those who are desperate to stay awake.[1]

There are sound-themed dreams, too. Not a great genre, to be honest. Shouting is all right, 'Get down, get down,' was a sensible instruction. The closer you were to the deck, wherever you were on the ship, the less likely you were to be killed or wounded. Unless you were unlucky enough to be at the back of the 'death zone' of the tank deck. Everyone in the queue behind Welsh Guardsman Simon Weston perished. It didn't matter what they did.

But screaming, the noise men make who are dying or about to die, with no possibility of escape, was an awful, primal, desperate sound as loud and nerve-shredding in my dreams as on the day. Followed always by silence. No hope of rescue. Those who had been wounded calling out to their comrades in agony had either been consumed by the flames; or were too close to death and in too much pain to make any further sound.

Sight dreams are the easiest to deal with. Like many English schoolboys of my vintage, I was brought up on war films. *The Dambusters* and *Where Eagles Dare* remain on instant notice to move for rainy winter afternoons. Consequently, violence and sometimes gore had been present in my visual memory since the age of seven when I first went to prep school.

Life in the 1960s, except for a brief period around the World Cup of 1966, was still dominated by the war; many of our teachers had been combatants. The headmaster of my prep school had been a badly burned Battle of Britain Hurricane pilot, and one of the famous plastic surgeon Archibald McIndoe's 'guinea pigs' at East Grinstead. So, in a strange irony I was used to seeing someone nearly every day for five years of my young life who had been badly disfigured by flames.

I particularly remember his hands—gnarled and discoloured. Plenty of Welsh Guardsmen with those to this day.

He didn't talk about the war much but would occasionally grant us eager schoolboys an anecdote or two. Vera Lynn singing at the Royal Victoria Hospital in East Grinstead has stuck in my mind, as has the emblem of the Guinea Pig Club which he showed us one day—a guinea pig sprouting RAF pilot's wings set on top of a burning aircraft.

And every time I see the spire of Salisbury Cathedral only a few miles from where we live, I am reminded of him—one day at twilight after many hours in the cockpit he became disorientated, anxious to find somewhere to land before darkness fell and not quite sure where he was. He feared he would crash or be forced to bail out in the middle of nowhere. Then, as darkness was almost upon him, he caught sight of an object on the horizon which he turned hopefully towards—the spire of Salisbury Cathedral from which he was able to calculate a course to the nearest RAF airfield and put down safely.

Because sight is so dominant in the senses it loses the power to shock the unconscious; the dream re-runs the cinematic reel that recorded an event which is pre-loaded anyway. The memories that lie deeper in the cerebral cortex, like smell, produce a more powerful and disturbing effect. With the added hazard of acting as triggers. It was the sweet, seductive fragrance of a newly baked *madeleine* that triggered Proust's nostalgia fest.

Touch dreams have been limited, thank God. I doubt if it has been the case for those who were wounded—even light burns on the hands are hugely painful, as anyone who has burned themselves in the kitchen knows. A few times, touch has been the theme for the night. Oddest of all was the squeezing sensation required in using a morphine syrette; a bit like emptying a small tube of superglue or crushing a large wasp in kitchen towel. Not a bad memory, as morphine works quickly. A casualty writhing in agony will be at least slightly comforted and become easier to handle in less than a minute—though not for long. There wasn't enough morphine for the multiple doses required.

The stickiness and slipperiness of burns casualties as we carried them was something I hadn't expected on the day—the awful sensation that the leg or arm you are holding isn't as solid as it should be. The liquid stays on your hands—persistent and difficult to remove. Turning the volume up on a radio set was a shock—the human fat on my hands slipped on the dial. The same effect is produced in everyday life by picking up a slug. At first the fingers feel sticky in a routine way, but slug slime is more difficult to remove than expected. As every gardener knows, a good scrub plus some gel is usually required to get rid of it—and you can feel it reducing layer by layer. Same with the fat dripping from burned human flesh. It doesn't really come off—at least not in the conditions we experienced. And it decays, smelling worse as it does.

Mr Trumper's Extract of West Indian Limes along with all my other kit was destroyed in the attack—it would have been useful to sprinkle about in the days that followed. Smelling a bit smoky wasn't too bad but starting to smell like a decomposing corpse was a trial. Months later we were all sent letters informing us that we could make a financial claim for any non-military kit destroyed. The Ministry of Defence kindly paid the full replacement price of my Minolta camera (borrowed from my father) and a couple of books—by Agatha Christie and P.G. Wodehouse. But it refused to stump up for any more Trumper's. Everyone has these odd experiences in war—even small wars. Admiral Woodward has an amusing passage at the end of his Falklands book *One Hundred Days* where he receives a letter from the Director of Royal Navy Pay and Pensions cutting his admiral's entertainment allowance because he has failed to use it in the previous quarter. It entertained me that the first letter I got after 8th June was a curt and angry missive from the manager of my bank in the Strand telling me I was overdrawn.

But the strangest aspect of the touch dreams in my experience is a feeling of being under-dressed. In London, the various uniforms worn by young officers were always something of a concern—have I put my plume in the wrong side of my bearskin? Have I got the correct sword knot and sash? Were my boating jacket (blazer) buttons properly polished? And so on. Even off duty we were expected to be smartly turned out.

Not something I worried too much about on the Falklands. In any case, it was difficult to look that sharp in the newly issued kit we received. Nearly all the guardsmen in the Prince of Wales's Company were over six foot. Our nickname was 'The Jamboys' because at the front in the Great War special arrangements were made to supplement the rations of the taller men. All the quartermaster could find in the circumstances was some extra jam—one tablespoon per man once a day.

The problem for us sixty plus years later was that the cold and wet weather kit issued to us—reluctantly—by the Army came in a standard distribution of sizes; but everyone in the company was long. I ended up with a giant combat smock (supposedly water-resistant but, as Guardsman Simon Weston puts it, merely 'sprayproof') and a set of 'waterproof' trousers so tight they would have embarrassed Elvis.

By the end of the evacuation of the ship these cheap and nasty bits of kit had found a more useful secondary purpose as improvised stretchers, and remained with the casualties as they were loaded onto helicopters, or lowered into boats. As a result, many of us ended up in shirt sleeves. June was the heart of the austral winter, and, although 8th June 1982 was a fine day, the wind never abates much on the islands. Just south of the Roaring Forties, there is no significant land mass between East Falkland and both Antarctica and Australia. It is always cold.

The guardsmen wore thick, hairy shirts, as I had when in the ranks at Catterick Garrison. I was 24499493 Trooper C.N. Black, 14th/20th King's Hussars, sir! On issue a little uncomfortable and prickly, they softened down nicely after a few washes—just the thing in a Boden catalogue. Difficult to iron—they didn't take a crease too well and guards uniforms are all about creases. But I wish I had kept mine. They were warm and absorbed sweat. In contrast, guards officers' shirts were made of very thin cotton—soft, easy to iron—a task normally split between mothers, girlfriends (if you had one), and whichever guardsman in your platoon (28 troops) was appointed to help you with your kit, for which he received extra pay quite properly (from the officer himself, not Her Majesty) and useful perks like being excused many ceremonial duties.

These kinds of dream-flashbacks never go away completely, although in my mid-thirties I thought they had. They may go into abeyance or remission but they are still there, evolving and waiting eagerly, I always think, to be triggered.

There may be a physical explanation one day about their nature and function. There's a lot of high-priced medical work going on currently looking at the experience of our servicemen and women in Iraq and Afghanistan. Or it may be that flashbacks slither away to take cover somewhere in the soul.

2

Doubts

On 8th June 1982 there were eight young Welsh Guards officers aboard *Sir Galahad* from two different rifle companies. Only six of us are still around.

We have met for a few memorable lunches in recent years. On 8th June 2021, five of us left made it to a restaurant on the King's Road in Chelsea. From the Prince of Wales's Company: Jan Koops, our esteemed company-second-in-command; Hugh Bodington; Johnny Strutt; and me. From Welsh Guards No 3 Company just Ollie Richardson. Their company-second-in-command Tony Ballard, couldn't get to Blighty from Holland where he lives because of Corona travel restrictions. Sadly, its other platoon commanders Hilarion Roberts and Peter Owen Edmunds, who were sons of Welsh Guardsmen and also brothers-in-law, were no longer with us.

We were all connected in so many ways and have remained so. Like the characters on *The Bridge of San Luis Rey*, we all found ourselves in the wrong place at the wrong time. Peter, Ollie and I were at school together—our most famous school song is 'Forty Years On'. Tony was at school with Johnny. Jan was connected to everyone by rugby. Tony to quite a few through polo. Peter and Hugh stood as godparents to each other's children. Johnny and I were best men to each other and mutual godparents. And so on. But above all we remain connected by having shared the same experience—the Argentine air attacks at Fitzroy on East Falkland as the Falklands war was moving to its climax.

Fate has treated us differently. Jan, who was always entrepreneurial, went on to manage his own businesses with great success. Hugh stayed for a full career in the Army, serving in both Iraq and Afghanistan. Johnny inherited an estate and a peerage. I left the Army at 42 and re-invented myself as an author and television pundit. I remember getting a message from Tony a few years ago—at that stage he was a tea-planter in Sri Lanka. Ollie went into insurance in London and South Africa. His son is currently serving in the Welsh Guards.

Hilarion, who was badly burned in the explosion and fire, went into the insurance world as well, but tragically died in a car accident in 1985 on his way to join a group of us at a party in Pirbright. Peter became fluent in

Russian and set up a telephone company in St Petersburg. In 2016 he had the rotten luck to die of cancer. His obituary in the *Telegraph* said this, 'In later years he was heard to remark more than once that after what he saw and experienced that day most of what life threw at him could be faced with some equanimity'.

It was certainly true of him. I hope it's true about the rest of us. But, as we discovered together at the lunch in 2021, the one development that none of us had any equanimity about were the existing accounts of the war.

Having blanked 8th June 1982 from my mind as much as I could for as long as I could, I had a few days before our lunch to read for the first time an account by a journalist who was embedded with the task force.

This account, although not by an eyewitness, makes clear, indeed *stresses* that *Galahad* was met by a landing craft as she sailed into Fitzroy, East Falkland. All the other accounts I have read since say the same.

The problem is that when I raised this odd fact at the lunch, the five eye-witnesses together recalled that there was a delay before anyone appeared to meet us—more than an hour. The stern door of the *Galahad* was lowered; we could see what was going on. I had managed to sneak on deck for a quick fag break.

There was no one there to meet us. But the 'established' story in these books says something different.

Much has been said and written about the conflict from different per-spectives, many of them from a Royal Naval/Royal Marine point of view. Talking about it, we realised that none of the Welsh Guards officers on board had ever put their recollections together in a memoir. Key facts about our involvement and that of our brigade—5 Infantry—were just simply wrong. But unless you were there as an officer—seeing and knowing just enough—you would miss these errors.

I never liked the feel of events that fateful day when the *Galahad* was bombed. Not the bombing or strafing itself—they are a routine part of war—but rather the odd circumstances of the Argentine Air Force's success: a modest number of bombs inflicted an unparalleled loss on Britain.

Hilarion and I spent part of our generous post-war leave with my brother in Athens where he was a banker. He had a lovely flat with a view of the Acropolis. Hilarion's burns were acting up in the heat and so he spent much of the day in a lukewarm bath drinking Mythos beer. I hung around on the balcony drinking Retsina. We talked—quite loudly for the words to be heard from bathroom to balcony and vice versa. He was a Balliol history graduate and probably had the sharpest brain among us. He didn't like the circum-stances either. The number of things that had to go wrong simultaneously for the Argentine attacks to be successful seemed strange.

At veterans' lunches of this sort there is non-stop laughter and teasing; youthful embarrassments are gloriously resurrected. No one's blushes are spared. Industrial quantities of wine go down the range. But I remember the silence when we all realised that even the basic, critical, widely-accepted details of what happened that day were wrong and that, to quote more Shakespeare, thereby hangs a tale.

At some point during this long lunch, I seem to have been 'volunteered' to write this book which I had been thinking about in any case for some years—with others contributing their own writing (included later).[2]

We have become so accustomed to events as they unfolded down South in 1982 and as presented to us over the last forty years by a tide of at times boastful accounts of the campaign (a *Blob* if you like 1960s movies)[3] that even our historical judgement, and in some cases common sense, have been misled.

It is difficult, today, to make the imaginative leap away from this version of what happened (which I will henceforth label the 'orthodoxy') and identify what did and did not happen or should have happened—the war could have been won earlier at less human cost. Not only the *Sir Galahad* tragedy but the tragedy of the civilian casualties in Port Stanley would have been avoided.

Captain Koops puts it elegantly further down. I will probably explain in less literary terms. I hope he doesn't mind—if you annoyed him back in the day he was in the habit of 'inviting' platoon commanders to go on a long run and his legs were longer than ours.

Clearly, in this book I am making judgements and criticisms in the knowledge of what happened. My arguments, however, do not rely primarily on hindsight and our shared first-hand recollections.

My main source of interpretation is a synthesis of this first-hand experience with established British military doctrine and practice of the time—something that all the senior officers involved in both planning and executing the campaign would have known, or could reasonably be expected to have brought into play. There is also, crucially, the more than revelatory treasure trove of 1982 documents released by the National Archives in Kew, which finally unveiled the true story after some four decades.

A long-time addict of detective fiction and thrillers, as may have become evident, I have found writing them instructive, particularly laid over the top of the habits of analysing language in intelligence work. My novels always contain the puzzle of whodunit and conform to the idea of fair play. What I aim for in my detective novels is to be fair, indeed to tell the truth. But I leave key facts out or shade them in such a way to put the reader off the scent. Ultimately, I'm trying to present an image of cast iron reality that isn't quite real. A useful skill if you are trying to work out what hasn't been said in a report.

The main title for the book is taken from experience, as will become clear later. But the subtitle, *The Last Untold Story of the Falklands War*, obvious enough in some ways, was inspired by two books written by West Pointer Colonel Archibald Gracie IV, early in the previous century, both of which are relevant to my task.

His first, *The Truth about Chickamauga*, concerned an obscure but bloody battle in the American Civil War, where his father had commanded a brigade of the Army of Tennessee under General Braxton Bragg (one of his fellow Confederate brigade commanders, Ben Helm, was oddly Abraham Lincoln's brother-in-law).

It was a ghastly and controversial two-day battle resulting in 4000 dead and 35,000 wounded, producing possibly the bloodiest day in American military history, except that no one was able to separate those killed on the first day from those on the second in the official butcher's bill (the Duke of Wellington's term for casualties) that followed. General William Rosecrans, the Union commander, was held by Lincoln to have been useless—'like a duck hit on the head'. But the victor, Bragg, also stirred up intense controversy. Senior subordinates had been unimpressed by his style of command. Slow to follow up on his attack, he blamed everybody but himself, dismissing three of his junior generals, including Gracie's father, Archibald III.

Hence Gracie's book to set the record straight. It was selling well when he decided to treat himself to a European trip (without his family, luckily) travelling out on the Cunarder, *RMS Oceanic*. Refreshed by his European stay, he booked passage home on another Cunarder, leaving Southampton on April 10th, 1912, *RMS Titanic* (First Class Cabin C51). Southampton, same port of embarkation as us, same shipping line.

There is an additional thread between Colonel Gracie on *Titanic* and us guardsmen en route to the Falklands on *Queen Elizabeth 2 (QE2)*. After crossing the Equator, *QE2* had been sailing at full speed in order to get us there as quickly as she could, zig-zagging in a classic counter submarine manoeuvre.

As we sailed into the Southern Ocean, approaching South Georgia in the shelter of which 5 Infantry was to tranship to the liner *Canberra* and the North Sea ferry *Norland*, the temperature dropped dramatically. Suddenly, one afternoon our speed dropped. We felt it and wondered what had happened. Going on deck we could see icebergs, small ones—called 'growlers' according to the crew—and much larger ones that the eye had difficulty in sizing or scaling. They provided an amusing and interesting short break from training. Many of the guardsmen on deck were making jokes about *Titanic*, but I noticed one or two were silent. I certainly felt uncomfortable. Soldiers are superstitious and some sensed a bad omen.

I got hooked on the whole *Titanic* saga soon after. But it wasn't so much because of parallels between an Act of God in the North Atlantic in 1912 and an air strike in the South Atlantic seventy years later. One was a human tragedy on a great scale with 1503 men women and children perishing in water at minus 2.2 degrees Centigrade, the other a military engagement on a much smaller scale—49 dead of whom 38 were Welsh Guardsmen or Army Catering Corps and Royal Electrical and Mechanical Engineers posted to us (legally, most were recorded as 'missing, presumed dead'). These were major casualties for the British Army of the time and since, even with the ghastliness of Afghanistan and Iraq. What really intrigued me—the connections later alarming me—was that an agreed unfolding of events was a constant subject of debate.

Colonel Gracie was present throughout the drama helping passengers into lifeboats on Deck A, Port side. He was probably also the last person to leave *Titanic* who survived. Leaping into the water, he was dragged down by the suction of the sinking vessel but managed to break free, eventually swimming towards Collapsible B, precarious and upside down and under the command of Second Officer Lightoller (played wonderfully by Kenneth More in the 1958 film *A Night to Remember*). He survived the sinking, just—dying a few months later from the effects of hypothermia and all the rest of it.

Gracie knew he was on borrowed time. In what was left to him, he devoted himself to writing an account of the tragedy, *The Truth about the Titanic*.

His book was the first to try to establish the facts as they were rather than as people wanted them to be. In the months after *Titanic* foundered, drawing on his West Point training and experience as a military historian, he became a human truffle hound sniffing out exaggerations, evasions, shifting of responsibility and all the other human weaknesses exposed in extremis as they always are. The interesting thing about his efforts to record what happened on the ship that fateful night was that the most basic facts of what had happened were the hardest to establish.

He was checking the proofs when he died in October 1913 and the book was published posthumously. 'Make sure they get to the boats' were his last words.

I am not a graduate of West Point but of the Royal Military Academy,

Sandhurst, where I also instructed. And I apply to the events of 1982 a set of skills and experience that I didn't have then. I later attended the Army Staff College at Camberley and served on the Defence Intelligence Staff, at the same time studying for an MA in War Studies at King's College. After a year on a defence fellowship at St John's College, Cambridge, my final military appointment was as a lieutenant-colonel on the Cabinet Office Assessments Staff—flying a mahogany bomber in Whitehall, writing papers for the Joint Intelligence Committee and Immediate Assessments for Number 10. The Assessments Staff also provide the analytical firepower to COBRA—where I was on duty on 9/11.[4]

I, too, was an eyewitness. I, too, am a colonel. Though, unlike Gracie, I escaped from our own much smaller drama unharmed, many others did not. With 56 deaths and 150 wounded, the 8th June 1982 was Britain's most lethal day since World War II. The accidental loss of half a battalion was in fact unprecedented. So, like Gracie, I would like to know exactly what happened, who took the key decisions, who said what to whom and why.

'Untune that string'
Troilus and Cressida, Act 1, Scene 3

Where better to start than with Brigadier Julian Thompson's *No Picnic*, first published soon after the war in 1985? His was an important role. He was the Royal Marine brigadier in charge of 3 Commando Brigade, consisting of three Royal Marine units (each of these 'commandos' is similar in structure to an Army battalion, consisting of some 650 men).[5] It is the only brigade under the command of the Royal Navy and, totalling some 2000 troops that normally deployed with a thousand vehicles of its own (in 1982), it is nicknamed its 'private army'. Today, 3 Commando still consists of three commandos. But its size and ample funding was under threat. Thatcher's Defence Minister John Nott had warned Parliament in 1981 that 'there is at present no intention to reduce the number of Royal Marine Commandos... However, we envisage there being one fewer.'

To reinforce his Royal Marines, the Army provided the 2nd and 3rd Battalions of the Parachute Regiment (2 and 3 Para), another 1300 troops. These two battalions were usually part of 5 Infantry, the brigade designated for what were termed at the time 'Out of Area Operations'—any required military activity or intervention outside the NATO area or Northern Ireland. In addition, the 22nd SAS Regiment, up to another 600 troops, commanded by Colonel Michael Rose was added. Thompson's brigade also had his own artillery, 29 Commando Regiment, supplied by the Army. In addition, he had the Commando Logistic Regiment to organise frontline support. This regiment was a mixed Army/Royal Marine outfit commanded at the time by Colonel Ivar Hellberg from the Army's Royal Corps of Transport. In all this added up to around 4-5000 troops.

The idea had been to force Argentina to the negotiation table with this show of the Army and Navy's toughest forces sailing across half the world. For the longest time, it was thought that a diplomatic solution would be found for the stand-off with the Argentine *junta* as the Task Force sailed forth towards the Falklands: a face-saving way out, like a plebiscite. Despite the fact that the bulk of Britain's military force was tied down with NATO tasks, Mrs Thatcher had ordered the mobilisation of everything available on short notice.

When US support to broker a deal did not materialise, the only option open for Britain was to recapture the Falklands by force or risk losing face. Thus, assisted by civilian ships, Thompson's brigade was landed by the Royal Navy, into San Carlos Bay 65 miles west of Port Stanley, East Falkland, on the night 22-23rd May. Luckily there was no opposition to the Army and the Royal Marine battalions that landed.

Once the negotiation route failed, the Chiefs of Staff convinced the War Cabinet that another brigade was needed to guarantee success. Initially, the head of the Royal Navy had argued that the expanded Royal Marines brigade was sufficient, telling the Defence Minister that 'this was an amphibious operation suited to the Royal Navy's experience'. Nott did not believe him and thought he wanted to make it 'the Royal Navy show'. The head of the Army Field Marshal Bramall privately didn't agree and always thought two brigades were needed to win a landwar on the Falklands and that the Navy would come round eventually.

At this point, 5 Infantry's remaining Gurkha battalion (1/7G) was mobilised with its commander Brigadier Tony Wilson, a highly decorated Light Infantryman. To replace its two Para battalions lent by 5 Infantry to the Royal Marines, Bramall allocated the Scots Guards (2nd Battalion, '2SG') and the Welsh Guards (1st Battalion, '1WG') to 5 Infantry. The Welsh Guards had just stood down from nine months of Operation Spearhead training as the battalion in a high state of readiness to be deployed anywhere.

This ongoing Operation Spearhead was part of a joint-agreement with the US to have a 'rapid deployment force' ready for deployment around the world. John Nott told Parliament in March 1981, that the UK's contribution to such a highly-trained force would consist of 'a spearhead battalion, on 72 hours' notice... and in two weeks' time it will be the 1st Battalion the Royal Regiment of Wales'. Presciently, he had added that the Spearhead battalion was also there to 'undertake national tasks such as reinforcement of British dependent territories or the protection of British citizens overseas.'

Unlike Thompson's Royal Marines, Wilson's 5 Infantry—which had only be formed very recently—did not have much movement, supply or other logistical support of its own, nor was it given one, though he was allocated an artillery regiment. What had been scrambled together as logistics at short notice was geared towards garrison support and lacked battle capability. It was argued by Northwood planners that battle logistics for the two brigades would be merged by General Moore. He never did. The one exception to the rule was 5 Infantry's petroleum troop—91 Ordnance—that the Army brigade brought along. This unit Moore did bring under his divisional command in order to support Royal Marines' battle logistics.

The orthodox view given in many books about the Falklands is that all was well from the moment Thompson's 3 Commando went ashore on Thursday 22nd May, 1982, up until the Army's 5 Infantry landed on Tuesday 1st June. It was then that things began to go wrong.

Nothing, however, could be further from the truth as I discovered four decades later while I worked my way through the books and war memoirs, and, finally, newly-released dossiers at Kew. By the time we landed, the war had come close to being made much more difficult than it needed to be.

It began even before the Task Force sailed. The most startlingly odd aspect of the arrangements for Operation Corporate, the codename for the military effort to retake the Falkland Islands, was the command system put in place by the Chief of the Defence Staff in London, Admiral Sir Terence Lewin, a decorated veteran of the Second World War. He was supremo over all three armed services and constitutionally the senior military adviser to the government (Mrs Thatcher's War Cabinet in this case) with the right of immediate access to the prime minister.

Unfortunately, Admiral Lewin's was a complicated, bureaucratic way to control the military side of a war.

Overall operational command was exercised by Admiral Sir John Fieldhouse, Commander-in-Chief Fleet, from his headquarters at Northwood in suburban London. He had a string of commanders under him in the theatre of war.

Most of the ships in the task force would come under the command of Rear Admiral 'Sandy' Woodward flying his flag on the aircraft carrier *HMS Hermes*. But not any of the submarines that would still be controlled from Northwood, London. And not any ships involved in amphibious logistic support. The latter would be controlled by Commodore Michael Clapp, Commodore Amphibious Warfare (COMAW), flying his smaller flag on the landing ship *HMS Fearless*. He would return to the rank of captain after the war.

The on-land troops would initially be commanded by Brigadier Thompson, the commander of the Royal Marines. But this would change to Royal Marine General Jeremy Moore when he landed just ahead of the arrival of 5 Infantry's reinforcements. From that moment all land forces would come under him as Commander Land Forces Falkland Islands (CLFFI, colloquially referred to by us as 'cliffy').

Mrs T did the exact opposite from Admiral Lewin's Rubik's cube. On the advice of Harold Macmillan and others she created a 'War Cabinet' of just a few trusted ministers.

The first fundamental error was obvious to me straight away as I immersed myself in the published accounts of the war four decades on. In the South Atlantic, the scene of the action, no one officer was in charge.

The Navy's Private Army

The second mistake took some time to sink in—until 5 Infantry landed there were in effect three commanders of apparently equal status: Thompson, Clapp and Woodward. In seniority, a rear admiral (Woodward) outranks both a brigadier and a commodore (the naval equivalent to a brigadier). It was a recipe for confusion. Especially as senior naval officers back at Northwood appeared confounded by their own arrangements.

Admiral Fieldhouse became very frustrated soon after the landings at what he saw as Brigadier Thompson's general lack of offensive action. So, he instructed Woodward to get a grip of him—but Woodward wasn't in command of Thompson and declined. The only person who could grip Thompson at that stage was Fieldhouse himself—from Northwood, London.

Furthermore, in a departure from amphibious doctrine at the time, once Moore landed the command triumvirate continued and now consisted of: Moore, Woodward and Clapp. Again, Clapp is still up there but is, as commodore, now inferior in rank to both a general and a rear admiral. Clapp is still an equal commander, though. And there's a serious flaw—Clapp's responsibilities are not precisely defined. Neither he nor his staff is in the other two commanders' chain of command and obliged to do Admiral Woodward's bidding on naval matters or General Moore's on troop landings.

Making a part of the military machine independent from another has important consequences. With three separate local chains of command dispersed across water and land, room is created for each top officer to do his own thing because he is a commander. Informing others becomes merely a courtesy rather than the building block for action. This is not normally the case. The Allied invasion during World War II, for example, was directed by Dwight Eisenhower as supreme commander. Everything that happened then was part of an order and all the precision of information that comes with it to avoid confusion. The official Falklands dossier of 23rd September 1982 at Kew spends a lot of time digging into these three separate spheres in exhaustive narrative detail in an 8-page document.[6]

In practice, the three independent Falklands commanders worked together in an informally created pattern. General Moore and Commodore Clapp worked together closely. They were next door on HMS Fearless and met twice a-day, as well as sharing dinner together. They 'went direct to CTF 317 [Fieldhouse in Northwood, London] for main decisions keeping CTG [Woodward on HMS Hermes] informed'.[7] In case something was needed from Woodward, Clapp would talk to him directly to receive information or agree between them on a course of action. In practical terms it meant that, after the Task Force had landed, Moore was the senior commander.

While all this cooperation took whatever shape it took, orders within each of the chain were treated very differently. Orders were transferred with an arsenal of the latest technology to avoid misunderstandings within the chain. Thus operations were 'run by signalled instructions, secure voice conversation, by personal visit and discussion'.[8]

These were not independent means of communication, but were meant to be layered on top of one another to create maximum clarity for recipients as it was found that a single means could cause confusion, particularly within the amphibious group. 'Whenever possible signalled instructions were used to supplement verbal orders and instructions', the Board found.[9]

There were two remote voice systems in the Falklands: the US NESTOR system and DSSS secure speech. While this sounds a lot better than what Admiral Nelson had had at his disposal, it wasn't quite so great. There was a general dislike of DSSS (whose use was therefore restricted by commanders) because the system didn't generate hard copy of what was said and so it was not easy to share with those not on the call. Nor was it necessarily clear whether both sides were talking about the same thing.[10] It took a lot of advance preparation to make sure that DSSS communication did not add to wartime confusion.

One particular problem in all this was that Royal Fleet Auxiliary (RFA) staff of supply ships such as Tristram and Galahad—called Landing Ship Logistics or 'LSLs'—had not been combat-trained in Royal Navy standardised operational instructions (OPGEN). They were an ancillary naval entity with different training and different staff. Although otherwise part of the amphibious group, RFAs were not normally included when instructions were sent out widely by amphibious staff. Even if they were included, the report found, Navy instructions were not 'well understood by LSLs'.[11] Clapp's team were aware of this and 'by personal visits by staff officers to LSL's [sic] this was averted as far as possible'.[12] As we will see, even these measures failed when things got complicated. This would prove pivotal on 8th June.

The lack of formal structure bonding the three command groups showed. Between the three staffs, some 1300 signals (secure electronic communications) flew every day that communication officers had to parse for sending on down their chain of command to the right person. It inevitably led to delays and time-lags when things changed, even for 'flashes'—the highest priority signals. They took 'approximately 1 ½ hours to get through, with OPERATIONAL IMMEDIATES taking some 6 hours'.[13] And that was not taking into account that apparently signals could get lost. By this time, the amphibious-logistics group had twenty six ships under its control.

Not only the lack of OPGEN training on LSLs (effectively meaning that Royal Navy shorthands did not have the same meaning to the crew on these supply ships) was a Falklands problem leading to potentially botched orders. The entire Task Force—hastily cobbled-together—was by nature an amphibious operation across 8000 miles. There was, however, no existing drill Operation Corporate could rely on, as, unfortunately, due to budget shrinkage even Royal Navy training of these types of operations had been cut to the bone. In order to save money, Britain was focusing on submarines only at the expense of strike carriers or amphibious operations training.

In a 2018 Falklands seminar sponsored by the Australian Army, Clapp observed candidly on his lack of amphibious experience, 'Certainly, we in the Navy were almost all amphibious logistic amateurs'.[14] Such was the financial pressure at the time that only minor exercises and deployments were allowed.'[15] What little practice there had been, involved landings of Royal Marine battalions on a friendly beach that were as highly choreographed as large-scale ballets. There was no Royal Navy training, however, in panic-room scenarios of a fast-moving hot nature as they exist during an amphibious assault on enemy territory under constant attack such as in the Falklands.

This lack of amphibious training went right down from the Admiralty Board top and would react adversely in the Falklands with the lack of training on LSLs in communicating efficiently with Royal Navy staff. Regrettably even at this lower level, Royal Navy staff did not bear this in mind when issuing orders. They tended to treat respondents as if they were Royal Navy rather than Royal Fleet Auxiliary.

None of this meant that there wasn't an authoritative rulebook on how to mount a major amphibious attack. Britain's occasional friendly landing training exercises had been executed further to NATO's doctrine, also called the Allied Tactical Publication, or ATP. This rule book was based on ample, real US experience with aircraft carriers and amphibious assaults. Britain's own doctrine was, moreover, covered by ATP 5, 8, 36 and 37. However, neither Fieldhouse nor any of his Whitehall overlords had declared that ATP (or these British sections at least) applied to the Task Force.[16] In fact, it looks as if none of the admirals in Whitehall had any in-depth or operational understanding of its significance. It would prove a crucial flaw not to rely on ATP's standardised and concentrated military knowledge. Without, second-guessing of rules on location in the Falklands became the norm.

Mortars and All That

The third fundamental error (and in my view the most serious) was the absence of a senior Army officer in the command set-up as the first convoy set sail and 5 Infantry prepared for its role down South. The 'Land Adviser' to Admiral Fieldhouse on the Task Force was General Moore. For all his virtues, he was a Royal Marine general with little knowledge of military operations involving more than one brigade or general (non-naval) warfare.

And so, the planning and equipping of our 5 Infantry before it left had little input from the Army. Nor did the beefing up of Thompson's 3 Commando—at sea, but still in the Northern Hemisphere and due to stop at Ascension Island (with its huge airstrip) for a period of training and refitting. The hastily devised plan of the Task Force envisaged the effective use of the weapon systems available to the Royal Marines but nothing outside their limited naval experience. There was also no Army counterweight to the elite point of view of the Navy's 'private army' in the system from the very start.

As it happened, once Moore himself departed by air for Ascension in May to join us on *Queen Elizabeth 2*, General Richard Trant—a Light-Infantryman-turned-gunner—replaced him as Fieldhouse's land adviser. It's a shame it wasn't the Army general who left for Ascension. Trant was a seasoned Army officer who had served in the Korean War, extensively in the Rhine Army and had commanded 5 Infantry a few years before. Trant would, at the very least, have understood the need for more light tanks. And not necessarily more artillery (heavy equipment), but at least a battery (the military term for a group of six to eight guns and all the soldiers and kit required to fire them) of something light-weight with more range and destructive power than the 105mm light gun with its limited range of 10-11 miles.

We needed more than something to keep the enemy's head down: artillery that would ruin their day and shred morale. In service with the British Army since 1980, a single battery of FH70 towed 155mm (light-weight) guns with a range of 15-18 miles would have silenced the Argentine 155mms around Port Stanley that caused so much harassment in the closing stages of the war. 105mms and 155mms don't sound so different. But they are when it comes to guns. A 105mm shell weighs 40-45lbs and has 5lbs of explosive in it. A 155mm shell weighs 95lbs but has 14lbs of explosive inside it—two times the weight but with nearly three times the bang. Big difference.

If the weapons side was decidedly thin in Army terms, the human side was worse even though the five top commanders in the war were Royal Navy or Royal Marines, part of the navy. I hadn't realised that they did not see eye to eye, to put it mildly. Admiral Fieldhouse, the Task Force's Commander-in-Chief, for example, and his subordinate Thompson of 3 Commando had a strained relationship throughout. It is illustrated by the American general and logistician Kenneth L. Privratsky who recounts in his book on the Falklands Campaign that 'Shortly before noon on 26th May, Brigadier Thompson was summoned to speak to Fieldhouse via the satellite phone newly linked to London from Ajax Bay. During the call, Fieldhouse ordered him to attack Goose Green or be replaced.'[17]

The scene is regarded as a detail illuminating the tensions and difficulties experienced by senior commanders during a small war far away. Fieldhouse and the War Cabinet in London were keen to get moving on the agreed battleplan to attack Port Stanley across two axes: from the north and from the south. Goose Green was nearby and the first bridgehead of the southern flank.

But such an order, backed by such a threat, is still highly unusual. Commodore Clapp described meeting the Royal Marine commander afterwards as 'ashen-faced and very bitter' about what Clapp terms the 'kick in the arse'.[18] 'I don't think he wanted to see any naval officer ever again!', he adds. Obeying the admiral's order, Thompson, then still in command of all the troops on the Falklands, went on to organise the attack.

The Battle of Goose Green (Friday 28th May-Saturday 29th May) has become legendary—rightly. People even today know that Colonel 'H' Jones was killed in action during the battle and posthumously awarded a Victoria Cross. His personal gallantry and the quiet, cool-headed competence of Major Chris Keeble, his second-in-command, underpinned 2 Para's determination.[19] They fought with sheer, bloody-minded courage and skill, eventually overwhelming an Argentine Garrison more than twice their strength (600 overwhelming 1200). Fifteen other paratroopers were killed in action.

When we first heard news of the battle at sea on *QE2* we assumed it had been fought by the Royal Marines themselves rather than the Army's 2 Para. After all, the Royal Marines had bravely taken San Carlos in the first place with the Paras and would surely be eager to obtain first blood in revenge for losses.

Thompson's intelligence reports about Argentine strength were mixed. Reports available to him suggested a large garrison of an infantry battalion (650 troops): three companies of infantry, plus a further platoon (28 troops), one amphibious platoon, one engineer platoon, two 105mm howitzers, up to six

35/30mm anti-aircraft guns, up to six 20mm anti-aircraft guns. However, the SAS Squadron that had attacked Darwin on the day of the landings briefed Colonel 'H' that the whole area was held by about one company (up to 250 troops).[20] In cases of this sort, it would be customary in the Army to adopt a worst-case scenario, or at least split the difference. Intelligence reports can never be by their nature completely accurate if only because the enemy tends to favour the element of surprise.

In the general area, the British had by now landed five battalions (over 3000 troops) at San Carlos some 20 miles to the north of Goose Green. Darwin and Goose Green are two small neighbouring settlements on a narrow isthmus connecting the main area of East Falkland to the landmass of Lafonia (East Falklands furthest southern landmass). In other words, on the day of Goose Green the British enjoyed overwhelming local superiority even if they were keen to get going towards Port Stanley with the bulk of Argentine forces 65 miles away to the west.

Thompson declined to use this superiority. His own brigade also initially declined to deploy any Royal Marines at Goose Green, in the end despatching a single company of 42 Commando that arrived too late to make a difference.

Troops to task proved not to be the only problem. Reading accounts of the support available to 2 Para is a puzzling affair. Thompson's brigade allocated them just a single battery of half a dozen 105mm guns taken forward by helicopter.[21] During the final battles around Port Stanley a fortnight later most units had the option of calling on no fewer than six available batteries, if necessary. At that later point in the war, they had to share and General Moore had to work out priorities. But if a battalion or commando was unexpectedly outnumbered, as 2 Para were at Goose Green, all available guns could have been directed in support of them. In the case of 2 Para that day, however, no further artillery was available apart from that one battery.

In addition, since the Great War, the British Army has always ensured that its infantry battalions have their own very light artillery—muzzle-loaded mortars manned by their own soldiers. 81mm in calibre, they can fire high-explosive and illuminating bombs out to 4.5 miles. The point about this is that mortars go everywhere with you. They are an integral part of a battalion's defence perimeter. If something goes wrong, or you run into trouble, at least an infantry battalion has some firepower in addition to its rifles and machine guns. Generally, they are manned by more experienced soldiers who have served for a couple of years in the rifle companies: Guardsman Simon Weston was a mortarman.

These 'very light' mortars are still heavy and just about man-packable—commonly only for short distances, not 20 miles. Army mortars are usually transported in rather dinky light wheeled lorries, or in Germany in armoured personnel carriers—neither of which were available. Thompson's brigade had its own movement regiment, including helicopters and Bandvagn tracked vehicles which normally transported the Royal Marine mortars. However, 2 Para were not given mechanised transport for their artillery at Goose Green.

As a result, they were able to carry with them just two (of their regulation six) mortars, because they had to carry them on their backs to Goose Green from their original positions outside San Carlos. Far from ideal. The failure to understand the function of Army mortars, incidentally, also proved to be a factor in the Welsh Guards story later on.

Naval Gunfire Support for 2 Para was allocated from frigate *HMS Arrow* steaming on a gun line in Brenton Loch, a water way leading to Goose Green. It was a proper and sensible provision, but crucially in defiance or ignorance of the military maxim 'belt and braces'. Despite a plethora of possible replacements— every destroyer and frigate mounted at least one 4.5-inch (114mm) gun, similar in fire power to the Army's 105mm guns with a 10-11 mile range—no back up in case anything went wrong seems to have been thought about on *HMS Arrow*. Sure enough, just an hour into the battle, its 4.5-inch gun turret developed a fault and couldn't fire. As no other ship had been brought forward in reserve, the 600 paras were on their own from that moment against 1200 enemy troops.

It was even worse. Colonel 'H' asked Thompson's staff if he could be supported by the Scimitar and Scorpion tanks of the two troops of the Blues and Royals light-armoured regiment with the task force who had also landed at San Carlos. A Scorpion fires a 76mm shell and a Scimitar is equipped with a 30mm cannon that can fire 6 rounds in quick succession without reloading. Both vehicles mount a co-axial 7.62mm General Purpose Machine Gun—the gun is controlled by the same fire control mechanism as the main armament. It is used to supplement or replace the main gun on the tank—particularly useful against infantry. The crew inside the tank enjoy absolute all-round protection against bullets and shrapnel and chunkier protection across the frontal arc against light-anti-armour weapons.

But Thompson told 2 Para's Colonel 'H', no. 'I refused his request because I did not consider that these armoured vehicles would be able to negotiate the boggy ground between Sussex Mountain and the Darwin Isthmus.'[22]

The reason given above is strange to read. Most Army officers know well that light armour can go almost anywhere. Indeed, the vehicles were specifically designed on procurement to cope with 'boggy ground'. A reconnaissance vehicle that cannot cross such conditions would be nigh on useless. Such capabilities are demonstrated to us Army officers both at Sandhurst and to infantry officers at the School of Infantry. Many of us had friends in armoured regiments.

The key movement characteristic of both the Scorpion and Scimitar is the low ground pressure of their wide tracks—5lbs per square inch. A person, depending on weight and size of feet averages over three times more at 16lbs per square inch. And what about troops with heavy kit who have to negotiate boggy ground? The Tank Museum at Bovington made a lovely video a few years ago comparing the ground pressure exerted by a Scorpion to that by a professional ballerina *en pointe*. They both had to do their stuff on some ordinary sheets of polystyrene mimicking 'boggy ground'. The Scorpion left a track 8mm deep—the ballerina's pointe shoes dug in 13mm. An Army brigadier would not likely have refused Colonel 'H' light armour, he would have allocated him both available troops.

It was the same with movement support. 2 Para had seen and—like us a few days later—rather envied the Bandvagn vehicles with which Thompson's Royal Marines were equipped. Their Commando Logistic Regiment had 76 of them in all. But no movement support seems to have been provided to Colonel 'H's 2 Para. The Bandvagns later made it all the way to Port Stanley, more than 65 miles over much more difficult ground than the route to Goose Green for 2 Para—as did the light tanks of the Blues and Royals covering the distance in 6 hours of the 36 they had been given. 'Even as I landed on June 1 with 5 Infantry Brigade, The Blues and Royals had been making a name for themselves with everyone they worked with', recalls Roger Field, who commanded a scimitar. They were 'floating over the sodden peat like speedboats', said Troop Leader Lt Mark Coreth.

In any case, 2 Para's 600 soldiers unexpectedly faced the Argentine garrison of some 1200 troops and, at this point, the British had little idea of its ground fighting capabilities. All they knew was that the enemy had a highly impressive and aggressive air force; and a less impressive navy that had been completely out-manoeuvred by Admiral Woodward.

The Army approach to battle is to hit a nail on the head with an anvil—unless you are forced to use a hammer. It gets the job done with minimal room for mistakes. The most logical course of action for an Army officer would have been a two-battalion attack (1300 troops) supported by the light tanks of the Blues and Royals, six mortars per battalion rather than the two mortars man-packed by 2 Para, two or three batteries rather than a single battery of artillery; and properly organised Naval Gunfire Support. The anvil was available. So use it.

This would have produced a rapid and crushing victory with fewer casualties than sustained by 2 Para. The frightened messages from the Argentine commander of the Goose Green garrison to Port Stanley as the red (2 Para wear red berets) and green (the Royal Marines wear green berets) killing machine overwhelmed them would have unnerved the Argentine high command.

Instead, despite 2 Para's success, Britain showed a chink in the armour. The lesson the Argentinians learned from Goose Green was that it was possible to defend fixed positions effectively against British paratroopers—the cream of the British Army as Colonel 'H's valour showed. If Argentinian intelligence had been slightly better about numbers of British troops attacking, they might, if not defeated them, have at least beaten them off.

A British attack on Goose Green executed according to British Army doctrine in force at the time would instead have exposed the relative weakness of the enemy. The truth of it was that the Argentine Army wasn't up to much except in a few places where it could pack quite a punch: Goose Green certainly; Mount Longdon and Mount Tumbledown being the only other land engagements where they fought with significant skill and courage. And, of course, its air force.

This was the state of land operations before 5 Infantry—we, the Welsh Guards, Scots Guards, Gurkhas and our artillery regiment—even got there on 1st June.

The leading Royal Marines brigade seemed to be struggling with the requirement of early offensive action, a principle of war. In the end, it happened after five days because Admiral Fieldhouse gave a direct order. Yet even after the fact, Thompson writes in 1985, 'The question remains why the battle was fought in the first place, as it undoubtedly slowed down the advance on the main point of effort, towards Stanley. At the time I had not the slightest idea why.'[23]

Brigadier Thompson continues, 'The battle was to have a profound effect on the conduct of the rest of the campaign. It signalled to the Argentines the determination of the British to succeed.'[24]

This signal is a debatable interpretation of the situation. Although Argentine forces had lost Goose Green, they had killed the commander of one of the world's most famous regiments. This had made the Argentine garrison see a glint of victory. All of a sudden, British forces transported over 8000 miles by an Armada of over one hundred ships didn't seem that invincible to the Argentine generals.

As mentioned, the orthodoxy of the Falklands War histories is that things began to go wrong when we landed on 1st June, seven days before the bombing of the *Galahad*. In fact, the different style of warfare of the Royal Marines and Royal Navy—initiated by Chief of Defence Admiral Lewin's complicated top command structure without Army commanders—was starting to cause serious unforced casualties.

Thompson himself concedes he should have mounted a two-battalion attack of the five at his disposal: 'Had I done so, it would have been over far quicker, at less loss.'[25] Unfortunately, 2 Para was given 'inadequate support', as he writes.

6

South

'The best way to crack a nut is with a sledgehammer.'
Field Marshal Viscount Slim

The original plan had been for us, 5 Infantry, to go ashore at Ascension Island, some 4000 miles from the Falklands, for a short period of training, and to take the opportunity of a pause to restow equipment. The Royal Marines (including 2 and 3 Para battalions) had done the same earlier. But the urgent need to reinforce the troops soon to go ashore—if British troops were to have a large enough force to take Port Stanley—meant that after taking on fresh water at Freetown, Sierra Leone, *QE2* headed south at top speed.

Anticipation is not a principle of war. Maybe it should be. But it is certainly a useful, probably vital characteristic in military commanders. Vice Admiral Lord Nelson was always looking many moves ahead and expected the same of his captains.

Admiral Sandy Woodward (whom we all admired at the time and since), who commanded most of the Task Force's ships, was the same. He was helped by something Nelson never experienced: submarine training. The rigours of commanding one of Her Majesty's Submarines and, in Woodward's case, having run the submarine captain's course (the famous 'Perisher', after periscope), gave him the habit of creating in his mind a three-dimensional moving picture of the tactical situation at any given time, and then rapidly working out a course of action several events ahead. It's this quality that allowed him to deal so effectively with the Argentine Navy when it was trying to trap Woodward's fleet in an air-sea pincer movement. It culminated in their defeat with the sinking of *ARA General Belgrano*. After that, the Task Force enjoyed sea supremacy.

With troops landed and in control of San Carlos from 23rd May, it quickly became clear that Argentinian ground forces on the Falklands far outnumbered the 4-5000 Royal Marines, Paras and additional troops.[26] The numbers spoke for themselves. Intelligence suggested that the Argentines had positioned about 10,000 or so troops in the Falkland Islands (in reality, it was 11,500 plus); with the majority in and around Port Stanley but with a strong garrison in and around

Goose Green-Darwin, and some minor units on West Falkland.

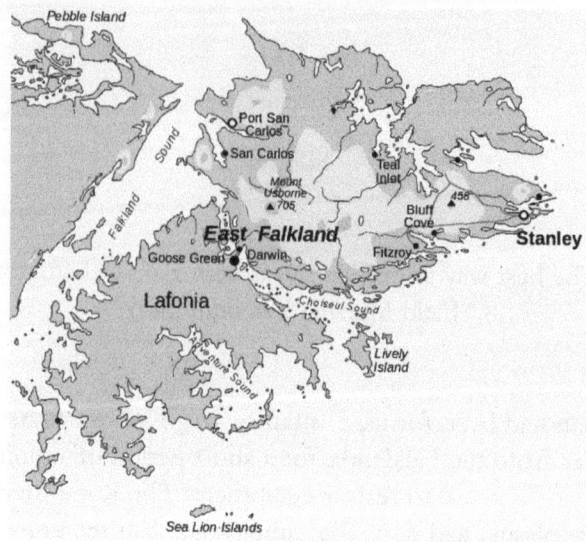

Junior officers like us weren't briefed on such matters, but it came both as somewhat of a surprise and a disappointment to the War Cabinet. Though the standard measure for numerical superiority is three to one, it was still reckoned by commanders at the top that an equal number to the Argentinians was sufficient to achieve victory. Hence the fact that we, 5 Infantry, were ordered straight down without further training from Ascension with the approval of the Chiefs of Staff in London. British military doctrine, again, was clear. One brigade, no matter the number of special troops, was not enough to win a war on land half the size of Wales. 5 Infantry's arrival would increase the forward force available to take Port Stanley dramatically. Instead of hurling a maximum of Thompson's four battalions at the Argentines (holding one in reserve at San Carlos), there would be seven to launch in the attack. If correctly and speedily deployed, it meant that the Argentines would be defeated in short order.

The size of the British land fighting force wasn't the only concern. Speed was also vital. The Argentine Army had to be defeated as quickly as possible—rapid execution is part of the doctrine of all military forces. Leisurely build ups went out with the campaign in 1850s Crimea. Given conditions in the South Atlantic, every extra day the campaign lasted meant further demands on and dangers for the ships of the task force, particularly in view of Argentina's airforce. There was also a danger the *junta* might play for a draw—stalemate or perpetual check in chess terms.

There was another imperative considered by the Chiefs of Staff in Whitehall. If the Argentines decided to make a stand inside Port Stanley and fight street by street, even three brigades would not suffice. In the process the town would be destroyed with the possibility of civilian casualties—British civilians. It would get very ugly very soon. And what exactly would be the point of winning back the Falklands if Port Stanley was razed to the ground? It was of the utmost importance to gain the upper hand over the Argentines as quickly as possible and to make sure they were defeated, losing the will to fight, *before* it became necessary to clear Stanley.

It didn't help that General Moore remained out of contact until 30th May—something that would repeat itself with devastating consequences on the night of 7th June. Part of the problem was that from the moment he embarked on *QE2* at Ascension Island until he left the ship on *HMS Antrim* off South Georgia that day, there was a technical SNAFU. The complex and expensive communications equipment installed on *QE2* so that he could give secure orders to Thompson and Clapp failed and would not respond to the repair efforts of specialist engineers. While the Falklands triumvirate got on with it, he kept up-to-date as best he could by listening to the BBC World Service and by enthusiastically strategising with 5 Infantry's Brigadier Tony Wilson, who was on board with him.

But Fieldhouse in London was on call as Commander-in-Chief to the Falkland commanders to sign off on any advance forward until General Moore came online. One can understand the War Cabinet and Fieldhouse's frustration at lack of further progress after the 23rd May capture of San Carlos and why Fieldhouse stood in for Moore to issue direct orders to attack Goose Green. The senior Argentine staff officers and commanders (both on the Falklands and back in Buenos Aires) had had nearly two months to prepare for the arrival of British forces. They had clearly thought long and hard about it and with each extra day we were handing them time to assess our strength and intentions. Although air superiority against Argentina had been expected it had not been achieved and each additional day exposed the Task Force to losses resulting from airborne bombings.

Just a day before Moore's arrival in San Carlos on 30th May in *HMS Antrim*, with 5 Infantry's battalions trailing him in *Canberra* (Scots and Welsh Guards) and *Norland* (Gurkhas), everything was ready for a rapid continuation of both flanks. After 2 Para's victory with heavy losses at Goose Green, the southern flank had already established its first bridgehead. Only Port Stanley was left standing as Argentina's stronghold on the Falklands. 'A southern flank would not only increase the pressure on the enemy who believed that the main attack on STANLEY would come from the south, but would also provide an option to swing the main thrust between the two axes', the Royal Navy's postmortem of 23rd September 1982 concluded.[27] It would immediately complicate the Argentine commanders' job as they would now have to track and fight in two directions.

This necessity for two axes of attack and all that it entails was realised well before Moore arrived on 30th May.[28] In preparation to develop 5 Infantry's southern position, teams to scout out and mine-sweep the anchorages near the settlements at Fitzroy as well as Bluff Cove were sent out—earlier assessments of all East Falklands' anchorages had in any case been made when the acting triumvirate selected San Carlos as its preferred landing spot.[29] Bluff Cove lay 3 miles further than Fitzroy Settlement towards Port Stanley.

Like San Carlos, Fitzroy Settlement was very suitable as a supply hub for ammunition and food and survival stores to the front line—in fact, plans were mounted on 7th June to move the San Carlos hub to Fitzroy.[30] There was just flat terrain ahead. Teal Inlet (at twice the distance from Port Stanley compared to Fitzroy) had been selected by the Royal Marines as the best location for their northern hub despite the screen of mountains towards Port Stanley. A recce by a newly-beefed up 'cadre' of Mountain Marines had provided intelligence that Port Stanley had weak defences on its mountainous north side—the Royal Marines were very keen to take advantage of this. All General Moore had to do on arrival was press the button and get 5 Infantry to exploit further forward from its bridgehead at Goose Green and get the Royal Marines—who were en route to Teal Inlet chivvied on by Fieldhouse—to insert in the north.

To this effect, General Moore had briefings from 30th May to his landing on 1st June at San Carlos with many of the senior officers now that he did not have to rely on BBC reportage. It was at this point, however, that peculiar decisions started being taken at the Task Force's military top. Instead of pressing the button for both, he seemed to press full-speed forward on the northern flank while creating the suggestion of a southern flank to Westminster. The War Cabinet had been persuaded at the end of April of the urgent need to send a second brigade to clinch military victory and were naturally expecting 5 Infantry to be deployed together with the Royal Marines.

Moore's first decision on 30th May was to be sanctioned by Fieldhouse and it joined them both at the hip. It was to be heavily criticised in an internal secret report distributed to a restricted number of six people in 1982. It is only now—almost four decades later—that the rest of us can learn about it for the first time.

Its main findings are dry and bureaucratic, but the message is like a grenade blasting through the building. Under ATP doctrine, Fieldhouse was obliged to terminate the amphibious assault phase of Operation Corporate once San Carlos was captured. From that moment, the land phase would start and doctrine stipulated that Fieldhouse as Commander-in-Chief had to redefine the role of the amphibious staff as their main task would now be transport and general unloading (cold) rather than assault (hot). No such signal was issued by Fieldhouse, however, and nor did he redefine Clapp's responsibilities. In effect, he tore up ATP by trying to run the operation in a new, informal and therefore untested way. The criticism levelled at Fieldhouse is shockingly direct. It led to 'degradation in the tautness of Command and Control', the report concludes. Attempts were made to patch this up 'by signal and DSSS conversation but no hard and fast new organisation was ever promulgated to all land and sea units concerned'.[31]

Predictably, deviating from ATP created a muddle that was impossible to fix in the constant state of planned disruption that is a military campaign. The southern flank singularly suffered from Fieldhouse's departure from doctrine. While its lead commanders, Moore and Clapp, met every day and 'could discuss and settle immediately by verbal briefings; to those further away, and indeed to some of those Commanders' staffs, the situation became more grey with time'.[32]

Moore concurred with setting aside ATP doctrine and did not insist on sub-ordinating the amphibious group to his own divisional staff. Had he stuck with doctrine, in a stroke, the trained precision of orders would have enveloped the amphibious staff. His position made little sense as there was not a chance of a hot amphibious assault being required to move the 5 Infantry Army battalions to Bluff Cove. Yet, Moore even mooted giving Clapp a new title of his own confection. Though it was to remain the same, Clapp 'suggested Commodore Falkland Islands or COMFI' ('comfy' to Moore's 'cliffy' and Admiral Woodward's 'foffy'—Flag Officer Flotilla 1—FOF1) instead of COMAW. In amphibious NATO training the Royal Navy would always adhere to doctrine and use 'CATF' (Commander, Amphibious Task Force) instead.

Fieldhouse and Moore's decision to continue the triumvirate structure, however, addressed a different problem. While they were not against a two-axes assault as such, they seem to have been persuaded by the provocative idea of a quick move forward of the 'navy's private army' in order to capture Port Stanley from the rear only since the Argentine occupier didn't seem to think it would be attacked from that side. In theory, it was a move akin to the one through unde-fended jungle that led to the fall of Singapore in 1942. The war would be over faster than expected and the Royal Marines would be able to finish the job with 3-4000 troops. In this scenario, the 3000 5 Infantry on the southern flank were still useful as a Plan B in case things didn't pan out as expected. However, Fieldhouse had by now primed the War Cabinet to expect two flanks during Moore's radio black-out on *QE2* and Moore, knowing only the state of play on the Falklands through the BBC, had groomed Wilson for a role on the south-ern flank.

Presumably, being upfront was an unattractive option because it would mean making a U-turn to the War Cabinet. Saying there would now only be a northern axis of attack risked having to make another U-turn later on if this plan failed (it did) and having to explain why precious time was wasted on a single axis of attack (it was). Suspension of ATP offered a way forward that masqued in London what happened on the ground in the Falklands. 5 Infantry had little mechanised transport of its own to exploit forward and most of what it had now lay at the bottom of the ocean as a result of an Argentinian Exocet strike hitting *Atlantic Conveyor* on 25th May. It meant Wilson would always have to ask the divisional staff for help, who would need to ask the amphibious staff in turn. The amphibious group was the spigot through which the southern flank could be controlled. While the Royal Marines' attack through a single northern axis was being pursued, support to Wilson could be withheld for the time being. 5 Infantry's advance to the southern front line was effectively delayed until such time as Clapp's amphibious staff decided to allocate support to the southern flank. All that Wilson's staff could do off its own bat was speak to Moore's divisional staff (which had little mechanised support of its own to offer anyway). They could not go directly to Clapp's staff since—in contravention of ATP— Clapp answered directly to Fieldhouse in London under a separate chain of command.

As for the Royal Marines, ATP doctrine was adhered to in practice where the northern flank was concerned. Despite the fact that the amphibious group theoretically fell under a separate, independent chain of command, their officers did have to follow orders issued by Royal Marine staff. This was because the Royal Marines were given 'temporary' tactical control (TACON) over all amphibious assets assigned to the northern push. That is to say, amphibious independence was in effect 'terminated' (for the time being, technically) where this brigade was concerned. Instead of the departure from doctrine applying to both brigades, it really only applied to 5 Infantry.

Next, Moore, a Royal Marine general, decided on 30th May to assign ('chop' in amphibious parlance) practically all available helicopters[33] to the Royal Marines in the north despite his promises made to Wilson on *QE2*. He had brought at least 28 additional support helicopters with him. Teal Inlet was a lot further away from Port Stanley and the distances alone to the frontline meant it needed greater effort to be sustained.

It was a momentous decision. The plan to develop the southern flank ostensibly determined that 5 Infantry would be moved forward by 'marching, helicopters, or shipping'.[34] But by 30th May it was already clear that unsupported 'marching' over long distances through the Falklands inhospitable terrain was not an option. The only way either of the first two were now going to be meaningful options was if the amphibious or divisional staff—both of which had spare helicopters of their own—were agreeable to lending a hand to 5 Infantry. As you will see, our battalion paid the price for this twisted situation on 3rd June. We were aware of none of this.

Moore's next decision that turned the spigot down further on the southern flank was to land 5 Infantry's battalions way back at San Carlos. Goose Green-Darwin was the better option as it was far nearer to Port Stanley: 45 miles as the crow flies as opposed to 65 miles. Furthermore, as part of its 28th May victory, 2 Para had captured the *MV Monsunen*, an Argentinian coaster, for 5 Infantry to use. Even if 5 Infantry had no helicopter support, this vessel was ready-made for moving its battalions forward to Bluff Cove along a direct coastal water-way—Choiseul Sound—that was easy to patrol. *Monsunen* would only need to cover 40 miles instead of a ship having to round Lafonia, the large, flat protu-berance that forms the south of East Falkland, which made a journey starting from San Carlos 170 miles long. Moore's poor decisions kept 5 Infantry vaguely 'on-hand' (not a military term at all) at San Carlos without ever declaring to Wilson or the War Cabinet that he wanted to deploy a single-pronged attack through the northern flank.

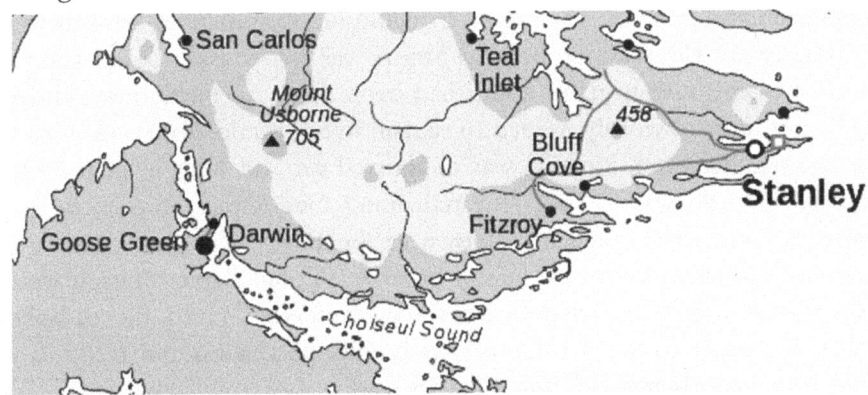

Another decision Moore sanctioned was postponing the move forward of a key piece of air-protection armoury. An essential element of having a brigade stationed south of Port Stanley was having the supply hub right behind it. To deter attacks by the Argentine air force, it needed a protective dome with a crucial piece of artillery called Rapier, a sophisticated radar guided system that could respond to signals even after the missile was launched—much like a com-puter game. It supplemented the far less effective Bofors anti-aircraft artillery and automatically avoided ugly accidental 'blue-on-blue' shoot-downs of British jets through a coded signal system. A single Rapier unit had four missile firing points and each unit covered 90 degrees, with four placed together creating arcs in a full 360 degrees circle.

While clever pieces of machinery, Rapiers were fragile and sensitive like fridges and needed settling before they were operationally reliable. Twelve units landed with the Task Force on 23rd May but they were not designed for sea journeys through Antarctic storms. 'It would not be until D[-day]+4 that eleven out of the twelve Rapier firing points would be operational',[35] Commodore Clapp recalls in his memoir. Once operational, though, they proved invaluable. They helped inflict losses on the Argentine air force, discouraging the Argentine air force from mounting further assaults on the Task Force's main hub in San Carlos as fifteen enemy planes were downed a day—taking a sizeable chunk out of the Argentine air force. At the time, twenty hits were claimed for Rapier but subsequent analysis suggested fewer. Nevertheless, it is clear that the missile system formed an essential part of Britain's air defences against the Argentine air force because Argentine pilots were afraid of it. The flash of a missile being launched was enough to discourage some of them from pressing home their attacks. We may not have had the 155mm mortars needed for an effective land war, but at least Rapier missiles had the desired aggressive effect on the Argentine air force in spades—regardless of the number of actual hits.

After the arrival of additional RAF missile batteries, on 3rd June four Rapiers were immediately helicoptered to the north to protect the Royal Marines' hub at Teal Inlet. Their third battalion (42 Commando) leapt forward by helicopter on 30th May, the first day Moore was able to issue orders and two days after Goose Green in the south had been taken on Fieldhouse's orders. Four Rapier units obviously needed to remain in San Carlos for its protection. Once the southern hub location was conquered on 2nd June, all that Moore now needed to do was to order the remaining four Rapier units to be helicoptered (or otherwise) post haste down to the Bluff Cove area to secure a dome over 5 Infantry's forward hub at Fitzroy. Without Rapier units, it would be open season for the enemy's air force. Preferably, given the diabolical weather, the order to get 5 Infantry's four units packed up and ready to go should have been issued on 30th May. Instead it took until 8th June for the southern flank's hub to receive its Rapier.

It is clear from the newly-released Kew documents that it took until 4-5th June before the penny started dropping that a single attack via the northern axis only was not achievable. But not for want of trying by Operation Corporate's top commanders. On 4th June, Fieldhouse personally iced a plan to move 5 Infantry forward to the southern axis's frontline at Bluff Cove at last. Instead he ordered Moore and Clapp at noon to 'CONSIDER TEAL INLET'[36] as the location in the north to where 5 Infantry should be transported from our holding pen at San Carlos.

In actual fact, Mount Kent's icy wind-blasted terrain was even more horrific than the rest of the Falklands. Unlike Singapore's jungle, it was, if not 'impassable', at least impossible to sustain troops for long. Teal Inlet could hardly support another brigade. And so the Royal Marines' HQ signalled Moore eight hours later that the situation was getting desperate: 'SURVIVAL CONDITIONS IN MOUNTAINS. SHORT OF RATIONS'.[37] Despite having dominion over practically all of the Task Force's mechanised land transport, the Marines' brigade was already running out of its own supplies and rations at this point. It robbed Moore of the idea that inserting 5 Infantry in the north alongside the Royal Marines could work.

Two hours later, Moore signalled Fieldhouse that their northern flank idea had hit its first hard buffer. 'TEAL PLAN WOULD LOSE INITATIVE' if 5 Infantry were inserted there, he wrote.[38]

However tough and well-trained the Marines were, the northern approach soon started claiming their men without the Argentines having to lift a finger. One report suggests that ten marines a day were succumbing from cold injuries. The Argentine generals, who knew the Falklands rather better than their callers, reckoned that, since the north was a nigh impenetrable climatological blizzard-tortured barrier, an attack would come from the south. And they were right.

Even so, the southern flank's build-up—which would position four Army battalions (Scots Guards, Welsh Guards, with 2 Para and the Gurkhas right behind) on the opposite axis to the two Royal Marine units and 3 Para—would still only creep forward. Moore continued to drag his feet.

It wasn't until the evening of 5th June that he would finally greenlight one of the two Guards battalions to move from San Carlos to Bluff Cove. But they would only replace 2 Para, whose battalion would fall back 3 miles to Fitzroy. Despite the bad news regarding Teal, as late as the evening of 7th June Moore still clung to the idea of a single northern attack by the Marines and wanted to speak in person to his commanders there—presumably to make a final decision, at last. As we will see, the new Kew documents reveal just how caught up he was in this long-drawn gamble that day.

7

The Waiting Room, 2nd June

The Scots and Welsh Guards disembarked from *SS Canberra* in the morning, 2nd June, into landing craft manned by Royal Marine cox'ns and then onto the jetty at San Carlos in a well-planned operation. It was stormy winter weather. No one fell in, luckily. The water around the Falklands is around 4 Celsius in winter—survivable for between 10 and 20 minutes. No Argentine aircraft turned up to disrupt our arrival. It was a big day for us, an even bigger day for 3 Commando ashore since 22nd May, and the fleet at sea offshore. Also, for those back in Blighty and, if they knew, the inhabitants of the Falkland Islands.

The safe arrival of 5 Infantry with all its equipment meant that at last we had enough troops ashore to defeat the 11,500-man enemy occupying garrison. The enemy's best chance of winning was gone. I led my platoon ashore and in an act of bravado threw away my ludicrously ill-fitting steel helmet.

To my relatively inexperienced military brain, it seemed strange we were being landed 65 miles to the west of Port Stanley—a bit of a wasted opportunity. But I assumed there must be an overriding military reason for this; and, in any case, arrangements to get us forward ASAP would be well in hand since Moore had given orders that we were to be deployed rather than held in reserve. 'Theirs is not to reason why, theirs is but to do and die', says Tennyson in 'The Charge of the Light Brigade', 1854.

My thoughts were not so much on our arrival, although I was keenly aware of its military significance, but on what might lie ahead. I had been training for the best part of two years since joining the Army in the ranks. This was my first military operation—and it wasn't patrolling the streets of Belfast or Derry—I was in the middle of a war 8000 miles from home. How should I conduct myself in these circumstances? Who were the best shots in my platoon? Who were the best machine-gunners? Were the medical kits going to be enough? If life got rough, who could I rely on most?

I had gone through these details and a host of others on *QE2* with my platoon sergeant—a no-nonsense veteran of Aden and three tours of Northern Ireland. We had worked it all out together. But most of all I had taken to heart something he said to me during our last private chat before we landed. I knew it already, had understood from the very start of my officer training. Yet it's very different when your platoon sergeant says it to you as you disembark into a war: 'Remember sir, we'll all be relying on you.'

Privately, I also recalled famous historical parallels to our arrival as reinforcements. The reaction of the Lucknow garrison in 1857, as they heard bagpipes in the distance playing 'The Campbells are coming', is one of the epic moments of Victorian military history, the subject of countless paintings and prints. As you climbed the stairs to the first floor of my preparatory school and reached the landing there was a huge representation of the great moment. My parents who had met and married in Calcutta had a series of smaller prints of the event—weary sentries smiling, women clutching their children applauding General Havelock as he entered the Residency. Soldiers from different regiments—different armies even, shaking hands. Wellington, Havelock, Haig, Montgomery, and Slim—all of them at one time or other were overjoyed to receive reinforcements.

That day we went ashore proved to be an icy shower of reality. We must have been the first Army reinforcements in a British military campaign ever not to be welcomed with relief and open arms. With the arrival of the 3000 troops of 5 Infantry, the number of soldiers had almost doubled. From a hammer, the British force on the Falklands had turned into, if not an anvil, at least a sledgehammer. Reason for celebration.

Not so. At San Carlos, we were received by 40 Commando, one of the three Royal Marine units in Thompson's brigade. They watched and muttered. The other two of the Royal Marine units (42 and 45 Commando) plus 3 Para were already well forward closer to Port Stanley that day. The 650 troops of 40 Commando had been left as a reserve to protect what was now merely a divisional landing and a Transport Administrative (TA) area. Should things go pearshaped at the front line or from the rear, they were held back to tilt the balance back in Britain's favour.

They were clearly very unhappy about this. No one smiled, offered to point us in the right direction, or made any attempt to communicate. I noticed no compliments were paid to officers—not that I cared but it's one of the tell-tale signs of poor discipline. If one of my guardsmen had failed to salute or stand to attention in front of a Royal Marine officer, or omitted the word 'sir' while addressing him, my non-commissioned officers would have 'intervened'. And if I'd been there, I would have apologised for their disrespect.

This unexpected attitude surprised me and I began to worry about my men. If an Argentine shell had landed among us or we'd been shot at by the enemy I think I would have taken it in my stride. But there was an oddness and hostility about the feel at San Carlos that I found unnerving. Looking back now, I suspected the commandos were not only unhappy about being reserves but also about not being used to attack Goose Green, the task Thompson, their brigadier, had given to Colonel 'H' of 2 Para—some four days before Moore landed and took over as land commander.

It seemed as if a large element of the troops at San Carlos were indifferent to the arrival of 5 Infantry down South. I knew enough about military life to understand that attitudes flow from the top down. Even so, it was with a measure of complete surprise to read almost four decades later the following in the memoirs of Brigadier Thompson, the Royal Marines commander of all troops on the Falklands (until General Moore assumed that role on 30th May): 'We neither bothered ourselves with what the other brigade [5 Infantry], or any other "outsiders" were doing, nor cared what had happened to them, unless it affected us directly.'[39] To discover that we were branded as 'outsiders' by a former land commander of Her Majesty's troops on the Falklands was a baffling statement that I find hard to understand to this day.

In 1982, all we junior officers wondered about was how would 5 Infantry now be incorporated rapidly into the assault strategy to form a sledgehammer against the enemy with the Royal Marine forces already close to Port Stanley?

The most direct way from San Carlos meant getting 5 Infantry to Goose Green-Darwin via Brenton Loch. The loch was an approach which had been considered and reconnoitred for 2 Para's attack a week earlier. It was then rejected because of the possibility of Argentine armoured patrols on the shoreline: 2 Para would have been sitting ducks. But the Argentines had long gone and the area was defended by a ring of aggressive, impenetrable steel, 2 Para and subsequently 1/7 Gurkhas. They shot at anything that moved, asking questions later, unless they recognised who passed their cross hairs.

Brenton Loch itself was deemed by experts too shallow for any large ship to drop us off directly. Be that as it may, the means of getting us ashore would have been at night by one of the six LCUs (Landing Craft Utility, capacity 120 fully laden soldiers) at San Carlos along this relatively short stretch. After the surrender of the Argentine garrison at Darwin and Goose Green on 23th May, the Royal Marine officer in charge of the landing craft had 'offered to take as many LCUs up Brenton Loch as was necessary to collect the prisoners, plus any wounded and civilians.'[40] If it was possible to get prisoners, wounded and civilians *out* on LCUs it would have been possible to get us *in*, we reckoned. The Task Force's two Royal Navy tactical landing ships, *HMS Fearless* and *HMS Intrepid*—called Landing Platform Docks or 'LPDs'—each had four LCUs that could be loaded inside the hull and then floated into the sea. Two of *Intrepid's* LCUs had already been handed over to the Royal Marines at Teal after an emergency run to deliver 250 tons of critical stores on 31st May by the ship as the first snow fell, so that left six LCUs available in San Carlos to take us forward to Goose Green.[41] Six LCUs would eventually be involved in taking 5 Infantry troops forward at night. But this happened only many days later and in a trickle over days. These nightime moves were in addition so convoluted that they ended up moving all six LCUs the other side of the island where they lay idle not doing much of anything instead of being used for the many loading tasks during the daytime in San Carlos.

Goose Green was preferable in other ways as the base for all 5 Infantry troops. The Gurkhas landed the day before us at San Carlos and then immediately had to march the seventeen miles to relieve 2 Para still stationed at Goose Green after their victory. Moore had ordered the Army battalion of Gurkhas to be given the Task Force's single Chinook (the largest type of helicopter) for an hour. It air-lifted their heavy equipment that could not be man-packed from San Carlos to Goose Green-Darwin. 2 Para had meanwhile discovered that there were no Argentinian troops at Fitzroy and Bluff Cove, under 20 miles west of Port Stanley and asked their commander, Brigadier Wilson, for permission to move forward on 31st May. He did so after 48 hours and when a Chinook arrived at Goose Green for his HQ, 2 Para deployed it to capture the two settlements without opposition on 2nd June.

It was as good as it got. Both axes—north and south—were now held by Task Force troops on 2nd June. Compared to the super-sized support on the northern flank, not much support was needed to have all the battalions ready on the south side. Reducing the weight carried by the troops to around 60+lbs per man, the entire Army brigade could have marched to 2 Para at Bluff Cove in a couple of days (even in our nearly useless DMS boots) with some helicopter or other mechanised vehicle support for our heavy equipment. From 4th June we would have been battle ready: a sledgehammer of 2 brigades ready to liberate Port Stanley. Or so we thought looking at our Falklands maps.

The Army has a sarcastic saying, 'Rush to wait'—a good description of the frustration, boredom and inconvenience sometimes associated with our attitude to time. We all had to be early for everything, very early. A detachment mounting guard at Windsor Castle, say, at eleven o'clock would arrive in Windsor two hours before. No bad thing. A perfectly sensible practice deeply ingrained in us. To this day, I am early at airports and stations to the occasional irritation of my family.

General Moore had the opposite attitude—'Wait to rush.' Our two Guards battalions of 650 men each were to idle at San Carlos for between four and six days, after which there was a panic about moving us forward to Port Stanley, a long way away. With helicopters and cross-country vehicles especially stretched, the poor logistics and poor communications, this precipitous and chaotic move was the next unforced error in the Falklands campaign.

8

March to Nowhere

On 2nd June, the whole southern coast of East Falkland had fallen into British hands without contest thanks to the extraordinary initiative of 2 Para. No doubt fired up by their narrow victory at Goose Green and mourning the loss of their commanding officer and others, they were still seeking the enemy—though now dug in and tired. 5 Infantry needed to get to the front line, 40 miles away, as soon as possible. By appearances at least, that is what it must have looked like in Whitehall.

And to us. We started to march out of San Carlos towards the enemy on 3rd June via a track 2 Para had used the week before on their way to Goose Green. They negotiated the Falklands winter mud and sleet in light gear of 80lbs. On 3rd June each guardsman, however, carried at least 120lbs on his back. I was six foot three and a bit and according to our family weighing machine records 185lbs in my New and Lingwood boxer shorts (in blue-red-blue guards colours, of course). I could hardly stand up with all my kit on, struggling to carry two-thirds of my bodyweight very far. Smaller men would have been carrying close to their entire body weight. We slipped and slithered in our useless boots—fine on the streets of Belfast or in the back of an Armoured Personnel Carrier in Germany but not quite the thing in the South Atlantic tundra.

I was reminded at the time of that wonderful 1970s television programme *Jeux sans Frontières*. Teams of contestants competed against each other in absurd physical competitions often involving thousands of gallons of mud to the huge amusement of a live audience. There are echoes that the modern generation would understand in the Bushtucker Trial element of *I'm a Celebrity, Get Me Out of Here*. The guardsmen behind me were stoic but cursing as we tried to get up Sussex Mountain (I heard some swear words that made me blush a little—the ones in Welsh at least I didn't understand) towards Goose Green. We all slipped and slid but in a general upward direction.

We had been promised support by our brigade commander, Brigadier Tony Wilson, especially of 'some Snowcats' (a less reliable, older Army model of the Royal Marine Volvo Bandvagn BV202 tracked vehicles—of which the Royal Marines had seventy six on the Falklands, which it shared between its units only).[42] What we ended up with to move our battalion of 600 men and thousands of pounds of kit was as follows:

One tractor and trailer (borrowed from civilians by our
second-in-command)
Two Snowcats (of a total of six attached to 5 Infantry).

That was it.

We—troops and officers—found it incomprehensible at the time why no
logistics were lent to us from our fellow brigade or the amphibious team. We
were, after all, heading for the front-line against the same enemy. Only a direct
order by Britain's land commander on the Falklands would have got our battalion in place on the double. We found it very difficult to understand what
General Moore thought he would gain from withholding airborne or land logistics from half his troops. It seemed to create a low bar for our arrival at the front
line to be blown off course by, for example, the 'wrong kind of orders', winter,
exhaustion and illness, communication failure, mechanical failure, chance, etc.
And what about Argentine military commanders?

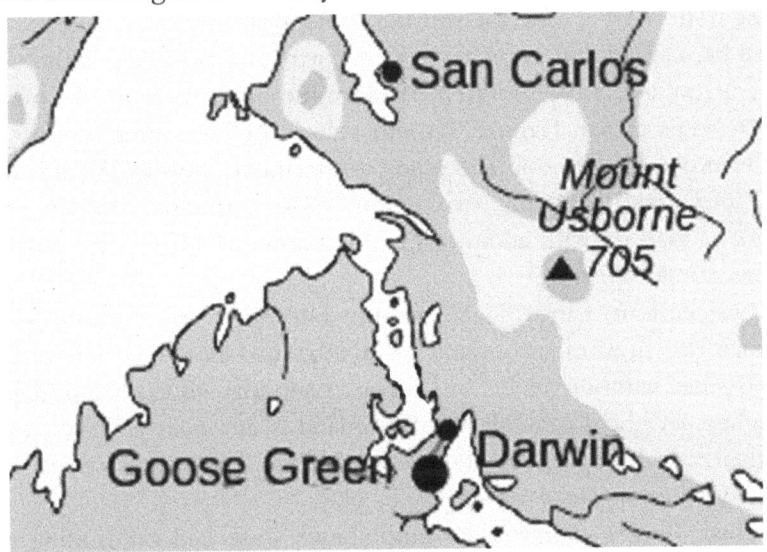

The tractor/trailer broke down almost immediately and could not be
repaired. The more reliable farming vehicles had already been commandeered
by the Marines and Paras. The two promised Snowcats rendezvoused with us at
San Carlos. Their drivers said they would return once they had filled up their
fuel tanks. In the words of our Commanding Officer, Colonel Johnny Rickett
(always referred to by most of us as 'JR' but obviously not in his presence), 'that
was the last we saw of them.'[43]

I served a further twenty years in the Army—three tours of Northern

Ireland, three and a half years in the British Army of the Rhine, lots of exercises at home and abroad, instructing at Sandhurst and so on. I have never experienced anything like it since. Rendezvous can be missed (as we will see). Transport can be late. Mechanical problems can cause delays. But for vehicles to arrive and then not return after going to refuel, knowing that they were the only movement support allocated to an entire battalion, was unnerving then and unheard of, to me and anyone else I know, since.

Something akin to it had happened once before to me, however, when in the ranks at the Royal Armoured Corps Training Regiment at Catterick—we finished a late-night exercise on the North Yorkshire Moors and spotted the lorry due to take us back to barracks with relief. As we wearily approached hoping there might be some hot tea, it moved off at a hell of a lick—we followed its progress hopefully as it was a 20 mile walk back to camp. Sure enough, it stopped a mile or so away and we caught up with it quickly. The Colour Sergeant in charge of our training laughed and bellowed as we eventually climbed onto the tailgate, 'just making the point, gentlemen.' The 'Strange Case of the Disappearing Snowcats' that day always puzzled us. The Welsh Guards tried to get to the bottom of it after the war but to no avail.

When he realised that no vehicles were forthcoming to help with our heavy equipment (especially the mortars), JR gave the order to return to our waterlogged trenches at San Carlos. Without vehicle or helicopter support, it was physically impossible for soldiers of any sort to move forward. Already carrying 120+lbs per man (including two 81mm mortar rounds jammed into our webbing), to load up with additional ammunition and heavy steel mortar base plates was not an option.

As I was curious, I investigated for this book the earliest moment when it was known that movement on land by infantry was extraordinarily difficult, if not impossible, without vehicle or helicopter support. 45 Commando, possibly the toughest of the Royal Marine Commandos amongst a strong cast, had begun their march ('yomp' in Marine slang) from San Carlos to Teal Inlet on 27th May with each man carrying 120lbs plus.

The Task Force's independent amphibious staff laid on landing craft to move 45 Commando from one side of San Carlos to the other—to make the march easier and cut a few miles from the distance they would have to walk. Within an hour of leaving San Carlos, the first Royal Marine fell out. By the end of the day, fourteen more Royal Marines had fallen by the wayside.[44] That brought the count to fifteen of some of Britain's toughest and best-trained military out of action from exhaustion or injury. The exhaustion of the ones that did remain standing affected their battle-readiness.

Their whole march was excruciating. Their commanding officer called a halt—asking for helicopter support the following day to lighten the impossible loads on his men. 45 Commando were carrying lighter loads than we were expected to carry a week later. They were not carrying their Milan anti-tank missiles destroyed in an air raid a few days before, each one weighing 53lbs. Nor were they carrying mortars (all-up weight, 86lbs) and mortar ammunition. Their mortar ammunition was taken forward in 4 Royal Marine Bandvagns—ours was mainly on our backs. So, when Moore gave the Royal Marines all helicopters, it was a lucky decision for them. All they needed to do was call in an order for helicopter support. It rapidly materialised to transport their kit and they continued their way to Teal Inlet in lighter (much lighter) order.

Captain Gardiner, a company commander with 45 Commando, rightly thanks his lucky stars that his men were equipped with proper mountain boots rather than our ludicrous DMS Army boots. Plus, they had all sorts of nice pieces of Arctic kit unavailable to us at 5 Infantry, like proper cold weather socks. Nonetheless, it was fiendishly difficult for 45 Commando to make its way forward—even with proper mountain boots, the help of a landing craft and its heaviest equipment (mortars and their ammunition) coming forward by other non-man-packed means.

No other Royal Marine unit, thereafter, attempted a similar march. In 2018, at a Falklands seminar sponsored by the Australian Army in Canberra, Royal Marines Brigadier Thompson described how unusual conditions were. Recounting the reaction by the uninformed, he said, 'We found that it was difficult for anyone who had not seen the Falklands to imagine what it was like. When we told people that the rate of advance of a battalion on foot carrying ammunition, weapons and equipment was about 1 km per hour, without any interference from the enemy, it was received with ill-concealed disbelief; bordering on contempt'.[45]

In Army campaigns it is inconceivable that such terrain and logistics information known from 27th May would not be shared instantly to all units by the divisional staff. The impossibility of man-packed movement without any transport assistance was, however, not shared by General Moore's staff with 5 Infantry. It is difficult to understand what could have motivated the decision not to do so. The only reason why Wilson ordered Rickett, JR, to get marching on 3rd June was the assumption that it was physically possible.

As it was, JR could not call in support from 5 Infantry HQ. The brigade had little vehicle or helicopter support available to it—with only light Gazelle and Scout helicopters (capacity three passengers) for recces and officer movement under its control. Everything else had to go through General Moore and his staff. There was no direct line to the amphibious group, as we saw.

There was an official inquiry soon after the end of the war, which I will go into some further detail later. This 1982 Inquiry makes clear that without any mechanised help forthcoming, JR took a reasonable decision to call our march off on 3rd June.[46] After we had returned to base, we were now to be moved by sea transport. It is unknown what informed this change, but under the circumstances it was another 'Wait to rush' which delayed the sledgehammer that was to flatten the Argentine garrison at Port Stanley with minimum casualties and maximum chance of success.

Once it was known that man-packed movements required vehicle or helicopter support, all Royal Marine moves were given such assistance. 42 Commando's 650 troops were transported well forward entirely by helicopter to Mount Kent on 30th May. After Stanley fell, this unit was even airlifted into the town by their helicopters rather than having to march like Army troops. In the closing stages of the war, in order to replace the two Welsh Guards companies blown up on *Galahad* (352 men including the mortar platoon), the two 40 Commando reserve companies of Royal Marines stationed at San Carlos were also taken forward by helicopter over 65 miles.

In the autumn of 1982 Professor Lawrence Freedman (later the official historian of the war) analysed it thus. The northern flank idea was sapping the Task Force's logistical strength and had little chance of success.

When it was realized that Mount Kent had been vacated, Royal Marines moved forward in appalling conditions to occupy it. This may have been a mistake, for Mount Kent was more suited to defence than for launching attack and the troops were bitterly exposed to the elements. It required the use of scarce helicopter resources to attend to their needs....

This had important consequences for the 3000 men of the British 5th Infantry Brigade who by now had arrived at Port San Carlos. They lacked the wherewithal for movement in sub-Arctic conditions and were in danger of getting stuck.[47]

After a few days in the San Carlos Transport Area, those of us further down the food chain had realised that there would be no help (or worse) forthcoming from an organisation controlled by Royal Marines who clearly considered 5 Infantry troops as 'outsiders'. JR, our colonel, however, didn't seem to realise this. He was a tough individual but underneath it all a gentleman and traditionalist. In his view of British military history, making life difficult for British troops advancing towards the front line was the exclusive prerogative of His or Her Majesty's enemies.

Accompanying 5 Infantry on *Canberra* and *Norland* was *Atlantic Causeway*, sister ship to the unlucky *Atlantic Conveyor*. It carried 20 Wessex (troop capacity

12) and 8 Sea King helicopters (troop capacity 28). Smaller helicopters but still with useful troop and kit carrying capabilities. Some, at least, of these, were earmarked to support our brigade offloading stores and assisting infantry forward. We knew that we had brought with us more helicopters—many more. We knew that the Royal Navy had re-tasked some of its anti-submarine helicopters to be support helicopters under operational control of the amphibious group. Just some helicopter support would have increased the speed of 5 Infantry's advance. We simply couldn't understand it.

We did see plenty of helicopters. They were busy supporting Royal Marines. But nothing was available to us. Not even additional reconnaissance helicopters were made available to allow units to send forward key officers to look at the ground. Rather like that disheartening experience most of us have had of waiting for a bus in a rainy and remote spot—the joy of seeing the lights and sound of transport coming towards you, only to see at the last minute the dreaded sign 'Not in Service' as it sweeps past, apparently unconcerned. 'Not in Service for 5 Infantry' was how we read the sky traffic above San Carlos.

While in transit to the Falklands on *Queen Elizabeth 2*, Moore intended that priority for the transport of supplies and troops should be given to 5 Infantry in order to get it forward as soon as possible—to catch up with the Royal Marines, the bulk of which was already forward on Mount Kent on the northern flank. This was not to the liking of elements of the Royal Marines. They complained that 5 Infantry had not arrived with suitable frontline-supply support and one of their own logistics officers 'protested loudly that his job was supporting 3 Commando Brigade.' Commodore Clapp, part of the triumvirate with Moore and in charge of amphibious transport, confirms in his book that commander of 5 Infantry, Brigadier Wilson, was 'clutching a promise from General Moore' but he also refers to us as 'reserves' as opposed to frontline troops. It was a messy situation that Moore was creating.

It cannot bear repeating enough that under Moore, Royal Marines had full use of virtually all of the Task Force's helicopters. It was to all intents and purposes their monopoly. Of all the helicopter movements of the Task Force, only three ever supported 5 Infantry troops moves. The Chinook moved the Gurkhas' equipment from San Carlos to Goose Green on 1st June, Wilson's to Goose Green and 2 Para to Fitzroy/Bluff Cove on 2nd June, and a mix took the Scots Guards to their start line for the Battle of Mount Tumbledown on 13th June. Far from a sledgehammer, the British Task Force was handled by Moore on the south axis like a complicated Swiss Army Knife with multiple moving parts at various speeds—a very different thing.

I'm sad to say that General Moore, instead of being the solution was at the heart of the errors from the moment he took over as land commander. Johnny, my equivalent in charge of another platoon (28 men), and I had bumped into him one evening as we took an evening stroll round the decks of *QE2*—he inspired our confidence and had just the right touch dealing with slightly startled young officers. He was a hero with a Military Cross and bar from Borneo, highly unusual in those days. But, after four decades I realise that the most he had ever commanded before was one brigade (3 Commando and its three units, 40, 42, 45). He was the wrong man to lead a two-brigade operation. He simply lacked the requisite experience, causing unwarranted delay in decisions with fuzzy objectives.

If we had been provided with the same level of movement support as 45 Commando on their deluxe 'yomp' of 28th May in comparison to ours of 3rd June, we would have got there. The idea that the (to the Army, at least) lavish arrangements available would be used only in support of one brigade would be absurd. But then again, Moore and Fieldhouse didn't really seem to want to move us forward yet.

Officers who were trained and qualified to command two brigades at the same time only existed in the British Army—divisional commanders or ex-divisional commanders from the British Army of the Rhine. They knew how to bring together the 8000 men split into two brigades that had never trained with each other and were different in many other respects as happens in NATO.

I already mentioned General Trant who succeeded Moore as Land Adviser to Admiral Fieldhouse. But the strongest candidate would probably have been General Geoffrey Howlett MC (originally from the Queen's Own Royal West Kents, subsequently a paratrooper), then serving at the 1st Armoured Division in Germany. He had climbed, against severe competition, the Army's *cursus honorum*—a process Julius Caesar would have recognised—with lots of operational experience. Moving up the ladder from battalion to brigade to divisional command, in the way the Army demands, working with and understanding the capabilities of all the various components of the 155,000-man British Army—not least the 55 different infantry battalions we then had in the field. He was probably the best Britain had at the time to fashion and wield a military sledgehammer with ease and skill.

There were others equally qualified of course. The individual would not necarily have to be an infantryman—there were several very sharp cavalry and h ery generals who could have done the job. What was needed was a strong oth to make sure that the two brigade commanders worked well with each briga nd that resources were equitably and efficiently distributed between the return. as laid down in Britain's core military doctrine—a point to which I will

With e arrival of 5 Infantry there were more Army soldiers in the

Falklands than Royal Marines (7 major units—5 infantry battalions, 2 artillery regiments—to the 3 major Royal Marine units). It must remain a mystery how the head of the armed forces, Admiral of the Fleet Sir Terence Lewin, and head of the Army, Field Marshal Bramall, settled on a Royal Marine general in the first place. At most, such generals had experience with its three elite units in a single brigade. Did Admiral Fieldhouse, chief of the Falklands campaign in London, not see the problem?

The world was shocked to discover after the war that Argentine officers were given different ration packs from their men—how very decadent and selfish. Yet 5 Infantry was dramatically less well equipped than the Royal Marines—rubbish boots, polyester Army issue socks, spray-proof wetproofs, leaky, ill-fitting sleeping bags, bergens bought in a hurry from civilian camping shops, some of them in civilian colours, difficult radios. And less well fed. All the units of 3 Commando enjoyed Arctic ration packs stuffed with treats, chocolates, cocoa—more than 4000 calories per man per day. 5 Infantry had standard NATO ration packs at around 2500 calories per day. Army troops were to pay a far higher price than fewer calories a day for Moore's muddled wavering and his ingrained parochialism.

9

Towards Bluff Cove
June 4-6th

And so, after a delay of three days, the two Guards battalions of 5 Infantry based at San Carlos were to be landed by sea at the front line, 11 miles from Port Stanley. The approach would have to be made at night as the anchorage was visible from the high ground around Port Stanley and the Falklands Task Force had not yet established air superiority over the islands from its aircraft carriers. By now, two of the brigade's battalions—2 Para and forward elements of 1/7 Gurkhas—were already in advanced positions for days.

On 4th June, waiting in the wind and pouring rain, the Scots Guards and half of the Welsh Guards stood by during the day to get down to the San Carlos jetty and be lifted forward, as our commanding officer JR records. At short notice, in the late afternoon, two Welsh Guards companies, hungry after waiting in the cold for a day, were loaded onto *Intrepid*. The other half were meant to transport on *Tristram*.

It was my first time on a Royal Navy ship, and rather exciting. Otherwise, though, HMS *Intrepid*'s Royal Navy crew weren't much different from the Royal Marines at San Carlos—a surly bunch. They stood and watched. As we sat in the wardroom, which we eventually found (there was nowhere else to go), my platoon sergeant arrived asking for a word. The Navy's chefs wouldn't give the guardsmen a hot meal: 'Your men have been issued with compo rations and they should eat those.' The prospect of hundreds of hexamine burners boiling up tins of chicken curry in the corridors brought about a swift change of mind.

The game plan wasn't clear to us junior officers. Within a few confusing hours the whole thing fizzled out and we were turfed off back to the beach at San Carlos. No reason was given. We were non-plussed, our guardsmen growing cynical.

JR, our commanding officer was incandescent—all our support weapons and heavy equipment had been lugged down to *Intrepid* to prepare for the move. As he was about to embark, a detachment of Royal Marines who ran the jetty told him and the Scots Guards that all forward movement was to stop. JR hitched a helicopter lift to *Fearless* and describes that there was 'a fairly short exchange of views between myself and some rather startled staff officers, who were left in no doubt as to the feelings of my battalion'.[48] He had no line of communication to 5 Infantry at Darwin, hence his desire to hear first-hand about orders on the Flagship.

It is extraordinary to read at Kew the sequence of events behind the scenes in the newly released files. The amphibious staff had completed a straightforward plan on 3rd June for the single-day move at 5.10pm by securing a frigate escort and Harrier air protection from Admiral Woodward. However, eighteen hours later, at 12.37pm the next day, Fieldhouse curtly stayed this proposed move and ordered Moore to consider Teal Inlet instead for both brigades as we saw.

Did Moore order Wilson to have the Scots Guards and us embark and disembark *Intrepid* for naught later that night, and why? On 4th June we thought that what happened was hardly a good omen, though even we—cynical as we had become—would scarcely have been able to believe the truth if we had clapped eyes on these communications. The amphibious staff's signal on 3rd June asking Woodward for escort and air support isn't for the 4th June: it plans for a landing two days later at 'APPROX 061039 [6th June 4.30am]'. It is hard to picture what General Moore had in mind when he ordered 1200 troops of Scots and Welsh Guards to assemble and wait at *Intrepid* in the freezing cold that day and, in the late afternoon, forthwith to board—a stillborn move to Bluff Cove in the future that Fieldhouse had already aborted half a day earlier—and then disembark us precipitously hours later, with Royal Marines brusquely blocking Colonel Rickett's access and the Scots Guards to *Intrepid*.

After this peculiar day, lengthy top deliberations with London continued meanwhile on how to move the southern flank troops forward in actual fact. It was decided to split the two Guards battalions and send them separately, each leg organised by the amphibious group. None of these moves went according to plan with chance creating ever more delays along the way.

On the night of 5-6th June, following the false move of 4th June, the battalion of Scots Guards with whom we had journeyed down on *QE2* eventually moved forward on *Intrepid*. This move, the first actually to put to sea, escaped by a whisker being a disaster two or three times the size of the Welsh Guards on *Galahad* two days later.

It should have been straightforward enough, like the first plan. The amphibious staff had only one serious operational detail to tie up. Royal Navy ships cruising on a gunline offshore while bombarding Port Stanley with their 4.5-inch guns needed to be warned about the movement of friendly forces by night in landing craft.

These ships were under the control of triumvirate commander Admiral Woodward, not Commodore Clapp (who was in charge of amphibious inshore vessels). Clapp checked verbally with the admiral earlier in the day. Woodward said there were no plans for a naval bombardment that night. And that was that. The conversation as recounted by Clapp echoes the famous scene in *The Return of The Pink Panther* where two people talk past one another:

> Clouseau: 'I thought you said your dog did not bite!'
> Hotel Clerk: 'That is not my dog.'

It turned out there *were* ships on the gun line that night astride the Scots Guards' route. They were totally unaware that there were LCUs on the way. *HMS Cardiff* opened fire on the storm-tossed convoy of the four Scots Guards landing craft. Luckily, the captain was more cautious than he had been earlier that night and decided to use illuminating shells before opening fire with high explosives: he realised in the nick of time the convoy was British.

Commodore Clapp writes that the admiral apologised profusely. Admiral Woodward deals with the incident in some detail, blaming it on 'heavily over-loaded… communications.'[49]

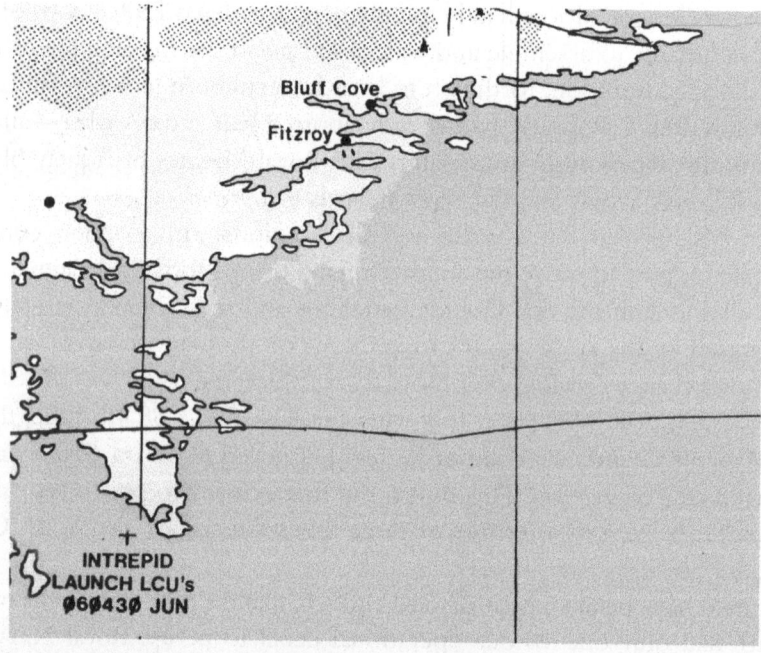

Had a signal from the amphibious group confirmed the route of the Scots Guards none of this would have happened. It would have been displayed in Woodward's operations room aboard the carrier *HMS Hermes*, as a result of their signal. Two Royal Navy captains alternated in twelve-hour shifts throughout the Falklands campaign to process information. It would have been passed as a matter of course to any ships ordered onto the gunline. It is ironic that

Commodore Clapp later criticised the most senior commander of the triumvirate at his 2018 Falklands seminar for the Australian Army, 'I doubted if Sandy, a submariner with very limited surface navy experience, knew much about amphibious operations and it worried us'.[50] Unfortunately, the amphibious staff would also have their own signalling problems that day. In addition, the new reports at Kew cast a very different light on *Intrepid*'s manoeuvre—as we shall see.

Just an hour before, *HMS Cardiff* had shot down (in highly controversial circumstances) Army Gazelle helicopter XX377 from 656 Squadron Army Air Corps, the air element of 5 Infantry. It was carrying signallers with fresh batteries to supply the rebroadcast station on Pleasant Peak (they were meant thereafter to do the same at 2 Para's radio station at Fitzroy). This peak was halfway in between 5 Infantry's HQ in Goose Green and the Paras at the Advance HQ at Fitzroy. By this time, 5 Infantry still had no secure communication link between the two places for six days and counting—something that was to play its own role later. All aboard were killed.

This was not clear, however, until well after the Falklands campaign. An initial technical inspection of the wreckage by the Royal Navy hastily concluded that it wasn't brought down by friendly fire—there were no pieces of a British Sea Dart missile among the wreckage, the inspection concluded. It was assumed for years that 5 Infantry had made a mistake of one kind or another by not clearing the flight with the Royal Navy (a view that is still perpetrated in some histories of the Falklands).

The relatives of the killed soldiers were not convinced and demanded a full military Inquiry, which was eventually held in 1986. It turned out the helicopter *was* downed by a Sea Dart missile from *HMS Cardiff*—the exact opposite of the original technical report.

Who was at fault, then? The Board of Inquiry Report had already concluded in 1982: 'As the sortie was to be flown within the airspace of 5 Infantry on a Brigade mission in accordance with Standard Operating Procedure there was no requirement for a report to be made to any outside authority.'[51]

The new Inquiry established four years later, in addition, that the helicopter had been misidentified by *HMS Cardiff* who thought the radar signal was that of an Argentine Hercules transport propellor plane heading supplies into Port Stanley. Overland was the preferred route for these planes, as they were more likely to be picked off over sea than when skirting the East Falkland mountains. The Argentine Hercules flights posed no immediate threat.

While the Scots Guards in their four LCUs had a very narrow escape from *HMS Cardiff* hours later, their icy-water soaked journey was extraordinarily unpleasant and far longer than planned by Clapp's staff. They were unfortunate in that the ship taking them forward to the point where they transferred to landing craft was troop carrier *HMS Intrepid*—the same ship that denied an evening meal the night before.

Intrepid's Captain Dingemans dropped them early in their landing craft—'strangely far short of their destination' in the words of Admiral Woodward[52]—into a stormy night ocean at 12.30am. Dingemans then headed home for safety from the Falklands winter weather. It was very different from the textbook emergency run to Teal Inlet that Dingemans executed for the Royal Marines on 31st May, past a suspected Exocet envelope in the north.

Woodward doesn't conceal his low opinion in his memoirs: 'She [*Intrepid*] dropped her LCUs before heading rather too quickly back for the relative safety of Carlos Water. Some 650 guardsmen set off unarmed in *Intrepid's* four LCUs on a fifty-mile one-way trip inshore. It was to be an horrendous journey, one which should have taken half an hour but in fact was to take more than five, with many of the troops very seasick and all of them soaked through to the skin.'[53] In his own memoir, Clapp himself concludes more mildly the morning after that *Intrepid's* captain, his subordinate, 'had clearly had a very worrying night and two weeks in San Carlos were proving a strain'.[54] Either way, the battalion of Scots Guards landed in diminished fighting condition as a result of this unexpectedly early dump.

The scene was uncannily reminiscent of Captain Queeg's early abandonment of US Marines in their landing craft depicted in Herman Wouk's novel, *The Caine Mutiny*, and the 1954 film in which Queeg is played by Humphrey Bogart. As the *USS Caine* guides the marines towards a beach on a Pacific Island held by the Japanese, Captain Queeg gets nervous—instead of taking station at the exact spot the marines should start their final assault run into the shore, covered by *Caine's* guns, he orders a yellow marker to be dropped and turns his ship away from the Japanese defenders. The Kew documents suggest there is a lot more to say about this peculiar voyage that endangered the lives of 650 Scots Guards—an entire battalion—and the crew on the four landing craft.

Dingemans took over from Clapp as COMAW on 25th June 1983 and went on to become a Rear Admiral.

10

EYEWITNESS: CAPTAIN JAN KOOPS
2nd-in-Command, The Prince of Wales's Company,
1st Battalion Welsh Guards

After our strange interlude on *HMS Intrepid* on 4th June we ended up back on shore. On 6th June we were moved onto *HMS Fearless*. That evening we received orders from our company commander, after he returned from the Battalion Orders Group. The orders from Moore were short and clear: 'Land at Yellow Beach (Bluff Cove, western bank), move through 2S[cots]G[uard]'s position on foot to Grid Square 2167. Dig a defensive position astride the track to/from Port Stanley. Await further orders there.'[55]

The ship was to sail to a rendezvous point north of Elephant Island where we were to collect LCUs. Along with the two LCUs on board *HMS Fearless*, the battalion (with full kit) was to be inserted under cover of darkness into Bluff Cove to link up with the Scots Guards who had carried out the same journey the night before on 5th June.

No LCUs made it to the designated rendezvous point. JR was faced with a very difficult decision: either split the battalion in half, against all his most deeply ingrained military instincts; or return to Falkland Sound and hope the Royal Navy could get its act together the following night.

The problem was compounded by the fact that one of the available landing craft, in anticipation of two more arriving imminently, had been pre-loaded with all kinds of kit from Headquarter Company to ensure the quickest turnaround possible. That meant that only one rifle company could go forward. It was the wrong way round. The troops who made it to Bluff Cove that night became the closest British troops to the Argentine front line on the southern flank. Their order of battle was 'unbalanced', a worrying military term describing in this case the absence of the second and third rifle companies in the battalion—us. If the Argentines came out to play, we wouldn't have sufficient troops to fight them off.

At this point our commanding officer was assured in person by General Moore whose Headquarters were on *HMS Fearless*: 'I'll get the other half of the battalion to Bluff Cove tomorrow night.' Which meant we would only be split for the shortest possible time and, we assumed, that the arrangements to get the rest of us forward were already urgently underway. This forced JR's hand and he made the difficult decision to disembark from *Fearless* with half the battalion on the two LCUs available. This was both an unwelcome and a possibly dangerous situation. Before he went, he issued specific orders to Major Sayle in formal military language—'You are to land at Bluff Cove and under no circumstances are you be separated from your kit,' making absolutely sure we knew what the plan was and what we were expected to do.

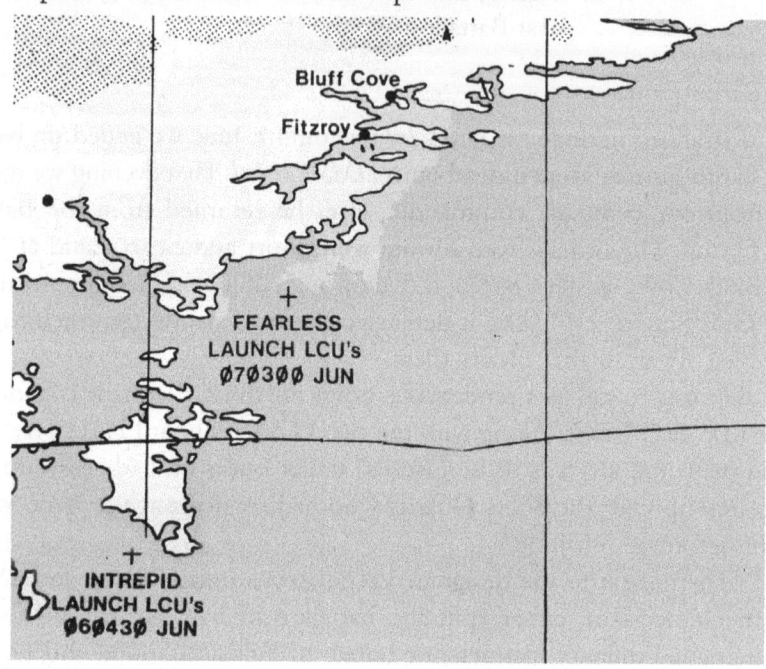

The final words that night of our commanding officer to Major Guy Sayle, my immediate superior, as he left us are still ringing in my ears:

'I have been promised by General Moore that you will be taken to Bluff Cove tomorrow evening. Make sure that this is what happens, OK boy?'[56]

It was a tense time. The guardsmen groaned when they were told.

Consequently, my half of the battalion returned to Falkland Sound on *HMS Fearless* but with the personal word of the general to JR that we would be taken forward to Bluff Cove within 24 hours.

11

Exocets and All That

The first half of the battalion of Welsh Guards made its way successfully to Bluff Cove on 6-7th June, but as Captain Koops has pointed out, with only one out of three rifle companies—down to just a third of its 'bayonet strength' in Army terms. Worse than that, each rifle company fields nine General Purpose Machine Guns (GPMGs) which meant our commander JR was short of eighteen GPMGs if ambushed by Argentine troops. Though half in number, the 300 troops assembled at Bluff Cove could only project at most a very modest fraction—not even a quarter—of their standard defensive power at a one mile range.

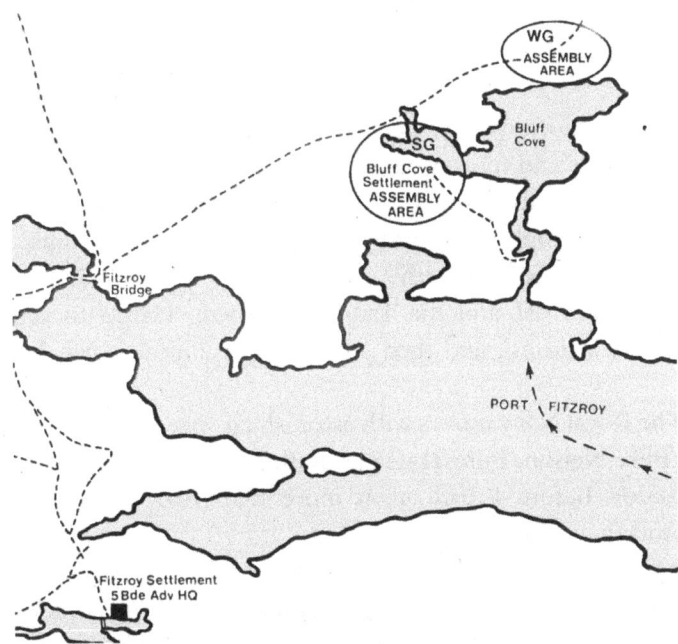

The first half did have with them their anti-tank missiles—quite useful against vehicles but not so much against Argentine infantry. Crucially, their six mortars and their crews and ammunition had remained with us on *Fearless*. In the event of an attack, mortars can engage out to more than four-and-a-half miles. It is probably the most important piece of kit a British infantry battalion is provided with to break up a sudden attack by enemy infantry. They are not a nice add-on or optional extra—they are integral to the way the British equip and train their infantrymen to operate in war. Hit the enemy with mortars which produce very nasty shrapnel as far out as you can. Then the GPMGs at a mile or so plus. And so on. Effectively, they were now dug in, stripped of the standard 4.5-mile layer of defence against the Argies.

From dawn, 7th June, the Welsh Guards were the closest British unit on the southern flank to the Argentine forward positions—just a few miles. Any half decent Army scenting a massively below strength infantry battalion hastily dug in astride a road a few miles away would have attacked.

Thank God they didn't. The situation the Welsh Guards found themselves in because of sea transport difficulties constituted a severe military emergency. The risk might have been worth taking for 24 hours—there appears to have been little choice. But not for much longer. To re-unite the two halves of the Welsh Guards as quickly as humanly possible had priority as a matter of core military doctrine. If only because of Moore's week of delays, we now risked the enemy wiping out the forward Welsh Guards (some 300 troops) before the Task Force's assault on Port Stanley had even started.

Back in San Carlos, 7th June

A rather exciting morning followed for us in San Carlos on HMS *Fearless* after our two companies and mortar platoon (half a battalion) got back early on 7th June. Having by now abandoned my noble intention of giving up smoking and feeling a little claustrophobic (hardly surprising given our circumstances), I was taking a turn round the deck with a gasper.

The alarm went off and the Tannoy boomed, 'Hands to action stations, hands to action stations', and then something technical which I didn't understand.

Wow! The Royal Navy moves with astonishing speed and confidence in these situations. Pure Nelson. Pure Trafalgar. Rather splendid. Everyone was in their proper position before I had taken more than two or three puffs of my cigarette. And then I heard my name,

'Crispin? Is that you? What on earth are you doing here?' A young naval officer in anti-flash gear and a helmet manning some sort of ack-ack gun was talking to me. I recognised the voice, a very old friend from school with the same Christian name who had always had his heart set on the Navy.

'Crispin, old boy, how are you? I didn't know you were on this ship.'

'Crispin, old boy, I had no idea you had even joined the Army. I thought you would go on stage.' (I had spent most of my time at school acting—mainly Shakespeare.)

We shook hands and had a laugh. Then he got serious and told me to get below quickly and not to smoke during an air raid. We listened to the Tannoy as *Fearless* fired her missiles. One Argentine plane was shot down, in naval parlance 'splashed'; another turned for home.

Later in the morning, we were told that *HMS Fearless* would not, after all, be taking us forward for a second go that night—7-8th June. We would be handed over to the *RFA Sir Galahad*.

Everyone on board, from Captain Jeremy Larken down to the most junior sailors, were very helpful. *Fearless*'s friendly crew were slightly embarrassed by what was happening.[57] We were being handed over to the Royal Navy's services outfit. I was offered a shower and cigarettes by a *Fearless* officer and the men were being looked after by its crew.

It was nerve-wracking for us—the forward half of our battalion was now exposed to possible annihilation by the enemy. We officers knew about General Moore's promise to our commanding officer and began to wonder what the hell was going on. As young platoon commanders during our Sandhurst training and in our first months serving with the battalion, we had come to understand the core bargain between officers and the soldiers they command. Our men followed our orders and in war their lives were in our hands. Death, disfigurement—all the horrors of a military operation were out there and if needs be we were all prepared to lay down our lives for Queen and country. But not squander them.

This bargain is deeply ingrained up and down the chain of command. Moore certainly had this instinct as far as the Royal Marines were concerned. But did he consider the lives of Army troops, particularly 5 Infantry, that he was putting at risk? I doubt it. Even after an entire battalion of Scots Guards was almost destroyed thanks to poor naval communications on 5-6th June (in a hurried move forward five days after landing as a result of his prevarication)—no alarm bells rang in Moore's head. He should have gripped the situation like a vice but didn't.

Knowing what I know now, I find Moore's string of orders from 4-7th June beyond difficult to understand or justify. The forward move of the Guards to the frontline was the single largest movement of troops during the whole Falklands campaign. It was the reason why—going against ATP doctrine—Moore had allowed the amphibious staff to continue working independently rather than subordinated to his own staff's orders. What followed were yet more plans that one by one were either shredded or fell by the wayside. Army troops' lives became subject to the vagaries of the weather, the availability of LCUs, mechanical failure on the way, 'blue-on-blue' hits, all the rest of the confusion I have described (and we will see below)—never mind Argentine attack. Moore's intentional procrastination had precluded a riskless advance through area that was controlled by the Task Force. Instead, however, we were moved around Lafonia, the longest way to reach the frontline.

The risk that is most often mentioned in connection with the Lafonia route is the stockpile of French-built Exocet rockets that Argentina possessed, apart from its sea mines (of which there had been no occurrence in the Falklands including at Teal Inlet since May). They were extremely costly and Argentina only had five of the most expensive air-launched AM39s. These were spent with some success against the Royal Navy in May and none were left in June. The Argentine military had positioned a land-based firing platform in a container on Port Stanley's furthest promontory with the cheaper surface-launched AM38s. It became clear after the war that it had eight of these (four having been smuggled in on hospital ship *Bahia Paraiso* flying a Red Closs flag) in stock on the Falklands. Though the couple that were launched misfired because of technical failures, this of course didn't make the potential threat any less real within its firing envelope. It was also suspected that Pebble Island in the north might have a similar platform with an envelope that could touch the route to Teal Inlet. This proved not to be the case after the Port Stanley fell, but that wasn't known then either. Exocetitis never gripped the northern flank in the discussions, however, as much as the southern route.

On my visit to Kew, one of the many surprises I found in the trove of new documents was a graph of Exocet's arc or 'envelope' that could be reached from its launch platform at Port Stanley. Its range was severely limited by the Falklands craggy coastline, leaving a wide 5-mile corridor along the southern coast that could be sailed out of harm's way. Another surprise was that this envelope was well-known many days before the use of ships was said to be restricted for reasons related in various ways to this Exocet location. The Board gives a precise time stamp for the intelligence regarding Exocet's range. 'Between 27 May and before 2 Jun[e], the enemy had deployed a land based EXOCET system. The exact location was not found but was believed to be roughly in the vicinity of HORSE POINT [just outside Port Stanley]. This gave it significant coverage to seaward to the S/SW/SE and E.'[58]

Woodward's frigates and destroyers—the prime targets for Exocets—were nonetheless free to move eastwards provided they stayed away from the Exocet arc reached from Horse Point. It was also clear by now, in case there was any real doubt, that the shoreline from Bluff Cove (Scots Guards), Fitzroy (2 Para), Darwin (Gurkhas), away from Port Stanley in other words and down to San Carlos, was not enemy held.[59] Clapp verified with Fieldhouse whether his Royal Fleet Auxiliary LSLs were to be excluded from the Lafonia route. He signalled to his Commander-in-Chief, 'PLEASE CONFIRM USE OF LSL FOR STORES. FEW BAYONETS

ACCEPTABLE'.[60] The response that came back from Northwood authorised their use. An upgrade of Fitzroy Settlement to become the entire Task Force's logistical hub even lay on the drawing table in the days ahead. The location was considered to be as safe as San Carlos.

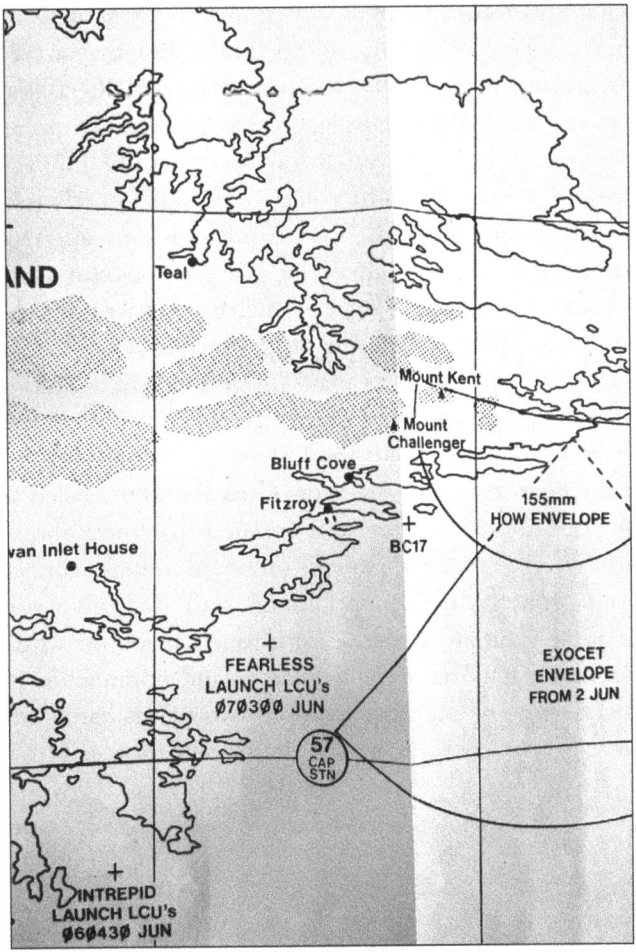

There has been a lot of talk about Fieldhouse's involvement from Northwood and that of the War Cabinet in view of what happened next. But in truth the map makes clear that the military situation didn't change much as far as the chosen troop exploitation along the southern flank was concerned. To that extent the Exocet discussion has been a red herring. Movement of battalions at night by a Royal Navy LPD along the southern flank remained unaffected by whatever London said. The facts bear this out. LPD *Intrepid* sailed on the night of 5-6th June with the Scots Guards, LPD *Fearless*, the amphibious and land force's Flagship, did so on the night of 6-7th June with the Welsh Guards.[61]

The decision to deviate once again from doctrine and to allow frontline troops to be transferred by a civilian organisation rather than by the Royal Navy on the same night of 7-8th June did have an enormous influence on everything that was to follow. With Fieldhouse's consent, we were being handed over to the Royal Fleet Auxiliary (RFA)—like sending ignition keys to be delivered by Amazon into a combat zone. This is not to question whether RFA staff were worthy and brave seamen. They were, no doubt. But they were not military. Their role was non-tactical and, so, were not trained in Royal Navy modes of assault. More to the point, their ships lacked the dependable sophisticated communication equipment that allowed Royal Marine LPD *HMS Fearless* to be General Moore's HQ from which he could safely and securely issue orders.

I wonder today what the Royal Navy would think of an Army outfit that decided a military front-line task involving Navy troops was too risky for the Army unit and should be handed over to civilians to carry out. As we will see, the evidence at Kew is clear in this respect—fear was the sole argument (Dingemans seems to have been its main proponent). In addition, what would they think if the Army had marked the contractor's means of transport down as 'disposable', as was the case with the LSLs?

Even after the near-miss with the Scots Guards and the failed Welsh Guards rendezvous, neither Moore nor his staff insisted that there should be a Royal Naval 'officer-in-charge' to accompany us on board to make sure landing orders were carried out properly by the amphibious staff and other services troops. This was of course standard in any case if one carried on with independent chains of command. It is hard to imagine a land commander with multiple brigade experience who would have exposed two of his battalions (1300 men) in this cavalier way both en route and at their destination as pre-disaster chaos gathered.

12

EYEWITNESS: CAPTAIN JAN KOOPS

Port Pleasant/Fitzroy

Within a few hours of General Moore's exchange with Colonel Rickett on *HMS Fearless* south of Elephant Island (three quarters of the way towards Bluff Cove), about splitting the Welsh Guards, it transpired that *Fearless* would no longer be available to take us, the second half, forward. On the orders of Admiral Fieldhouse in Northwood, Royal Navy landing ships would henceforth, so we were told, remain in Falkland Sound.

We 'crossdecked' by boat once more on 7th June to the *RFA Sir Galahad*— a cargo ship with a rear landing door that could be opened, a bit like a small roll-on/roll-off ferry. Our departure from Falkland Sound to Bluff Cove was delayed by the amphibious staff. 16 Field Ambulance, a field hospital, had failed to sail the night before on *Tristram* because of a lack of landing craft to load them, and they were added to *Galahad*'s cargo at the last minute with some of its manpower. They took ages to embark, again, because of a lack of landing craft.

We were given little information through the afternoon, but could see that the operation wasn't proceeding smoothly. More and more people and equipment were crammed onto the ship. As time crawled forward, our unease rose. The split from our battalion increasingly looked as though it would be more than just 24 hours.

The medics were ordered to Port Pleasant, the sound south of Fitzroy (a spit of land with 5 Infantry Advance HQ and 2 Para), as was a Rapier anti-aircraft battery—also added to be packed aboard *Galahad* rather than *Tristram* (sailing the previous day), at the last minute. We on the other hand, of course, remained under Moore's direct orders to land at Bluff Cove, north of Fitzroy, through a sound called Port Fitzroy, to bring up to full strength the Welsh Guards, at that point 5 Infantry's forward left battalion astride the road to Port Stanley. The entire operation was meant to be completed during the hours of darkness—like the previous Guards transports on 5th and 6th June.

In a change of plan, the amphibious staff, however, ordered Captain Roberts to sail to arrive at dawn. My superior on board, Major Guy Sayle, was not told that Roberts intended to skip Bluff Cove, despite having been in touch constantly during the afternoon and evening with *Galahad*'s captain. If he had been, Sayle would immediately have referred the matter up the chain of command to Moore. Nor was anyone else. It was a very strange omission.

In the moonlight, *Galahad* steamed into Port Pleasant, Fitzroy's harbour around 7am. We anchored next to another cargo ship, *Tristram*. Coming up on deck at the crack of dawn, we were astonished to find ourselves looking at Fitzroy rather than Bluff Cove—itself visible across the narrow spit of land in front of us and Port Fitzroy sound beyond. It was almost touchable. It was a clear morning for the first time after five days of relentless winter storms. We could clearly make out the enemy-occupied hills around Port Stanley. If we could see them, we were sure they could see us.

Sayle immediately went to Captain Roberts to seek clarification on the last set of orders that the captain had received. At the same time, he offered to man the decks with our machine-gun teams. Captain Roberts, however, was satisfied the anchorage was safe.[62] Britain's air defence arrangements provided a triple layer of anti-aircraft cover. First, there was an air-raid early warning system triggered by a Royal Navy destroyer or frigate on station as far west of West Falkland as was sensible—invariably giving about fifteen minutes warning of an attack. Two Combat Air Patrols (CAP) provided by Royal Navy Sea Harriers and Royal Air Force GR3 Ground Attack Harriers were in the air over East Falkland. Their protection was made continuous rather than episodic by the Harriers being able to fly from and refuel at a landing strip ashore at San Carlos, rather than having to make the long round trip from and to the carriers at sea for each sortie. Three, whatever ground fire was available in the vicinity—both Scots and Welsh Guards had machine gun platoons equipped with ½ inch Browning machine guns. And we had our own General Purpose Machine Guns (GPMGs) and personal weapons, the 7.62mm Self Loading Rifle. *Galahad* and *Tristram* also mounted two 40mm Bofors anti-aircraft guns each. Each layer had its own early warning requirements. On board, we could deploy our guns in less than a couple of minutes—the same for *Galahad*'s Bofors team.

One of the pompous comments found in accounts of the attack by those who were not on the ship goes something like this, 'There were two types of people at Fitzroy that day—those who had seen what the Argentine Air Force could do around San Carlos and those who had not.' Captain Roberts had seen plenty of the Argentine Air Force, *Galahad* had been hit by a 1000lbs bomb (which failed to detonate) and strafed on the morning of 24th May. The damage was obvious when we arrived aboard. It's one of the reasons Sayle immediately asked Roberts's permission to deploy our machine guns on deck—we couldn't miss noticing what the Argentine air force had done.

While doing some background for my contribution to the book, I was appalled to discover another piece of pomposity, on the National Army Museum's website no less. Brigadier Julian Thompson, Commander of 3 Commando, is quoted about our predicament, 'If I'd have been on board that ship[,] I would have swum ashore rather than stay there.'

Other than the obvious points that he would both have been disobeying orders by abandoning his post, deserting in effect, and would have sunk without trace in the freezing water, dragged down by more than 100lbs plus of kit, I find it utterly inexcusable that a man in his position of authority and responsibility could come up with such an absurd quote about the guardsmen and others on board *Galahad*. When I travelled back to the UK in late June 1982 with the Royal Marines aboard *Canberra*, I met Thompson. I find it hard to reconcile our long and friendly one-to-one about 8th June with this crass and mindless sneer at everyone who found themselves aboard *Tristram* and *Galahad* that day. He should ask for it to be removed. Indeed, he should withdraw the comment entirely and apologise.

Our concern and tension that morning were rising by the minute, once again. Compounded by the fact that whatever plan had been put in place was not working, once again. It was clear to one triumvirate commander by late afternoon on the previous day that the latest plan was unravelling. Admiral Woodward regretted not intervening, 'I *could* have stopped it. *Should* have stopped it. *Didn't* stop it.'[63]

What about General Moore? The shambles unfolded only a few hundred yards away from him. The *Galahad*'s failure to get under way on time would have been bad enough as a single operation but this was the fourth failure in five days. Our prompt and safe arrival would secure his southern flank. If Admiral Woodward judged it a mess, why did General Moore not see it and intervene?

The guardsmen cooped up in the tank deck below were getting restless after we anchored in Port Pleasant and little happened. We officers had been taught about the 'fog of war' and 'logistic difficulties' at Sandhurst. They took a dimmer view that we were being 'f...d about—f...g again'.

Not only was our half of the understrength battalion at Bluff Cove's front line exposed, we were now in an even more precarious situation than they were—forward but still not dug in with the rest of the Welsh Guards as we had been expecting. Stuck on a boat with the enemy looking at us.

Having been told repeatedly in the previous few days that we would have to sail in the dark, it seemed inconceivable that the Royal Navy would be moving us to the front line in broad daylight if it was too high a risk. We were reassured by the thought of the Combat Air Patrols in the air; and the fact that we would receive an Air Raid Warning Red of any imminent air attack.

There was still no one in the bay to meet us.

After about an hour of being at anchor—a golden hour wasted—an LCU (*Foxtrot 1*), jammed with ammunition boxes from *Tristram* pulled in alongside the lowered stern gate. *Tristram* (I read later) had arrived from San Carlos the day before, a day late—with a cargo of mainly artillery ammunition. It had not been fully offloaded overnight, even though a large part of its intended cargo had been stowed last minute on *Galahad*—16 Field Ambulance and the Rapier Air Defence unit. The slow loading of the Field Ambulance was the main cause of the seven-hour delay in *Galahad's* departure from Falkland Sound and the reason why we now found ourselves at Fitzroy rather than Bluff Cove—and in broad daylight rather than at night.

A number of logistics officers stepped from *Foxtrot 1* and walked into the hull of the *Galahad* where he met Welsh Guards Majors Sayle and Bremner, and me. The LCU obviously was prepared neither for our arrival nor our transport to Bluff Cove.

Sayle pointed out to one of these service officers in simple, if caustic language, that three previous attempts by the Royal Navy to take us forward had already failed and, now on the fourth attempt in a civilian ship, we had been taken to the wrong place. Mindful of his unequivocal orders from General Moore and our direct commander Colonel Rickett to land at Bluff Cove and not under any circumstances to be separated from our kit, he made it clear that we expected to be landed there as soon as possible with all our equipment. Getting fighting troops along with all our firepower at the same time, by the quickest means possible, to an under-strength battalion was the obvious over-riding military priority.

Three nights before, one of the amphibious officers present had himself commanded *Intrepid's* four LCUs taking the Scots Guards to Bluff Cove during their long stormy passage after Captain Dingemans dropped them unceremoniously mid-sea off Lively Island, 50 miles from Bluff Cove. Two nights before, this major had also encountered the first half of the Welsh Guards as they landed at Bluff Cove.

The officer, however, seemed not to understand our urgency in us getting to our fellow Welsh Guardsmen on the front line. I was used to dealing with transport officers in Berlin and Crossmaglen. This seemed different. Whilst I didn't contribute to the discussion, I was present throughout.

That a major troop move to the front line had both been interrupted and diverted to address auxiliary issues at Fitzroy and allocated only a single LCU was simply unbelievable to us.

The smokescreen that has subsequently been thrown up around this ill-tempered exchange masks the fundamental point that, at daybreak, not one but two ships found themselves anchored next to one another at Port Pleasant: *Galahad* laden with troops, *Tristram* with ammunition—and there was only one LCU for offloading.

Even then, an empty LCU waiting for our arrival—6:50am that day, an hour and a half before sunrise at 7.52am—could have moved the three hundred and fifty Welsh Guards and their kit to Bluff Cove before the air attacks took place some seven hours later. The distances involved were small. Where the first half of the Welsh Guards had landed at Bluff Cove nearly thirty hours before was three miles north as the crow flies from the *Galahad*'s anchorage. An LCU routinely moves at about 10mph and it would have taken about an hour by sea around the Fitzroy headland via the 'Z' curve. A faster 'full speed ahead' can be coaxed out of the LCU's engines, if necessary—as Crispin discovered, it was the night 3 Commando landed at San Carlos as recorded by Brigadier Thompson.[64]

It was even more of a smokescreen than we thought at the time. Only ten hours earlier, there had been six LCUs at Port Pleasant/Fitzroy: more than enough to get everyone to where they had been ordered to go with plenty of time to spare. But, by the time we arrived only one had remained there. It bears repeating that if the *Sir Galahad* had made the night-time journey to Bluff Cove all of the Guards and equipment would have moved in the dark. As he and everyone else knew, the Argentine Air Force did not have the capability to attack at night.

The upshot was that the LCU departed to off-load the *Tristram* ammunition. Major Sayle went to get his orders confirmed. Sayle asked the captain for use of *Galahad*'s communications and, in his words, 'the orders came and they were: to go in the LCU round to Bluff Cove in two groups.'

As a result of the command vacuum that had arisen after the standoff, the colonel of the Medical Corps pulled rank on Major Sayle, his junior in the Army hierarchy, when the empty LCU returned at last. Taking two groups of guardsmen to Bluff Cove would have taken three hours, or possibly a bit less, and he wanted to wait no longer. The field ambulance had numerous vehicles and an array of heavy kit—all good life saving stuff such as generators, large tents and oxygen canisters. There were still some ambulance troops left to move the equipment. It was a short distance to shore.

We were extremely unhappy. I didn't understand on the day and still don't understand why the Royal Navy decided to load all these units with different destinations onto *Galahad* in this way.

When finally the empty LCU was available to get us, rather than anyone else, ashore with our equipment to Bluff Cove as ordered by General Moore, we began the off-loading of our troops.

Unfortunately, the front landing gate on the single LCU malfunctioned for some reason. Instead of the quick loading into the landing craft through *Galahad*'s stern gate it meant all the kit had to be taken up on deck first and the guardsmen loaded into the craft down scramble nets rather than walk along the ramp to the LCU. It took another hour.

It was at this point that *Galahad* was attacked.

There was no prior air raid warning.

Generals throughout history have sought to visit their troops on the eve of battle. At the same time as Woodward was becoming deeply worried, General Moore was holding a conference at his HQ on *Fearless* far to the rear, unaware of any of the difficulties at Fitzroy until the conference was interrupted later with news of the successful Argentine attacks.

It is frustrating and depressing to consider what might have been achieved that day in following General Moore's orders even with just a single landing craft—the lost opportunities to move us to Bluff Cove.

What two LCU landing craft would have been able to do is one of those thoughts I have to fight from my mind at four o'clock in the morning—even now.

13

10:26am, 8th June

At 10.26am local time, three hours and fifteen minutes after *Galahad* anchored next to *Tristram*, the Argentinian Airforce were informed of the presence in Port Pleasant of two large ships and a number of smaller ones. Argentine soldiers on top a nearby mountain radioed their Port Stanley HQ. On the northern flank a Royal Marines electronic warfare troop on Mount Kent intercepted their message. Like many other things, it is not clear what the hold-up was but the vital information was not passed on to Moore's staff on the Flagship before the attacks happened—almost three hours after the Argentine radio signal was sent.

Tristram had actually been spotted the day before by Argentine soldiers on Mount Harriet, situated at an equidistant 7 miles from Bluff Cove and Port Stanley.[65] The second sighting on 8th June, however, suggested to the Argentines that something bigger was afoot—a mass movement of troops towards the Argentinian positions at Port Stanley for D-Day. It confirmed that Britain's main assault to capture Port Stanley was imminent and would come from the southern flank.

The Argentine generals sniffed an opportunity and its air force sprang into action. Its military leaders had been on tenterhooks since they had lost Goose Green. 8th June looked like a unique opportunity to inflict substantial losses on British troops before they attacked the garrison.

Eight Skyhawks (a US-made light attack aircraft) from 5th Fighter Group and six Daggers (an Israeli made variant of the French Mirage) from 6th Fighter Group were loaded with bombs and scrambled from Río Gallegos, a military airfield on the Argentine coast at the same latitude as the Falklands. Both aircraft types were armed with parachute-delayed bombs—their mission to attack *Tristram* and *Galahad* in Port Pleasant, *Bahia Agradable* in Spanish. The first planes took off with an hour and a half of the message reaching Rio Gallegos. It was a massive effort (including a later, second wave of planes), involving according to the Argentines no fewer than three military airstrips: Río Gallegos, as well as San Julián and Río Grande, respectively situated south and north of the Falklands latitude.

Three Skyhawks (among them the flight leaders of the groups) and a Dagger turned back for various mechanical reasons.

In a wave a few minutes ahead of the Skyhawks and Daggers, four Mirages (the more advanced French-made version) from 8th Fighter Group were tasked to make a dummy low-level attack along the north coast of the islands to create the impression that the main anchorage in Falkland Sound or the forward base at Teal Inlet (both well-protected by Rapiers) were under threat—with the aim of attracting the attention of the Harrier Combat Air Patrols (CAPs) and their fighter controllers aboard the carriers. As soon as they thought the British had fallen for the trick they were to break off and return to base.

The Daggers aborted their mission to Port Pleasant when they spotted the frigate *HMS Plymouth* in Falkland Sound—an opportunity target as the Argentine air force's goal was to derail what they saw as the build-up of British troops towards Port Stanley. They turned to attack. *Plymouth* was hit by four 1000lbs bombs and badly damaged but none of the bombs exploded—no one was killed. The Daggers all made it home.

All Britain's CAP Harriers, including the pair earmarked to protect the landings at Port Pleasant/Fitzroy, had concentrated on the northern coast to see off the Mirages. The Mirages, content that the Harriers and their controllers had fallen for their ruse, turned hard west to escape. They also all made it home.

The Mirages didn't swoop out of nowhere for the Task Force. Our early warning system had been triggered the moment they first appeared within radar range. *HMS Exeter*, the picquet (early warning) ship, had sounded 'Air Raid Warning Red' some minutes before the diversionary Mirages appeared over Falklands air space.

Catastrophically, however, the message didn't reach or wasn't heard by *Tristram* or *Galahad* (more on this later). Two of the protection layers—Air Raid Warnings and CAP Harriers—around them had vanished without anyone in Port Pleasant realising it. The absence of the air-raid warning thus meant that the third layer—the five minutes it would take for the Bofors teams to man their turrets on the two ships and our machine guns to be set up on deck of *Galahad*—had also failed.

That left five Skyhawks looking for unsuspecting and therefore unprotected prey in Port Pleasant. They made a beeline for us in seconds and attacked with 500lbs bombs and 30mm cannon fire at 1.05 pm local time according to their records, 1.10pm according to British records. *Tristram* had few people on deck, but Welsh Guards were at that exact moment trooping up and crowding *Galahad*'s deck to load *Foxtrot 1* from above as the LCU's landing gate had stopped working.

The LCU, by sheer luck, was hidden behind *Galahad*'s hulk and invisible to the attacking Skyhawks.

Instead of taking us to Bluff Cove, it was undamaged and now started taking injured troops into Fitzroy.

Without hesitation the first Skyhawk aimed for us—at low-level, we could see the pilots' flying helmets. As we describe, they were bullseye hits even though the bombs slow-burnt rather than exploded. The five kept at nearly wave-top height to escape British troops firing back—those who could at any rate from shore and a few troops on board both ships. All Skyhawks made it home.

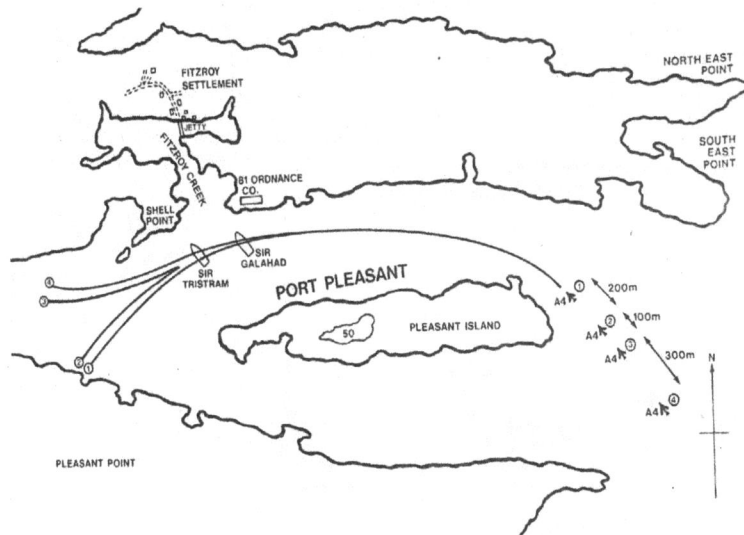

Admiral Woodward, triumvirate Falklands sea commander, observes in his memoirs, 'I suppose it was a ground-attack pilot's dream—two sitting ducks with none of the risk of missile, shell and bullet defences to face.'[66] After the 1.05pm attack, two additional formations of four Skyhawks each were despatched from Rio Gallegos as the Argentines tried to make the most of their unanticipated good fortune.

When I myself arrived ashore, I reported to Major Sayle. He handed me a rifle and some ammunition, a few minutes before the first new group of four Skyhawks attempted to attack troops around Fitzroy. As Middlebrook records, they were met with a hail of fire from every type of infantry weapon and functioning Rapiers.

It was rather satisfying for us to be firing back properly. The aircraft promptly broke off their attack—three of the four were badly damaged and made it back to their base by the skin of their teeth.

Later, by sheer chance, the second group spotted LCU *Foxtrot 4* on her way back from Goose Green—attacking the small landing craft with bombs and cannon fire. The crew of six were all killed.

It is some small comfort that within seconds of this attack a pair of marauding Harriers despatched three of the four Skyhawks. The first was blown out of the sky by a Sidewinder missile. The second was cut in half by a Sidewinder. The third, attempting through violent manoeuvre to escape a Sidewinder on its tail, crashed into the shore. All three Argentine pilots were killed. The fourth managed to get away, making rendezvous with a Hercules tanker which escorted him back to base.

14

EYEWITNESS: CAPTAIN JAN KOOPS

Air Raid Warning Red

In the process of off-loading, I was in a line of guardsmen crossing the mess room at the rear of the boat. From nowhere, Air Raid Warning Red was announced loudly over the Tannoy system. At this point time stood still as the ear-splitting roar of jet engines was closely followed by the devastating explosion of three 500lbs bombs ripping through the superstructure of *Sir Galahad*. I was a matter of feet away from one of the bombs as it tore its way through the mess room; the kinetic energy blasting me off my feet. The fireball that followed burnt everything in its path.

The diesel tanks caught fire and the ship was engulfed in flames and thick black smoke. In the darkness and surrounding carnage of the mess room, I got to my feet and took a breath, filling my lungs with an acrid mixture of burning plastic and diesel fumes. I choked on this lethal mix. My lungs, sensing this life-threatening lack of oxygen, instinctively caused me to sink to the floor where I was again able to breathe, quickly pulling a piece of clothing across my mouth and nose. I shouted out for everyone to do the same. My fellow rugby-team member Dai Graham's voice rang out above the mayhem, indicating where the exit was. Along with others in the room, I moved towards his voice, pausing whilst Guardsman Grimshaw 17, who had lost part of his leg, was pulled from the room.

Stepping out into the open air, the striking beauty of the clear blue sky was a breath-taking contrast to the pain and destruction that had been inflicted upon us. I ran to the foredeck where I gathered a few non-commissioned officers and instructed them to get the injured off the boat as a priority, into the landing craft alongside.

We had not trained for a situation like this. With the inferno blazing inside, igniting mortar shells that exploded against the hull on which the men were standing, it was a feat of extreme discipline and selfless bravery which enabled them to calmly assist the wounded, some in extraordinary pain, down the netting into the landing craft alongside or subsequently into helicopters and onto inflatable life-rafts.

Time was difficult to gauge but after what seemed a long and distressing period of helping casualties and trying not to think about the prospects of the ship blowing up completely, or another attack, the decks suddenly were empty. I was concerned that someone might have been left behind beneath the debris on the deck and was conducting a final check when I became aware of another officer nearby. Much of our clothing had gone to the casualties—I noticed he had just a shirt on his top half. He ran towards me, 'Jan, it's time to go.'

Having done all that we could, we departed the boat by climbing down the scramble netting at the foredeck onto a waiting mexeflote.

Tragically, 49 men were killed in that shattering hour of devastation—38 of them our own close friends and colleagues, the experience of which is burned deep into my inner subconscious.

From that day to this, a day has not passed without me in some way remembering and reflecting on those who did not return.

15

EYEWITNESS: HUGH BODINGTON
2nd Lieutenant No 1 Platoon, The Prince of Wales's Company,
1st Battalion Welsh Guards

Hugh, or 'Bod' as he is usually known to his brother officers, sent me this account for inclusion in the book. His platoon suffered three dead and twenty-two wounded out of twenty-seven, over ninety per cent casualties.

After the storms and heavy seas of that week, 8th June was a bright, calm, and sunny day when the stern ramp of *Sir Galahad* was lowered shortly after sunrise at about 8am local time. There was not a cloud in the sky and we could see for the first time the Jurassic dinosaur backs of the dominant hillsides and high ground of East Falkland, and once again breathe in the fresh air of the South Atlantic rather than the conditioned air of the tank deck.

We were fully loaded and ready, with a full complement of ammunition and spare radio batteries in our bergens and webbing; and our combat clothing was stuffed with military accoutrements. Weighing in at over 100lbs when on our backs, it was heavy—but we had become accustomed to it and it was certainly bearable by the strong Welshmen of the Prince of Wales's Company. This plus the rough boggy moorland and penetrating winter weather would further test us before we were to meet the Argentinians—but we were on the cusp of our moment to 'close with and engage the enemy in all terrains and all weathers' at our nation's bidding—the culmination of our training over the last nine months. We had been issued with oversize maps, difficult to keep dry or to consult in the wind and rain without ruining them. We were pumped up now. Number One Platoon, The Prince of Wales's Company was to be first in the order of march. We were proud of that and I took reassurance from my excellent section commanders (each eager to be selected for the SAS) who would all help to keep us on the right bearing on the next tab.

We had been lined up, sitting on our bergens, ready to disembark from the tank deck facing the stern ramp since well before first light. But the night before as we settled down in the tank deck the engines were silent while additional troops and equipment were loaded on the ship. They roared into life at about 10pm—too late for darkness all the way. By then we were used to delays, more delays followed by changes of plan and more changes of plan. We had time a plenty to chat amongst ourselves about all manner of things and to keep each other going. The banter was as good as ever—if there was a national banter prize, we would have won it hands down.

After several hours, the disembarkation plan changed again, as the landing craft that we would use had a malfunctioning front ramp. So, the stern ramp of the LSL closed once again and we were back in the murky light of the tank deck. The ship's staircases were too narrow and steep to take the heavy, wide loads on our backs; and nets and cranes were therefore used to lift them from the centre of the tank deck to the landing craft that had moved alongside. The deck roof opened to allow the crane to operate and once again we could see the bright blue sky as a stark backdrop to the Chinese crew that were clad from head to ankle in bright orange on deck for the crane operation. We turned around and lined up to disembark via the starboard stairs to the top deck and then climb down a scramble net draped over the side of the ship. As I had been in the tank deck with my men all morning, I did not know the route to the top deck (and it was surprisingly easy to take a wrong turn on your way up these unfamiliar ships), so took up the offer by No 3 Platoon Commander 2nd Lieutenant Crispin Black (who I think had sneaked on deck for a fag a couple of times) for them to lead the way to the top deck. As Numbers 3 and 2 platoon respectively filed up the stairs, we were shuffling nearer to the tank deck's side doorway to the staircase.

At about 1pm local time, the shocking, overwhelming all-consuming noise of unexpected jets flying close overhead coincided with distant cries of 'take coveerr!' and the sight of the man in orange way up above literally hitting the deck. The last time I ducked for a fly past was aged 8 at the Yeovilton Air Show and felt a fool; this time, instinctively, in front of my platoon, I hesitated, which gave me that unique moment to see a 500lbs bomb dive in through the top deck crane opening mid-ships—a direct hit.

Accelerating into cover, ironically behind a 45 Gallon oil drum, I was convinced that this was to be my last action. The ensuing massive explosion then dominated all senses for a few moments; and as the ringing retreated and the thick choking black smoke enveloped us, I was unable to see, nor hear, nor breathe, nor feel; and experienced an out of body sensation, confused whether I was still alive or experiencing the after-life. As we got to our feet, through the black smoke I could see Pentecostal tongues of fire all around me. The cries of pain and shock increasingly penetrated the blankets of smoke. All was not well. There was a surge of movement towards the starboard door and I was swept along in the crowd of desperate men, all aiming to survive.

Military order began to reassert itself over this infernal chaos as we, first of all, called for calm and order to get people through the door and up the stairs as fast as possible. The tank deck was clearly the wrong place to be; if we had taken a hole below the waterline, we would sink and we would be the first to go down, but immediately we needed air and we needed to get away from the mortar ammunition that was stacked in boxes on the tank deck. The idea of the effect of secondary detonations in that relatively confined space leading to the stern ramp where my guardsmen were was unthinkable. We also needed to be prepared to return fire on whatever came in the next wave of attacks. The damage seemed to be forward in mid ship.

What I did not realise at the time was that the most significant damage was in fact more towards the stern, in the narrower stern tunnel where my platoon and the mortar platoon were, and that I had been saved from serious injury or death from the blast of another 500lbs bomb to my rear, which ripped past us just around the corner. My buddy pair, my 52mm Mortar Man Guardsman Williams 25, was on my shoulder and seemed to be OK, so off we went in the surge up the stairs. As my senses returned, I felt OK and prepared myself for the next round of the fight for survival, whatever it was to be.

We held onto each other's webbing, as we groped our way up the stairs, gasping for air. But there was a blockage caused by bomb damage—and a clear, calm message came back down the line saying that we would try another way. They did and it worked. I thought of *The Poseidon Adventure* film, when the ship turns turtle and the survivors have to climb up to the hull. I hoped to God that would not happen to us now. Within a few minutes we were up on the top deck, clear of the choking black smoke and I knew then that we had a chance of survival. I checked behind me to find Sgt Lewis 01 of HQ Company. The skin of his face was detached and hanging down. Instinctively and lost for other words, I asked if he was alright. Instinctively he responded that he was fine.

Then we got stuck into treating the wounded from across the battalion; I recall my GPMG gunner Guardsman Grimshaw, whose severed leg took many more than the issued one first field dressing; Lance-Corporal Cordy struck dumb by shock (and for those that know this giant of a man, you would not believe this to be possible) and Guardsman Davies 39 coping with a large piece of metal sticking out of his foot, through the boot and galoshes that we had been issued. It must have been flying at speed to have got in there in the first place. All in pain, these men were brave and solid.

They were either flown out by courageous helicopter crews, who were in action before I got to the deck and if not, they were put on to life rafts to start their journey to recovery, starting some 8000 miles from home. I saw my platoon sergeant, Sergeant Jennings being attended to and evacuated; our Company Sergeant Major (Williams 500) was also in a bad way. But the true devastation did not reveal itself until we got to the shore and we were able to muster the company and see just how many had gone under the care of the medics and who had not. When I left the deck, that black smoke was billowing and gushing out of the doorway through which I had just passed and there was no way of going back in without some form of breathing apparatus, which some crew did have.

Having cleared the casualties, I scrambled down the net and on to a round, inflatable life craft, with various wounded and shocked members of the battalion on board including our attached Master Chef—four of his chefs had been killed. To my mind, would the ship sink and if so, would it take us down with it; or would it keel over and flatten us; or would it explode and consume us in a fireball? Fortunately, none of the above happened—and equipped with only one paddle we endeavoured to get ourselves away from the ship and to the shore just 600 metres away. I was tempted to swim it but having lost my bergen to the blaze I only had what I stood up in. Not a sensible option. The helicopters came back and helped us on our way with their downwash. This was great quick thinking by the air crews and provided so much relief to us.

I took great comfort from seeing my first fellow officer alive, Peter Owen Edmunds, when I reached the shore, for I had thought that No 3 Company may have taken the full blast. Little did I realise until we mustered a few minutes later that it was in fact our end of the tank deck that had formed the killing zone: at that point Guardsman Williams 25 was the only other unwounded member of my platoon I could find. I tried to go back to the ship but was told no. The risks were too great. Another wave of attacks came in and attention began to switch to what next with what we have.

I took over a depleted No 2 Platoon from Johnny Strutt who had been evacuated as a casualty—although luckily, he came back to us a few days later once he'd been sorted out by the medics—bruised, scratched, with his arm in a sling, dressed in a brand-new naval uniform that didn't fit.

In the days that followed, we learned from the various casualty stations both onshore and offshore that No 1 Platoon had suffered 22 wounded. Miserably, we were to discover some days later that three of mine were not amongst those evacuated, did not survive and were later to be buried at sea with the others on *Galahad*, which was sunk as a war grave. Lance Sergeant Carlyle, Guardsman Edwards 32 and Guardsman Marks would have taken the full force of the blast with members of the mortar platoon in the rear ramp approach tunnel, just behind my position.

May God look after them and their families for ever. Simon Weston is the best-known survivor of people from this area of the ship and his spirit during his recovery has inspired many across the world who have found themselves badly burned.

The Paras at Fitzroy were very good to us, throwing medics at our plight and helping with the ongoing evacuation and withdrawal. There was a secondary air attack, but on this occasion, various units' air defences were better prepared and many claimed hits. We could see that the Rapier Detachment could not lock on to the target and we felt exposed. A sip from my commanding officer's whisky flask was most welcome and I traded my galoshes in with a Para officer with trench feet for some cigarettes, to calm my nerves, as darkness fell around the sheep sheds of Fitzroy.

We flew back to *Fearless* that night in a clattering Sea King—our fifth ship in as many days—just where we did not want to be, but at least this time we were under the protection of their missiles which were launched at Argentine aircraft during our short stay; and we had the luxury of flash masks (a white cotton hood and gauntlets worn by all Royal Naval and Fleet Auxiliary personnel that protects against short duration intense burning), just in case. If only we had those on *Galahad*, our casualties could have been so much lighter.

We were so proud to deploy with the Task Force and eager to play our part, whatever that was to be, as the campaign unfolded—but our preference was to be in on the action. We were that but with a price. I personally had felt prepared for the worst, but not for so many of my men to die and to suffer.

Over my subsequent service I have learned and reflected that the air attack on *Galahad* was the result of a Joint Warfare military operation (involving all three armed services) being prosecuted poorly, with a litany of errors running through and across the chains of command.

The Welsh Guards more than anyone else paid the price. We should not forget the lessons nor the many people—soldiers, families, communities—who have suffered loss. May God bless them all. Cymru am Byth.

16

EYEWITNESS: JOHNNY STRUTT

2nd Lieutenant No 2 Platoon, The Prince of Wales's Company,
1st Battalion Welsh Guards

What happened to Johnny was recounted the day after to Max Hastings the London *Evening Standard*'s war correspondent in the Falklands. At the time they were on board *HMS Intrepid* where some of the walking wounded were being treated.

Max Hastings watched as hour after hour helicopter pilots ferried survivors to the doctors on warships in the Carlos Bay anchorage. Here is his report:

A corporal of the Welsh Guards, saved from the blazing *Sir Galahad* said to me 'I was told to get down and the next thing I knew I was on fire, like.'

In a seaman's mess aboard an assault ship, blackened and bandaged men sat and lay on stretchers as their injuries—and, above all, burns—were dressed.

A gaunt young man masked in mud and scratches nodded, and it was only when he spoke that it was possible to recognise him as a subaltern of the Welsh Guards to whom I had been talking in the wardroom two nights earlier. He wore a blanket wrapped around his shoulders—one of them dislocated—and sipped coffee as he described the ship's unloading, so violently interrupted by the air attack. 'Everybody was longing to get on to dry land'.

Next door to him a Guardsman stood with both arms plunged in a bucket of iced water to soften the pain of his burns yet all of them spoke of the extraordinary cheerfulness with which their comrades had endured their ordeal. 'I shall never forget the way everyone was joking on their way to the dressing station,' said Guards subaltern, 22-year-old Johnny Strutt.

Lt Strutt described how he was 'lifted about 10 feet by the explosion and woke to find myself lying covered by a great mound of stuff. Then I was helped up and escorted to one of the boats.'... This morning Lt Strutt, completely cleaned up, was having breakfast in the wardroom with only his shoulder in a sling to show that he had suffered any misfortune.

In the book Max Hastings wrote after the war Johnny is described as 'a charming, boyish-looking subaltern of twenty-two.'[67] He had turned twenty-two on 4th June at San Carlos.

17

'The valiant never taste of death but once.'
Julius Caesar, Act 2, Scene 2

This is a famous line by Caesar refusing to be afraid the night before the Ides of March. His views on war are still important to modern soldiers. *De bello gallico*, his account of campaigns in Gaul (conquered in double quick time with great skill—except Asterix's village) was often quoted by the directing staff at the Army Staff College, Camberley. As a young officer, Julius Caesar had received one of Rome's highest decorations for bravery in action and, as a more senior officer, he was never afraid of the front line. But if he ever did say something like this in real life, I suspect he knew it not to be true.

It certainly wasn't true for me on 8th June 1982. Each time death came intimately close, I found that I went quite far along the process of dying—even if each time fate failed by a slim margin to administer its *coup de grace*.

A few moments after I exited the ship's superstructure on the port side, alongside Johnny Strutt—No 2 Platoon's commander—my platoon radio operator grabbed me on the shoulder. Hard.

'It's red, sir, air raid warning red.' I replied, 'It can't be. It can't be. We can't go from no air threat to red, just like that,' and reached for the handset. That was when the tremendous overhead roar suddenly occurred.

Accompanied by a strange rattling noise. I could tell it was a plane but my immediate instinct was one of relief—it was a Harrier accelerating out to sea to intercept the raid. Only when something came out of its belly did it dawn on me what was going on. There was more rattling which I realised was cannon fire hitting the ship. I could see some of it was tracer—bullets with a small pyrotechnic charge in the base that light up like a firework when fired. The planes firing them could see where they were going. Those being fired at could see them coming towards them. A most uncomfortable feeling. It was only then that I reacted.

There's something impersonal about bombs, something very personal about being strafed—infamy, infamy, they've all got in for me. Cary Grant's Roger Thornhill clearly felt the same way in *North by Northwest*.

The blast coming through the door we had just left hit with tremendous force. I must admit, I thought it was game over, or in Welsh Guards speak

'Good night, Vienna.'

Other explosions kicking off, screaming, men emerging from the door behind in the most awful state, the smell of burning flesh—I just couldn't see how we were going to make it. The military side of my brain was also whirring—we had been uneasy but mainly about being delayed and messed around (yet again).

We had experienced an air raid the day before on *HMS Fearless*, quickly seen off by the Royal Navy. But it wasn't a top priority. And we had been ordered some hours earlier to get our General Purpose Machine Gun (GPMG) teams together so they could line the decks. Six rifle platoons with three GPMGs each would have meant nine each side of the ship—one every forty feet or so.

But our company commander checked with the captain of *Sir Galahad*, who said they weren't necessary and we were stood down. I was also acutely aware that I had not seen or heard the Rapier battery in the anchorage, a highly effective short range anti-aircraft missile system, engage any of the aircraft that had attacked us.

In summary, the military side of my brain concluded that something had gone very wrong and we were sitting ducks for further attacks—if we managed to survive the initial strike which, frankly, wasn't looking good.

But at this stage there was plenty to do—try to find the rest of my platoon, help with the casualties, give morphine and try to look as though things were not as dire as they were.

First time, it wasn't easy to remain calm and in absolute control of oneself. The non-military, non-Welsh Guards part of my brain was telling me in the strongest possible terms to get the hell out of there. But my platoon sergeant's words came strongly to me, 'Remember sir, we're all relying on you.'

Snatches of Shakespeare also came into my mind but I pushed them away. The only useful words at such a time are the Lord's Prayer in English and or Welsh muttered gently under the breath so the guardsmen around me couldn't hear. Roman Catholics have just the thing in the Hail Mary. Comforting, instinctive, functional, fortifying, used wonderfully by Robert Redford in *A Bridge Too Far*.

At that point I looked down at the landing craft tied alongside. A number of casualties had found their way aboard and there was space for more—a slight comfort. It was the only way off for the badly wounded at that point except jumping for it. At least some of the wounded would survive.

The bombs dropped on us did not explode but instead deflagrated, a technical term for common or garden burning after their casings had split.

Not that we could tell the difference from where we were standing. The intense heat produced started to cook off mortar and artillery ammunition;

which in turn blew up the fuel tanks in the tank deck; which in turn set off the explosive mixture inside the bombs; and so on. But that's why there were two or three seconds between the bombs being dropped and the blast—as if they had paused to catch their breath before unleashing their destruction.

I was standing opposite Johnny just outside the door to the superstructure on the port side. Close, very close to him. Trumper's Extract of West Indian Limes close. He was hurled up and into the bulkhead with such force it dislocated his shoulder. But the blast left me on my feet. Something hot, nasty, and fast pinged past my head. I dread to think what it was, certainly not a cricket ball or that staple of mess rowdiness and the Drones Club—the bread roll.

I thought at the time how odd the blast was—random, fickle, merciless. Recently, while researching background for my latest thriller *The Venice Archive*, set mainly in Venice but partly in Berlin, I came across on the internet the best example I have seen of its random nature—a colour coded map of the briefing room in the *Wolfsschanze* on 20th July 1944 that shows why Hitler wasn't killed by Colonel von Stauffenberg's bomb, and why others further away from the fateful briefcase perished.

By this time the non-Guards part of my brain was screaming at me to get out, get away. I caught sight of Captain Koops helping to carry casualties further along the deck. Captain of our recently victorious rugby-football team, Koops was six foot five (a couple of inches taller than me) and an all-round sportsman. One of these people who is just good with a ball and wonderful to watch on the pitch. Rumour had it that despite being educated elsewhere, he had been drafted in the year before I joined to play in both the Welsh Guards Field Game Team and our Harrow Football team. Jan told me the story was 'urban legend'.[68]

Captain Koops moved calmly amongst the guardsmen and the wounded. I was re-assured—at least someone was in charge. Perhaps I might make it after all. At that moment one of my guardsmen came up to me, bent double and in considerable pain, 'Are we going to be OK, sir?' I checked him over. 'Yes, of course. But get off as quickly as you can, anyway that you can. Now.' He was bruised and battered more than anything else—possibly a bergen had been blown into him. And he brought the welcome news that Sergeant B and the rest of my men who had been strung out behind me on the companion way had managed to get out.

Maybe, just maybe, there was going to be enough time. And then another huge explosion from the tank deck. I could feel the shudder going through my boots. The deck in some parts was hot, getting hotter. We were loading casualties onto helicopters and life-rafts with even greater urgency, if that were possible. More explosions, sinister rumbling from below. The decks were heating up even more, the paint beginning to blister. Would the ship just go up in one huge explosion? Would I be blown into small pieces or become a human fireball? Would it capsize? Would I drown in freezing water trapped under tons of grey painted steel?

Getting a grip second time round was more difficult. Despite the heat from the fires and explosions and the physical exertions of casualty carrying I didn't feel hot. It was a fine day but cold with a strong westerly wind that helped blow the smoke away. I should have been sweating. But then I realised I only had my shirt on, open at the neck. My tie had gone with a casualty. I think I must have given it to a medic for a tourniquet.

And then the explosions started going off the boil. Less frequent, less force. The deck was still hot but not getting any hotter. Hot but stable was good news. I could also tell that a lot of the crew and soldiers had managed to get off one way or another. Most of the casualties had been evacuated, but there were still a few guardsmen and crew members queuing up for helicopters which were shifting them as quickly as they could.

Captain Koops was still somewhere on the deck. I'd seen him a couple of minutes before. Again, hopes were rising. Casualties away. Remaining troops and crew close to being picked up.

And then, other than the wind everything went quiet. I started to feel cold. I could see Captain Koops still there searching through mounds of debris making sure no one had been left behind. I thought we might have to jump for it or at least go down the scrambling net and swim ashore. I stopped by an orphaned Clansman radio that was propped up against a bollard chattering away. The dreaded words 'Air Raid Warning Red' repeated, again and again were coming out of its speaker—like listening to a slightly hysterical dalek.

It was the final blow. Given that the original warning arrived simultaneously with the enemy aircraft attacking us—all seemed lost. What was the point? The guardsmen had gone. Maybe it would just be a better idea to sit down with a cigarette. A large gin and tonic would have been nice. Very large. Followed by a couple more. Maybe, I could retune the Clansman radio to pick up some Frank, or maybe Dean would have been more appropriate.

Grab one of the rifles lying on the deck. Go down with a few shots—just to keep the Argentine Naval Air Force on its toes. And wait the few moments before death arrived with some humour and dignity.

But there was no sign of any aircraft and the Scots Guards machine guns at Bluff Cove were silent. I ran towards Jan trying to look reasonably in control and hoping he wouldn't argue.

'Jan, it's time to go.'

We hightailed it to the side where to our relief a mexeflote, a floating steel platform with a small engine, had just arrived. Major Bremner, Company

Sergeant Major Neck, and Lance Sergeant Loveridge were in the process of clambering onto it. We followed quickly. I was cold and shivering. Partly the temperature, partly shock, partly fear, partly growing relief, but mainly because I was in shirtsleeves.

Major Bremner kindly handed me a spray-proof jacket. We headed for the shore. I didn't want to look back but I did, saying the Lord's Prayer under my breath.

Sceptical of religion at the time and slightly worn out by some of the more old-fashioned religious experiences of my schooling, I came to understand amongst other things that day that it is a strong human instinct to wrap dead bodies—out of respect perhaps, in dignified farewell, or as protection on the journey to the afterlife. The Egyptians started it—indeed perfected it. The Romans wrapped their dead and placed a coin in the mouth to pay Charon the ferryman who took the dead across the River Lethe into the underworld. It is customary in most countries whatever the major religions.

I remember watching a moving interview a few years back—the President of one of the Baltic countries was talking just after visiting the Queen at Buckingham Palace. The President was reminiscing about the ghastliness of the Communist years and then went further back in her life to in January/February 1945—as a young girl she and her family were attempting to flee across the frozen tundra on foot during one of the toughest winters in history. During their trek her younger sister, a babe in arms, died of exposure and malnutrition. The family stopped to bury her in the frozen ground, if they could. Her mother wanted to wrap the dead child in a blanket—but blankets were in short supply and vital for the survival of the remaining family members.

Somehow at the back of my mind I had been uncomfortable about the way I was dressed. It wasn't a Guards concern—shirt sleeve order is a mandated uniform in the summer months except on state ceremonial. And given the circumstances what could I have done. Combat jackets and Army woolly pullies as I mentioned earlier made serviceable improvised stretchers. My slow, reluctant shedding of my kit had been for the wounded.

The bombing and strafing of *Galahad* had been a group experience with many others—not all of them Welsh Guards. Those who were able to did 'bother themselves' working together to save lives, soften intense physical pain and get the wounded and everyone else the hell out of there. There are no 'outsiders' in these circumstances—not because of attitude or personal preference, but because of discipline—group and personal, humanity, and above all, courage.

Functioning, trying to help, trying to lead, is one thing. Instinct and training all play their part. But death is a personal matter. A crowd is not company in those circumstances—even if the crowd comprises friends and comrades and other servicemen bound together by strong bonds of loyalty to Queen and country.

For me on that day death had become a tease. Three times in forty-five minutes it looked for sure. I faced it in reasonably good order if (very) intermittent sangfroid qualifies for that description, remaining mindful throughout of my military duties.

It might have been the wind, the temperature, or the fact that I was plain terrified, but, as death approached—seemed certain—just a shirt on my back felt too thin for a shroud.

18

EYEWITNESS: CAPTAIN KOOPS

Upsetting an Apple Cart
Return to Blighty, Sunday 11th July, 1982

Those of us who had been on *Galahad* were taken on board *SS Canberra*—a P&O ocean liner in ordinary circumstances—where we were to be the guarding force of the broken and dispirited Argentine prisoners of war whom we offloaded in Puerto Madryn, Argentina.

I spoke with many of the prisoners and it was very evident that their history books quite clearly describe 'Las Malvinas' as Argentine territory. We obviously could not agree on the rights of ownership of the islands, but we did agree that taking it by force was not the solution. The guardsmen were good with them. I think, as always, rugby was a great uniter. Argentinians are a rugby playing people—as are the Welsh.

Canberra returned from Argentina to Port Stanley to load up with members of the Task Force to return home to the UK. The arrangements for our return to the UK were unclear and in this vacuum the men built up their hopes that they might be staying aboard for the homeward journey. This was not to be and the men were taken ashore to start the 'clearing up' of Port Stanley.

As mentioned previously, my commission was due to end. Therefore, during this disembarkation process our Commanding Officer came aboard to instruct me to stay aboard and journey home with the Marines of 3 Commando.

I said my goodbyes to the Prince of Wales's Company. It could not have been harder to find a starker finale to a career of active service—the Berlin Brigade protecting the western world's most isolated outpost; Crossmaglen countering terrorism in Ireland; and the Falklands fighting to free British subjects from the grip of an unpleasant fascist *junta*. Most guards officers' careers end with a smart dinner somewhere in London—mine ended with a few handshakes and best wishes 8000 miles from home.

The Marines quickly filled the decks of the *Canberra* and as we set sail on the ten-day journey, I was to be the only Guardsman on board. I was fortunate to befriend some of the junior Marine officers.

Together we started the unprompted process of filtering through the impact and meaning of our experiences. Exercise provided an important daily focus as we ran circuits of the deck followed by sit-ups, press-ups and a multitude of other exercises. Following this they would quietly recall and share some of the raw emotions experienced during the night-time attacks on the Argentine positions. The guts, bravery and expertise exhibited by all the infantry soldiers fighting through the Argentine defensive positions was humbling.

Canberra's Royal Navy Press Liaison Officer asked me to do an interview with Bob Bryant, one of the embedded journalists on board. A matter of hours after the interview I was called up to see the Senior Naval Officer—the larger-than-life Captain Christopher 'Beagle' Burne—to have an article written by Bob Bryant thrust into my hand. Incredulously, he asked me if I was happy for the article to be published.

I had been direct in my comments to Bob mentioning quite properly some of the points that are examined in this book and have been questioned and discussed amongst ourselves for forty years. But he had formed a very punchy piece around mis quotes and exaggerations concerning the bombing of *Sir Galahad* which, if released, would have only added further pain, anguish, and anger to families of the bereaved.

I was disappointed with the piece and told Captain Burne so. 'I suggest you do something about it, then.' I tracked down Bob Bryant in one of the bars and hauled him out, expressing to him very clearly my disappointment in the misrepresentation of my comments within the piece he had written. Together we penned a new piece to which I was happy to put my name. I'm not sure if it was ever published.

Without malice, I had upset the apple cart, which as the lone Guardsman, left me feeling isolated and vulnerable. It was clear that I needed to clarify my position, so I found the cabin of the Commander of 3 Brigade, Brigadier Julian Thompson. I knocked on his door and he invited me in, sat me down and poured me a gin and tonic. We had a long chat about my experiences during the war, with particular focus on the fiasco around the build up to and bombing of the *Galahad*.

As we ended our conversation, he sensitively and thoughtfully concluded that he and I had gone through two very different types of war. Royal Marine casualties had been extraordinarily light. Whilst he fully understood the frustration and impact of my experiences, he requested me not to talk further to any members of the press as he did not want anything to detract from the homecoming of the Royal Marines.

I respectfully pointed out that I had been asked by the Royal Navy press officer to give the interview. But added that I had no desire to have any further conversations with any members of the press corps on board. I was grateful and pleased that the brigadier had allowed me to openly clear the air with him, thus enabling me to relax and make the most of the remainder of the journey.

Thinking that this was the end of the matter, I was surprised when on the afternoon before we reached the Cornish coastline, I was again called up to see the Senior Naval Officer.

I was told that I was to be helicoptered off the ship in the morning with all my kit and flown into the Royal Naval Air Station at Culdrose, Cornwall. He allowed me to make a radio telephone call home to ask my parents to pick me up from there in the morning. I bless my devoted parents, who were expecting to meet me at Southampton not too far from our home in Sussex. They drove eight hours through the night to the tip of Cornwall to be standing on the tarmac to greet the arrival of the lone Sea King helicopter.

I stepped off the helicopter as the only passenger to a very emotional reception from my loving mother and my equally loving Dutch father, the survivor of two tours of duty with 320 (Netherlands Squadron) RAF Bomber Command in the Second World War.

Whilst this is a much-treasured memory of a deeply poignant moment, I was sad that it could not have taken place within the context of the wider homecoming. I had formed strong friendships with some Royal Marine officers for whom I had the greatest respect. It irked me then, and still does now, that the senior military officers on *Canberra* felt that they could not afford me the civility of sharing in the prize of the enormous public homecoming with which the ship was greeted into Southampton on 11th July 1982.

19

Stirrings

I took part in a documentary for the 25th anniversary in 2007. The producer was fair-minded, had known Hilarion at Balliol, and was genuinely interested in working out exactly what had been going on at Fitzroy on 8th June 1982. Others were also beginning to ask questions about the history that had been written about that day. Sadly, I myself was at that time still in blanking mode and not fully up to speed—not having read any of the published accounts.

The documentary researcher told me—a little reluctantly—that once the Royal Marine interviewees had got past their frustration at how the war turned out the way it did for them as minor participants in the land battles, they often moved on to criticising the Welsh Guards in intemperate and insulting terms. One key interviewee ranted so frequently about us that it was impossible to use his contribution in the programme.

It irked me, but I had myself noticed a rising tide of sniping at us. Reactions to the attacks on *Galahad* from those who did not experience them on the ship, or weren't there at all, can be complex. Most of us who survived the Argentine air attacks that day have experienced 'gaslighting'—being repeatedly told in subtle and less subtle ways how unprofessional or foolish we were; and that everything that happened to us was entirely of our personal making, even deserved.

Yet I have never heard any snide remarks over the years from the three Army units—2 and 3 Para and the Scots Guards—who did nearly all the land fighting down South. They had a grim time and bear losses, wounds, and sorrows of their own, which perhaps explains it.

3 Para: 23
2 Para: 19
Scots Guards (2SG): 8
45 Commando: 4
42 Commando: 2
Welsh Guards (1WG): 1

British casualties in the Falklands land battles by battalion

The most aggressive comments have always come from the Royal Marines units that experienced few casualties and were provided with the most generous resources.[69] By inverse proportion, however, it became clear to me in my research for this book that most history writing over the past four decades seems to have come from them. The Welsh Guards have come in for criticism down the years in the Naval and Marine memoirs with at times shrill protestations. The writing of this book elicited similar comments, discouraging its publication with the threat of negative stories about 'unhappy experiences' with the Welsh Guards. Or by threats that questioned whether our military training— which the Guards who were unharmed bravely put on display from *Galahad* when taking aim at the first wave of Skyhawks and very successfully to deter the second wave—could somehow have been different from other regiments.

Some of the accounts of us are just baffling. One Royal Marine was himself in Fitzroy the morning the Welsh Guards embarked on *Sir Galahad* in San Carlos. Yet I was amazed to read what he (not a witness in any way) writes about the atmosphere in San Carlos in a book called *Reasons in Writing* (1993).[70]

> The Welsh Guards embarked *content* in the *belief* that they would be dropped off first, and straight into Bluff Cove as *suggested* by a junior member of the Commodore's staff, which, *paradoxically*, confirmed the orders given by their own Commanding Officer as he left [HMS] Fearless earlier that day with the General's *promise* still fresh in his mind. [My italics.][71]

It is difficult to fathom what this passage is getting at with words like 'content', 'belief', 'suggested', 'promise' etc.

General Moore ordered the Scots and Welsh Guards to Bluff Cove and when the move of the second half of our battalion went awry on 6th, he gave orders to Colonel Rickett, and everyone else involved, for us to be taken to Bluff Cove on 7th June, the following day. It couldn't be more straightforward and less like Jane Austen. It is hard to picture anyone in a military chain of command who has an interest in paradoxes. Soldiers follow orders. Period, as the Americans say.

I was also surprised to read in one of the popular histories published soon after the war that the Welsh Guards were seven hours late embarking on *Galahad*, implying that it was epic tardiness by the Welsh Guards that led to the delayed sailing which in turn led to everything else. That such an error appeared in a published account was egregious, I thought, if not an insult to the memory of the battalion's 38 men who died, with its suggestion that the Welsh Guards were late, very late, for what turned out to be our own floating funeral pyre.

A moment's thought would have shown that this couldn't be true. We were transferred from *Fearless* to RFA *Sir Galahad* on the afternoon of 7th June as ordered by the amphibious staff on board the Flagship. There was no Army way of getting from one Royal Navy ship to another.

In a newly released confidential report in Kew, typed ten days after the event on 18th June, *Galahad*'s Captain Roberts confirms this in narrative, painstaking detail—taking stock of stores being loaded on his ship. He records the accurate loading timeline of his vessel in San Carlos on 7th June on three closely-typed pages alone.

His first orders from the amphibious staff that day were to sail no later than 5pm. Two hours before, by 3pm, the last of the two Welsh Guards companies were embarked—as were parts of 16 Field Ambulance. At 2pm parts for the Rapier batteries were on board. The latest to arrive, however, were Field Ambulance supplies. They did not arrive until 7:45pm and would take another two hours to load.[72] At 10pm, *Galahad* finally sailed. Stowed away on the tank deck, the 352 Welsh Guards had by then already been on board for at least seven hours as the first to arrive.

Such inaccuracies have a powerful effect, however. Historians, particularly those who have no first-hand experience of the Falklands during those days can, of course, only rely on what they are told by their military sources. And so, it leaves one to wonder how these basic but emotive errors of fact got incorporated into the public narrative of that day. We may never find out how these distortions arose exactly, but this one should also finally be expelled from all Falklands War histories.

20

The Southern Flank

Of the hundreds of thousands of recent words written about the Falklands War, few mention the findings of the official 23rd September 1982 Board of Inquiry into the loss of *Sir Tristram* and *Sir Galahad*. The Inquiry was ordered by Admiral Fieldhouse, Commander-in-Chief, Fleet, and even the first sections declassified fifteen years ago don't make comfortable reading for those involved in the decision-making of the tragedy—nor to those who were its victims.

A very important point to make is that there is not one word, or even faint hint of criticism, of the Welsh Guards on that day by the Board of Inquiry. This is not surprising. Today as then, following orders is the prime job description in the Army as well as the Royal Navy. Troops must go where they are ordered—'A' means 'A'. A shambles would follow if troops, companies, or platoons had room for invention or second-guessing clear front-line commands. They put their lives on the line, but have no say in the marching orders that are issued from military command centres etc—whether these orders were good or bad, or bore implications for other parts of the military. Not that you'd guess this from today's misleading orthodoxy of the events of 8th June.

Perhaps it is not surprising, however, that the Inquiry notwithstanding, a degraded story of the day has sprung up over these decades. The full proceedings—witness statements, supporting documents such as signals (secure electronic communications) and written operational orders, all the facts that form the basis of any investigation, remain secret to this day. The Welsh Guards did not even receive a copy of the Board's report in 1982. There was no official announcement about its declassification twenty five years after being treated as a state secret. It is heavily redacted, with the identities of key participants blanked out.[73] The bulk of the Inquiry's supporting redacted documents, annexes and maps were only recently declassified at Kew. Its only after some four decades that these establish the basic facts.

Straight off the bat, apart from being effectively just the tip of the iceberg, there are three crucial caveats to Admiral Fieldhouse's Board of Inquiry that were true even before he formed the board on 21st July 1982. Given that 39 of the 49 men killed in the raid of 8th June were Army soldiers (all but one from the Welsh Guards), the Army should have been properly included in a process that involved them. Specifically, from my experience at the Ministry of Defence, an Army infantry full colonel with operational experience should have sat on the board. As it was the six Board members were selected by Fieldhouse from the Royal Navy (3), Royal Fleet Auxiliary (2), and Navy Ministry of Defence (1).[74] There were no 'outsiders'.

On the face of it, the Inquiry doesn't appear quite a 'whitewash'—the words with which senior Guards General Sir Michael Rose (who was part of the Task Force as commander of the SAS) described it in April 2022—though unfortunately it is clear four decades on that he was right and that it undoubtedly was one. The Royal Navy and Royal Fleet Auxiliary officers who made up the board certainly *appeared* to try hard to put themselves in the minds of key decision makers that day and get to the truth.

Colonel Johnny Rickett, our 'JR', wonders in his unpublished memoirs if the regiment should have insisted on an official Public Inquiry into the facts at the time.[75] In December 1982 on behalf of 'parents and wives', the former Prime Minister, wartime Royal Navy officer and Cardiff MP James Callaghan asked some awkward questions in the House of Commons—about what happened that day. There was general euphoria about the victory and no further pressure on the government to investigate.

The second is that the Board of Inquiry focused largely on operational questions. It only touched on the pregnant question how much the failings of triumvirate leadership contributed to Britain's military scoring the equivalent of an own goal with entirely unnecessary loss of life and limb, ships and material—and financial costs. As we will see, they deployed that question with a very specific purpose in their whitewash.

The third and most important caveat is that the Inquiry was, from the word go, a Whitehall fig leaf for what should really have taken place. The proper forum for an investigation into the success of a single enemy air attack causing the loss of so many ships, lives and supplies would normally have been a Court Martial—a trial under military law very similar in legal procedures to a civilian court but presided over by military officers. In the circumstances, the civilian crews of the ships involved would have been subject to service discipline. Crucially, the plans were made and executed by officers in the Royal Navy, Royal Marines and Army—all fully subject to the regulations of their individual services and all under the command of Admiral Fieldhouse, Commander-in-Chief, Fleet. This is standard Royal Navy procedure except in times of general war. It was so in 1982, and remains so to this day.

With 56 deaths and 150 wounded, four vessels struck—RFA *Sir Galahad*, RFA *Tristram*, frigate HMS *Plymouth*, LCU *Foxtrot 4*—it was Britain's single greatest loss of military lives and equipment in one day post World War II. Moreover, the Argentine air attack had accidentally knocked out half a battalion in a single wave.

Commanders do not survive such mistakes. One has to reach far back in history for a general who actively squanders a battalion. After Rome's army was mouse-trapped in Teutoborg Forest in 9 AD, Emperor Augustus famously cursed its general: '*Vare, legiones redde*'—Varus, give me back my legions! Varus did the honourable thing and fell on his sword. There hasn't been an example since.

This means that the appropriate Court Martial is still due to (still must) take place. Major Guy Sayle, the senior Welsh Guards officer on board, once said of the attacks, 'Forget *all* you have been told [my italics] about *Sir Galahad*.' As the rest of this book will show, he was right even as to the basic facts and timelines of what happened. After four decades, crucial lessons remain to be learned and it should take place sooner rather than later while participants are still alive. A proper analysis of the failures of that day will save lives in the future.

It is important to stress that the convening of a Court Martial does not imply that anyone involved is guilty of wrongdoing or discharging their duties other than in an adequate way Her late Majesty would have expected at the time, or His Majesty would expect today.[76] A Court Martial is designed principally to discover the facts and then to publish the official record. In that sense, its function is similar to a Coroner's Inquest with the difference that its legal mechanics are as exhaustive as Statutory Public Inquiries. The first thing a Court Martial will have to construe is an exacting and accurate timeline based on all the witness statements and documents that are currently still treated as secrets. Timings are crucially important— when are they not? As with the helicopter that *HMS Cardiff* shot down (denied as friendly fire until proven by a Military Inquiry in 1986, whose findings were immediately made public), the detail matters.

What follows may be the most Sherlock Holmes-style section of the book— much like my Colonel Jacot. But it is necessary because in forty years no one has yet looked critically at the arcane behind-the-scenes stuff that led to the loss of half a battalion with the latest available information. I hope the reader will agree by the end that the published memoirs together with recently released trove of documents of the Board of Inquiry raise a mountain of questions about the probity of Admiral Fieldhouse and General Moore.

Although one plans to avoid fatalities and setbacks as much as possible, they are to be expected in wars. But here the object is different. The least we can do for those who risked and lost their lives on the frontline is try and put together a clear picture of the events that led up to them. Details in the memoirs discussed below have muddied that picture and we owe it to the dead and survivors to retrieve this clarity, much in the way Colonel Gracie did with the *Titanic* disaster. In the case of 8th June, we are surely also under a duty to troops risking their lives in the future (and their families) to ask in advance of the appropriate Court Martial of Britain's massive losses that day—what could we have done better so as to avoid repetition?

21

The Devil in the Detail

To understand what was going on in the amphibious section of the Task Force's operations room on *HMS Fearless*, it's important to start with the comparative scarcity of means of transportation to shore from ships. There were the LCUs—the Royal Navy's seaworthy landing craft. In most places in the Falklands, they were the Task Force's amphibious workhorse to get troops and supplies from ship to shore either in-harbour or beyond. *HMS Fearless* and *HMS Intrepid* each had four—making a total of eight in the Falklands. But because of the arrangement between Moore and Clapp, two LCUs were in the north under the control of Royal Marines (since Moore and Clapp respectively entrusted them with helicopters and landing craft) at Teal Inlet. That left six LCUs for San Carlos and the southern flank.

But they were not the only craft to get on shore. There were also a number of mexeflotes, supplied by the Army, that could be used in harbours, and four Royal Navy LCVPs—small landing craft that could be physically lifted by troops and stowed on deck and also only useful in harbours. Support helicopters were also deployed for heavy lifting, transporting troops or speedy recovery of the wounded. From 1st June, as the campaign geared up for its climax, the Task Force could deploy the one Chinook that escaped from *Atlantic Conveyor* (55 troops or 30,000lbs cargo): 21 Sea Kings (28 troops or 8000lbs cargo) and 23 Wessex (16 troops or 4000lbs cargo). Four of the Sea Kings had night vision which prevented them from flying during the day.[77]

It goes without saying that jigsaw precision in allocation and constant monitoring of objectives expressed in orders is of the essence in amphibious logistics. Here Clapp's staff had good Falklands form. They had flawlessly executed the highly complex assault landing of the Royal Marines and Paras as they took San Carlos from the open sea in the middle of the night on 21st May. The commander of the LCUs, for example, had played an important role in landing preparations. As an ex-commander of the Royal Marines Falklands Garrison for two years, he had a thorough knowledge of the beaches and sea approaches from slides, charts and sketches produced during coastline surveys from a professional and private yachtsman point of view.

As the amphibious assault phase had ended, the nature of support to the brigades also changed. The canvas on which Clapp's group worked changed to include the Falklands tundra. Julian Thompson, the Falklands land commander before Moore took over and brigadier of the Royal Marines, said about his fellow triumvirate commander: 'Mike [Clapp] was fascinated by the time land forces needed to pass orders down the chain of command. In a ship when the captain says turn left, everyone goes left. In a land battle if every marine/private does not know where the objective is and how to get there, it just does not happen'.[78] Thompson said this in 2018, at the Australian Army's Canberra seminar.

Clapp himself said then about Moore's arrival that he regretted he had remained part of the triumvirate. He wished, Clapp said in particular, that he had argued more strongly to be appointed 'on Moore's staff and not remain an independent naval task group commander'.[79] As part of Moore's planning staff, 'I should have then been able to follow his thoughts and influence his movements and logistics'.[80] A more succinct summary of Fieldhouse and Moore's doomed ATP experiment is hard to imagine.

Clapp's peers on the Royal Navy Inquiry Board, though satisfied with the commander himself, pull no punches about the operations of the amphibious group's staff as a whole. Normally, the staff tasked with amphibious operations was a team of five. However, because of the size of Operation Corporate, the amphibious staff was four times larger. The total was rapidly expanded to a number near twenty who were effectively learning on a stressful job with lives depending on them. The Board was surprised at the lack of previous amphibious training. Most of the group's staff lacked training in NATO's Allied Tactical Publication (ATP) doctrine.[81] By May, the 20 staff were exhausted, and 'this became particularly apparent when newly arrived officers impressed with their relative speed and clarity of thought.'[82] Lack of training also expressed itself in another way. Many of the staff 'did their own thing' and, due to their inexperience, didn't involve their colleagues where they should have. Of all Operation Corporate's casualties from April to June 1982, 68 per cent (173) of the total (258) occurred at sea. The amphibious group suffered the most with 48 per cent of the total (123), of which only a handful after the landing at San Carlos.

The Board singles out Clapp's 'Staff Officer Operations' (SOO), his second in command, who had no amphibious experience apart from some classroom instruction when joining the team in April and, as time progressed, 'became extremely tired and prone to "nodding off for a second or two".'[83] The Royal Navy did run an Amphibious Warfare Planning Course (AWPC), the most relevant training programme, but neither Clapp nor his SOO had taken it. Of the two, the one who should have taken it was the SOO, 'since he would require a close knowledge of amphibious operations if he was to act as Second in

Command.'[84] The experienced deputy officer who would have done most of this work and on whom the SOO would have relied was a US officer deeply versed in ATP doctrine. He was lent to the UK as part of NATO. However, because of his nationality, he was barred from joining the Task Force and sailing to the Falklands.

Meanwhile Clapp's own role was hamstrung by having to assume three hats despite the quadrupling of his staff. Under normal circumstances, one of the most senior officers of the Task Force on Flagship *Fearless* would act as his Chief of Staff (COS) and dominate all communications in the same way Woodward had two captains running contiguous shifts in his operations room on *HMS Hermes*, keeping track of all the moving pieces like air traffic control. However, given the enemy presence, this very senior officer had other things on his mind ('not as fully committed', the Board writes) in view of the frequency of air attacks and the Flagship being involved in day and night moves as part of the Task Force's 112 vessels during the amphibious phase.[85] Under normal circumstances, the Chief of Staff would pick up any slack left by Clapp's SOO. But given his main job, the very senior officer had not much time to spare for that ancillary responsibility either. As a result, Clapp had to cover both the work that would be done by his Chief of Staff ('most of the time') and the things left on the table by his SOO, his second in command ('part of the time').[86] Clapp's book bears evidence of the three hats he was wearing and refers at times to his busy log and personal occasional disconnects—for example, 'I did not immediately appreciate that the first wave of Welsh Guards had been taken to Bluff Cove from *Fearless*.'[87]

Only four of the twenty staff had taken part in a real amphibious training exercise. This was the administrative NATO landing just before the Task Force departed in April 1982. The four were Clapp, his Chief of Staff, a landing-craft expert and an 'LSL liaison' expert. The former was a Royal Marine identified as GSO1 and the latter was Major Guy Yeoman, an Army officer. Clapp was aware there were problems within the group and the Board recognises that he and his Chief of Staff tried to address them as best they could by 'constant and continuing efforts to ensure the smooth continuity of operations'.[88] Obviously the two were hampered by the fact that Fieldhouse had not officially ordered ATP to be Operation Corporate's rulebook. He had not even given a specific Operation Order that framed the Task Force's means and goals, the Board observed. Fieldhouse had in effect given licence to make up everything on the spot. At the 2018 Canberra Seminar, Clapp details some of the ATP corners that were cut by his superiors.

In the words of Clapp in 2018, the Task Force was 'a rushed and potentially shambolic effort'.[89] The Navy experts on the Board agreed whole-heartedly in 1982. When Westminster ordered 5 Infantry to join the Task Force as the gun-boat show of force had not led to negotiations, 5 Infantry HQ studied ATP to understand how they would work with the Royal Navy before and after landing in the Falklands. 'They were amazed to find Amphib[ious] Op[eration]s were not being conducted very much like the book. Responsibilities of Commanders were never clearly defined therefore as required [by ATP]', the Board concludes.[90] It appears they had to second guess what arrangements were in force rather than that they were able to rely on the clear and predictable framework in ATP.

Where did this Bermuda Triangle express itself most clearly during Operation Corporate? All this Navy informality worked generally in a satisfactory manner during the planning and assault phase. This was all Royal Navy run and whatever loose ends there were, sailors knew how to pick up despite three different chains of command. Problems started when the assault phase was over and the land phase began on 23rd May, the Board's experts found.

ATP doctrine is honed by NATO's different national military organisations having to work together in a coherent, predictable rather than 'shambolic' manner. From the moment the Army brigade landed, the Task Force no longer relied on sailors only. As in NATO, it had to cooperate and communicate effectively with 'foreign' command structures—outsiders. And so, the Bermuda Triangle was wide open after 23rd May. Instead of ATP integrating 5 Infantry smoothly into the next phase, events became 'obscure' in the words of the Board.[91]

In the Royal Navy memoirs there are clear echoes. Before Moore took over the land command from the Royal Marines' brigadier on 30th May and finally was able to communicate with his subordinates, the Marines had rejected the southern flank as their first choice. When Moore carried on with the southern flank, in accordance with the official strategy as sanctioned by Westminster, Thompson commented in 2018 on his superior's decision that southern-flank logistics were 'dumped' in the lap of Clapp's amphibious staff.[92] Here the political decision to prune the Royal Navy's involvement in NATO back to submarines only came home to roost. The NATO training exercise in which Clapp had taken part involved landing just two Royal Marine units of 650 men each. In theory, Whitehall had committed 'a secondary role of taking an Army Brigade but, in my time, there was little liaison and no exercises', Clapp said in Canberra.[93]

In effect, none of the Royal Navy commanders who ran the Task Force in London knew how to integrate an Army brigade, least of all their land commander in the Falklands, General Moore. It was another area of his inexperience which he did not fully grasp and where he failed to rise to the occasion.

2nd June

What is clear is that it was ultimately up to General Moore as commander of landed forces to maintain Bluff Cove as Britain's frontline after its capture by 2 Para—which he did. But, given their independence, nor did the amphibious staff have to accept this order through gritted teeth. If the amphibious team really thought logistically Bluff Cove was hopeless that pretty much meant curtains to any thought of deploying troops there. They didn't.

At crunch time, the commander's veto seemed merely to rely on what mine-disposal units recced in Fitzroy/Port Pleasant and Bluff Cove/Port Fitzroy. 'Until they produced results I could not decide if the operation was practicable', said Clapp in his 1996 memoirs *Amphibious Assault Falklands*.[94] Moving two battalions was more than just about moving men, there was also 'an immense amount of kit'.[95]

Clearly the move was considered 'practicable' from 3rd June.[96] Beach reconnaissances of the anchorages were ordered. It just so happened that Fitzroy Settlement was ambi-harborous. It could be accessed through beaches that were part of Port Fitzroy, the inlet closer to Port Stanley, as well as through beaches that were accessible through Port Pleasant, the inlet in the direction of Goose Green and San Carlos.

Specialists of the amphibious staff studied the charts of the area. Of the two sounds, Port Fitzroy looked ideal. Fitzroy Settlement was situated on one bank with Bluff Cove Settlement where 2 Para battalion was dug in on the other side. There was a bridge across the inlet further inland that the retreating Argentinian Army had bombed. But that didn't matter because any manner of landing craft would be able to ferry the short distance across the sound to Bluff Cove's Yellow Beach. It was perfect. The frontline on one side, the brigade's distribution hub on the other and a defensive moat of water separating the hub from the frontline just in case. On-site investigations were ordered and the beach reconnaissance of Port Fitzroy was 'more thorough' than those of Port Pleasant.

The inlets, however, were not navigable for all ship sizes. Both were too shallow for frigates, for example—though frigates could reach the waters in front of the inlets. Royal Fleet Auxiliaries LSLs such as *Galahad* and *Tristram* could enter, however, though neither inlet had a gradient suitable for hull-beaching for which their 'round-table' class of ships was designed.[97] The team soon came to the conclusion that an anchorage just to the east of Fitzroy Settlement was simply the best. 'Local people could suggest none better'.[98] The approach to this beach was quite satisfactory for LCUs.[99] Based on all the data, it was not a difficult choice. One was selected as fit for purpose and the other was shelved as awkward. Five days later, a move of the logistic base from San Carlos to Fitzroy Settlement was even considered.

As the Royal Marines were readying for attack in the north, lengthy discussions started on 3rd June, 24 hours after the capture of Bluff Cove, about organising 5 Infantry's hub. Moore ordered his staff to make sure that a scheme was 'worked out' with the amphibious team to move the two Guards battalions forward to take over from 2 Para. In contrast to the Teal Inlet 'emergency' completion on 30th May, the Bluff Cove scheme was to go through many, many permutations despite being more straightforward. From Northwood, Admiral Fieldhouse, too, weighed in on the matter as the plan of attack worked out before the landing in the Falklands was implented at a lethargic pace.

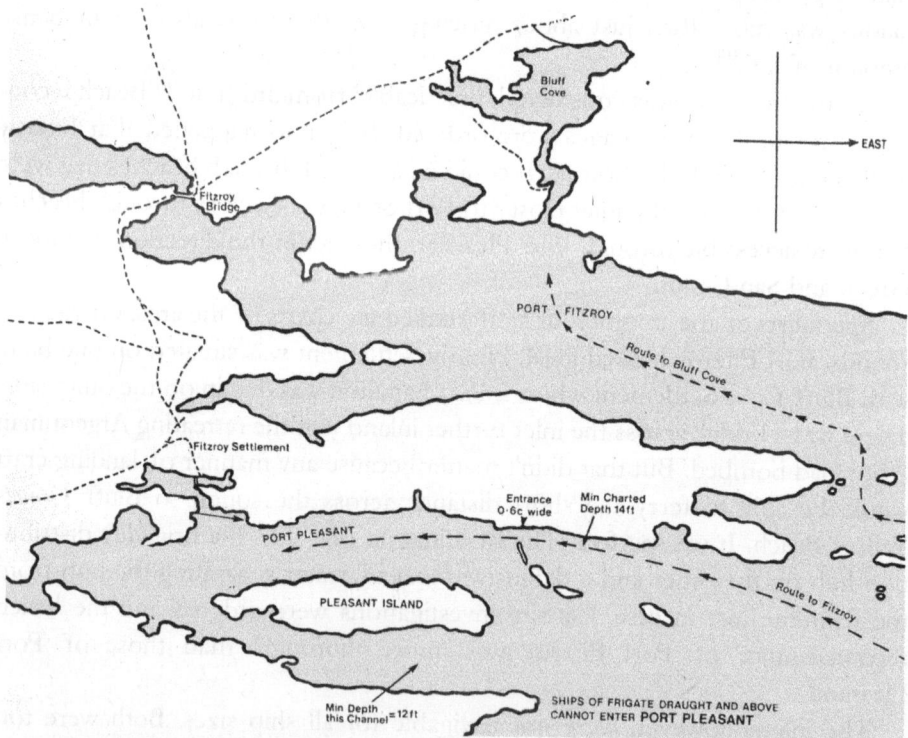

On Fieldhouse's leadership, the Board's findings are quite interesting. It had severely criticised the fact that the admiral never defined a detailed mission statement for Operation Corporate, or ordered his commanders to apply Britain's ready-made amphibious doctrine laid down in NATO's ATP. But, as to Fieldhouse's daily oversight, the Board said the admiral performed 'entirely satisfactorily'. Given that he was 8000 miles away, Fieldhouse didn't micromanage and allowed his commanders to get on with things. His method was 'command by negation'—he only took action by veto. His impatient direct order to Royal Marine Brigadier Thompson on 26th May to attack Goose Green-Darwin and finally get moving after three days was therefore an exception of the campaign.

The consolidation of the southern flank, however, became the subject of a lot of Fieldhouse's vetoes that slowed down its unfurling. Moore's prevarications and delays after Fieldhouse's bracing conversation with Thompson on 26th May were spared the same wrath. The admiral would in fact micromanage his subordinates several times over and his own oar seemed to be in every single decision exactly when things were poised to go. Presumably, the senior land commander had spoken to his superior in Northwood about his northern flank strategy.

On 3rd June, both amphibious and divisional staffs proposed Plan 1. Dingemans's *Intrepid* was to sail to the top of Port Fitzroy and land one-and-a-half battalions of Guards by LCU at Bluff Cove accompanied by a frigate for protection on 6th June at 4.30am. Half of the Welsh Guards would move by *Tristram* at the same time. Woodward offered stationing *HMS Yarmouth* close by. The return trip from Ajax Bay, San Carlos, around Lafonia to the inlets could be done in less than ten hours. Dawn to dusk was shortest in the Falklands in June, with 16-17 hours of darkness and dusk fell at 5pm. It left plenty of time for *Intrepid* to disembark everyone and sail back. If additional protection was necessary on the last few miles as it returned empty in morning light, CAP protection from the air could be offered as additional protection.

But Fieldhouse, looking over the shoulders of his subordinates in the Falklands 8000 miles away, decided it was not to be. On 4th June, he vetoed the troop move outright, 'mainly because of daylight risks to INTREPID and escort' at the tail end of its mission.[100] It would not be the last time that the Task Force's two top commanders were more interested in a hypothetical risk to empty Royal Navy vessels rather than in a real troop move to the frontline. Curiously the Board of Inquiry makes no reference to 4th June, the day the Scots and Welsh Guards were kept waiting in the rain all day and ordered on and off *Intrepid* for a few hours in the late afternoon and early evening.

Meanwhile, on 3rd June, the Royal Marines at Teal Inlet received their four Rapier units which were helicoptered in. As if the southern flank came under a different heading, its four Rapiers however were not air-lifted to the 5 Infantry hub at Fitzroy. And so, while Bluff Cove's anti-aircraft dome was postponed, it was also back to the drawing board for the amphibious team on Fieldhouse's orders.

Another plan followed on 5th June. It relied on no fewer than four moving parts over three days. The pressure Fieldhouse and Moore applied to get going with 5 Infantry was lighter than light. The Scots and Welsh Guards would be inserted at Bluff Cove over two days using night-time transport (*Intrepid*) and LCUs to Bluff Cove. One Welsh Guards company (150 to 200 men) would thereafter sail by *Monsunen* from Darwin-Goose Green to Bluff Cove. Separately, *Tristram* would kick off the build-up of 5 Infantry's brigade hub behind the front line. It created another day's delay.

It had already been decided that no Royal Navy frigate air cover would be provided to *Tristram* while it offloaded stores in daylight. It could be left to its 'own salvation'. The amphibious staff promptly cancelled *HMS Yarmouth*'s air protection: 'NEW PLAN INVOLVES NO LPD BY DAY ESCORT NO LONGER REQUIRED'.[101] *Tristram*, an LSL, would be on its own and were, effectively, 'expendable'. This decision on its own—though not very gratefully received on the LSLs who happened to be included on the 'own salvation' signal—was not entirely unreasonable. Single transport ships were, compared to battleships, not hugely at risk. There was not much strategic mileage for the Argentines to risk airplanes on sinking some supplies (troops were another matter, of course). But the absence of frigate escorts was to play its own critical role as the decision to treat LSLs as disposable—which may have made sense as to the plan of 5th June—became a constant in an otherwise increasing whirlwind of changes that chopped and fragmented matters in different hands over subsequent days.

The decision to split the insertion into many parts also meant that a new argument was brought into play that created delay—the worry that a repeat of insertions created a pattern that the Argentinians could exploit. It was specifically the delivery pattern of 5 Infantry's battalions, the fighting assets, to the frontline that was now used as a reason for further delays—*Intrepid*'s captain Dingemans, in particular, played the 'risks to INTREPID' card as a result of a 'pattern'.

Any hub will have a supply pattern by necessity, hence the facts that all such moves took place at night-time. His point of view, however, seemed to imply that an LPD with troops sailing along a supply route under the cover of darkness was defenceless as a sitting duck in broad daylight—even though LPDs were always accompanied by a frigate as escort, unlike LSLs. Suffice to say here that if that point of view was true, a simple plan from 3 June to deploy the captured *Monsunen* exclusively for Scots and Welsh Guards troops' night-time moves to Bluff Cove along the safe Gurkha-patrolled Choiseul Sound waterway would of course have made so much more sense. It goes without saying that this would be even more so the case, had 5 Infantry (the three Gurkhas, Scots and Welsh Guards battalions) been landed straight into Goose Green/Darwin on 2nd June instead of at San Carlos.

It bears repeating here that the two top commanders had pulled different levers on the two flanks as early as 1st June. In 2018, Clapp told the Australian Army regarding the move of the Royal Marines to Mount Kent on 30th May that '16 choppers for 5500 men, guns, ammo, food, etc. was clearly not enough'. On Moore's arrival 14 Wessex helicopters were transferred to the 'independent' operational control (OPCON) of the amphibious staff from 1st June. 5 Infantry's 3000 men were about to land a few days later. But by then tactical control (or TACON) of all the helicopters had already been handed on to the Royal Marines.

This was not for want of 5 Infantry's commander Wilson asking Moore and Clapp for such support. On 1st June, at a lunch in Clapp's cabin with Moore and the two brigadiers of the Marines and the Army, the latter (Tony Wilson) asked for all of them repeatedly to get the men of his two battalions forward into battle position on the southern flank in a swift orderly and risk-less manner.[102] Instead, a 2nd June log recorded, 'most, if not all, medium support helicopters [were] allocated to 3 C[omman]do B[riga]de to complete their investing of the northern flank. 5 B[riga]de left with legacy of 1200 prisoners of war and a great deal of unstable ammunition, including weeping napalm'.[103]

While not addressing this question directly, in his *Amphibious Assault Falklands*, Clapp provides the general approach of his staff to requests from Wilson or his staff. He writes, '[d]espite requests, I was not prepared to give tactical control of the landing craft to 5 Infantry for I was never to trust their command to employ them sensibly. On the few occasions they managed somehow to purloin vessels or helicopters they failed to understand the operational danger of independent operations.' This sentence is part of a discussion relating to 1st June, but, since 5 Infantry only landed in San Carlos on 2nd June, the 'purloining' seems to relate to a date before 1st June.

In fact, even when the brigade captured the *Monsunen*, the Argentinian coaster of about 30m, at Goose Green on 29th May, Clapp writes he quickly removed it '[as] I did not trust 5 Brigade'.[104] He adds, 'I quickly took her away from the *army* [my italics] after a discussion with Jeremy… As I did not trust 5 Brigade to operate the ship within my area of control'.[105] The not so rosy-tinted spectacles as to 5 Infantry seem to have been donned even before the Guards and Gurkhas landed on 2nd June.

In order for his staff to stay completely in charge of its subsequent movements, Clapp writes he 'sent aboard a Royal Navy Lieutenant and three ratings [sailors] from *Fearless* to provide communications and to act as crew' before returning *Monsunen* for 5 Infantry to use between Wilson's HQ at Goose Green and the advance HQ at Fitzroy.[106] He gave his crew strict orders, however, 'not to operate by day [as it might expose the vessel to an air attack] and to accept instructions from 5 Infantry only if they were agreed, and, if not, to report back to me immediately before sailing on any mission about which they were doubtful'.[107] Clapp continues, 'Tony Wilson probably found this difficult to accept but I remained adamant'.[108]

Moore aimed to attack Port Stanley on 6th June—despite not allocating the additional Wessexes to move 5 Infantry on 1st June—[109] but he clearly did not want to manage this brewing tension between his southern brigade and the amphibious staff. In the case of the captured vessel, Moore seems to have even enabled the mistrust by agreeing with Clapp's approach.[110] Moore fanned it even further by agreeing to the lop-sided landing-craft arrangement whereby Clapp 'would give tactical control to Julian [brigadier of the Royal Marines] for those in Salvador Waters' in the north, in contrast to 5 Infantry's hub in the south.[111]

The Port Stanley attack date of 6th June was by now none too soon for his northern brigade.[112] Royal Marine Brigadier Thompson made clear in 2018 how dire the situation was on Mount Kent. The 'total lack of cover and warmth away from the settlements, other than a few CP tents, meant that once a man was wet, he usually stayed wet. Most men's feet never dried, and many suffered from trench foot.'[113] Drinking water was another problem sapping his brigade's strength. 'By digging a shallow pit in the peat you could scoop up a brackish brew. Tablets sterilised, but did not remove the sediment, which inflamed the gut. As the war progressed, many suffered "Galtieri's Revenge" [the President of Argentina].'[114] There was the lack of food. 'On a number of occasions battalions and commandos went without rations for over 36 hours.'[115] In summary, the Royal Marines had now been exposed to the extreme weather in the Falklands 'for three weeks without any cover except ponchos, and there were several cases of cold injury, mainly trench foot caused by lack of any facilities to dry out'.[116]

Still Moore and Fieldhouse procrastinated. Meanwhile, Admiral Woodward was also starting to fear for his ships, which had by now been in intensive operations away from support for two months.

23

Basics

The amphibious staff had to stay on top of the nitty-gritty of logistics, how the weather changed things on the day, opportunities or delays, etc., and of course any tactical battle changes of Moore's ahead of D-day. In 2018, Clapp said about this 'I don't think it is boasting to say that once Admiral Woodward had established sea control, the ultimate success of the whole operation came to depend heavily on my Task Group and how we supported the Landing Forces. This not to denigrate the efforts of the Carrier Group, nor the SSNs [nuclear-powered hunter-killer submarines] *or land forces* [my italics]. They all played their part well but we were the pig in the middle from the moment we entered San Carlos Water until the surrender. Our game became mainly logistic but we had many more tasks both in defence of my task group and in support of the land campaign.'[117]

It is undoubtedly true that 'Good logistics win wars'.[118] In 2018 in Canberra, Commodore Clapp said the hostile capture of San Carlos with the Royal Marines was less complex to organise than the forward move of 5 Infantry along the southern flank from 2nd June.[119] About working with the marines, he said, '[w]ithout their heritage and knowledge of the Navy the landings would have been much harder to plan and execute.'[120] As to his own team, he concluded, '[m]y role would have certainly been far more difficult'.[121] When Moore decided to leave the rear defence of San Carlos in the hands of a Royal Marine battalion Clapp let out a sigh of relief.[122] An Argentine attack on the Task Force from behind remained on the cards, and the Royal Marines were now experts on the harbour.

Whether Army or Royal Marines, the Falklands posed the same problems for troops. One was simply the choice of San Carlos as the whole Task Force's hub. There were 53 Argentinian aircraft on the Falklands and another 164 on the mainland, and Britain's Harriers were still heavily outnumbered in June.[123] While San Carlos was the safest location, '[t]he obvious downside was the distance from Stanley over appalling terrain still with no roads, too few helicopters and very few tracked vehicles.'[124] As 'there were no roads in the Falklands; everything had to be lifted in helicopters, landing craft, or on peoples' backs', said Thompson in 2018.[125] For his own move to Mount Kent from 30th May, he judged the '[t]op priority for *helicopter lift* was guns, ammunition, people. Rations, packs came a long way down the list. Wheeled vehicles could not cross the peat bog. We took some of *our* oversnow vehicles with us in the hope that they could; they did [my italics].'[126]

Clapp himself understood the difficulties after the failed 3rd June march to Goose Green when the Welsh Guards' second in command wrung out and dried his sleeping bag in his cabin afterwards.[127] By Thompson's calculation, it would take a three-day march to get to Goose Green from San Carlos even without kit. Clapp says that Admiral Woodward favoured the 65-mile march from San Carlos to Bluff Cove till around 6th June and the admiral seems not to have been told about the terrain difficulties by Moore's staff before then— Clapp did so in their stead.

D-Day shifted three days to 9th June. Four Rapier units were due to be helicoptered from the San Carlos hills on 6th June destined for Fitzroy on *Tristram*. A troop lift by helicopter was not authorised due to the low cloud cover.[128]

24

Eyewitness

The most detailed description of the Guards battalions' actual first move to Bluff Cove is by an eyewitness: the LCU commander of the four *Tangos*. He provides first-hand narrative detail in *Reasons in Writing* (1993) of the night-time journey of the Scots Guards battalion on 5-6th June and the first kink in the scheme.[129] As we know, he never made it back from Bluff Cove with the four landing craft to *Fearless* by 1am on 7th June. The planned *Tangos-Fearless rendezvous* didn't happen as a result and only half of the Welsh Guards were transported with *Fearless*'s two LCUs (*Foxtrots 1* and *4)* to Bluff Cove instead of the whole battalion in these two landing craft and two of the *Tangos*. The LCU commander records thinking on the morning of 7th June (the next day) on Yellow Beach, Bluff Cove: 'I knew that the reason why we still had men "on the move" was the fault of myself and the landing craft crews'.[130]

On the morning of 6th June, after a five-hour long, unpleasant, arctic, water-soaked first journey, the Scots Guards battalion were deposited by him on Yellow Beach at 5.30am. As we saw, Dingemans's *Intrepid* had cast her *Tangos* off at sea in a different location from the one that had been planned—somewhere under Lively Island. After forty years, a map in the newly released Kew reports finally shows exactly where the Scots Guards were actually meant to have been launched in their four LCUs. The map itself details the Argentine Exocet radius from Port Stanley, but it includes 'Position BC17' that is identified in the written reports as the Scots Guards planned drop off. The LCUs' journey from there to Bluff Cove would have been a little over half an hour. *Intrepid* could have taken the LCUs in and back home that night as she waited briefly at BC17. In addition, the map shows that there was a wide corridor for *Intrepid* and its companion frigate to reach that position safe from the Exocet envelope—night or day—and the Argentine 155mm mortar artillery based at Port Stanley.

Why Dingemans didn't follow the plan is incomprehensible. Instead, the four *Tangos* had at least 40 additional miles to cover and took some five hours in rain, sleet and backwash, soaking all troops to the bone as they sat freezing in the landing craft. Instead of arriving fit to fight, the battalion had to turn houses at Bluff Cove Settlement into a temporary shelter and medical centre to deal with the consequences of Dingemans's decision. (They were excellent soldiers, recovered quickly, and would on 13-14th June go on to win the Battle at Tumbledown after heavy fighting.)

The LCU commander was put out, understandably. He did not have his own detailed maps or SATNAV because he had been told on *Fearless* that it would be a short journey from BC17, right under East Island (the small island to the right of the position on the map below)—through the short U-bend leading to Bluff Cove. He would have dropped off the Scots Guards in no time at all and returned the four *Tangos* to *Intrepid* before it had to sail back to San Carlos under night cover. But it was a very different proposition to navigate a journey from nautical memory that was ten times longer and with a magnetic anomaly that made the compass unreliable for a section of the route and with no defence against enemy attack to speak of during the long journey to reach Bluff Cove.

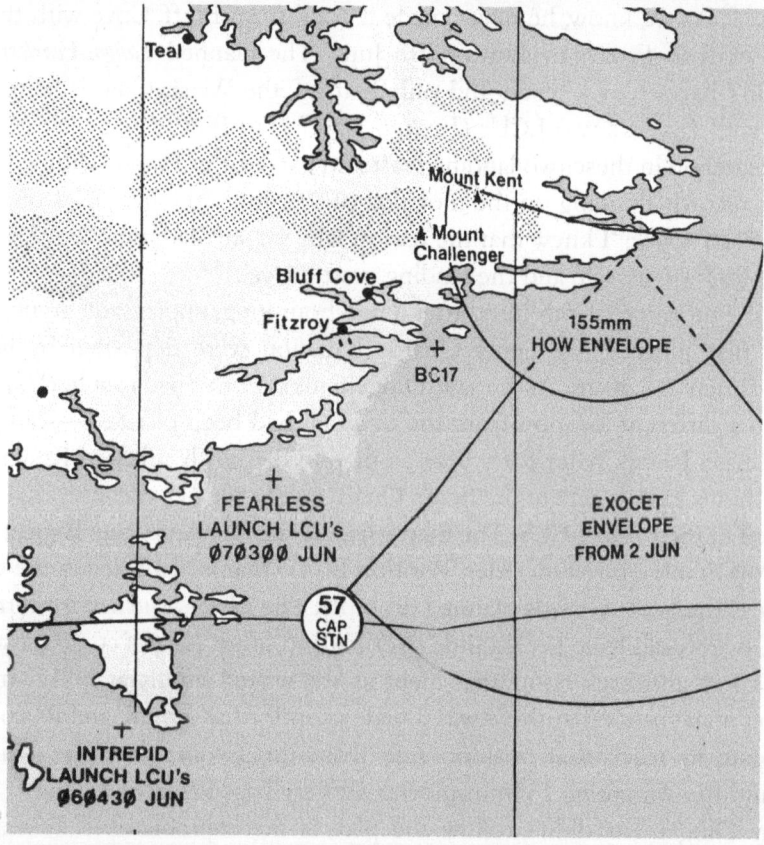

His seamanship both impressed and relieved the Scots Guards when he landed them safely at last at their destination after four or five hours. Despite their rough journey, they had survived and only one of their own needed to be casevaced to San Carlos. The map also makes clear why *HMS Cardiff* treated the four LCUs initially as hostile. If anything British, they were expecting to encounter *Intrepid* as per the DSSS discussion between Clapp and Woodward. Instead, because of Dingemans's off-the-cuff decision to dump the Scots Guards, they ran across four landing craft that might equally in the dark of night have carried Argentinian assault troops.

Next, the LCU commander decided to go to the Scots Guards HQ at Bluff Cove to signal the amphibious staff on the Flagship details of the dramatic events that had almost led to the sinking of his four landing craft. *Cardiff*'s star shell could have exposed the move to the Argentinians. On the way, he, in addition, paid a tea-visit to his local Falklanders friends Mike McKie and Tim Dobbyns. They owned the 'big house' next to which the Scots Guards were located in improvised sheds of canvas and plastic at Bluff Cove. At the Scots Guards' sheds, the LCU commander found that their communications were unfortunately down. At some point while at Bluff Cove, a Sea King helicopter en route to San Carlos touched down—the casevac for the injured Scots Guards, perhaps, or not. The Royal Marine decided to hop on board in the afternoon to make an unannounced visit to Clapp and his team on *Fearless* to appraise them of what had happened.

The LCU commander's helicopter lift to San Carlos was in part uncomfortable. The surly helicopter crew offered little help as they thought he was bumming a ride to 'comfort and safety'.[131] It would not have been unreasonable for the helicopter crew to think that there was a workable alternative available: hand the pilot a written message to be delivered to the staff on *Fearless*. This would also have meant that a second helicopter ride to take the major back from *Fearless* to Bluff Cove would not have been required.

In addition, a Para major on-board gave the major hell about the 'late' arrival of the Scots Guards. The Para wasn't aware of Dingemans's odd decision to launch the Scots Guards 40 miles early. When *Fearless* hove into view from the helicopter, the LCU commander himself writes that he saw 'a touch of peace, sanity, warmth, a hot shower, and a plate of food'.[132]

At dusk, when the Royal Marine was sent back from San Carlos in a return helicopter ordered by Clapp's team, the next horror unfolded before him. Though fully debriefed (but without time for luxuries) in San Carlos,[133] his LCUs appeared to be no longer where he had left them.

An atrocious gale was pummelling Bluff Cove and the crew of the *Tangos* had sought shelter further to his instructions. The major had to remain on shore until the weather passed sufficiently. As luck would have it, he could stay the night at Bluff Cove settlement and the same friends of the big house woke him in the morning. But the *Tangos'* latest sailing time from Bluff Cove—11.30pm— to meet *Fearless* for the pickup of the Welsh Guards battalion came and went as the weather did not let up.[134] With no sign of the LCUs under his command he waited further as Falklander Mike McKie of the 'Big House' at Bluff Cove provided him with a dram.

Whether the LCUs could instead have ventured out to the rendezvous with *Fearless* without their commander is unclear. It is a tantelising thought. They were experienced Royal Navy and Marine sailors and had already made the trip once. The Colour Sergeant of *Tango 1* was aware of the *Fearless* plan in outline. On 14th June, he would be dispatched to make the entire journey between San Carlos and Fitzroy on his own, rather than just the third to Elephant Island. The LCU commander wrote about this, 'I had been asked to navigate her but had declined for the reason that the cox'n knew the way and my continual involvement would undermine my crews' confidence.' He added, 'a landing craft Colour Sergeant is trained and capable of such journeys unsupervised. They certainly needed no wet-nursing from me on this occasion.'

But, apparently on the night of 6-7th June that was different. The cox'n had been given strict orders to stay put 'no matter what', and nor had the crew of the *Tangos* been provided with any charts it seems.[135] And so, none of the LCUs made the rendezvous with *Fearless* without the LCU commander despite their skilled competence.

Though what happened was a result of the weather, no wonder that the major still somehow felt that he was at 'fault' and that his crew was at 'fault'. It is one of the sharp vicissitudes of the Falklands War that, if none of the above had taken place as it did, the entire battalion of Welsh Guards would have been launched from *Fearless* in four LCUs as planned and would have been dropped off in the right place on Bluff Cove on 7th June—well before dawn and ready for Moore's attack on Port Stanley on 9th June. In military history, the deployment of the southern flank would have been considered as resounding an amphibious success as the deployment of the Royal Marines Brigade to Teal Inlet on the northern flank with its full panoply of amphibious supplies, Bandvagn and helicopter troop moves.

The Inquiry Board itself spends few words on this pivotal episode and not one of them critical.

25

The New Plan
Major Guy Yeoman

As it was, plans would have to adapt as a result of the situation in Bluff Cove. At 1am in the morning, the LCU commander was able to get a heads-up through to *Fearless*. Earlier in the day, the Scots Guards Bluff Cove HQ had not been able to get a signal to *Fearless* and he had jumped on a helicopter and back to speak to Clapp in person. But this time—ironically, as we shall see, given that it was night time—the signal was sent successfully via the Gurkhas at Goose Green who in turn forwarded his message on to *Fearless*.

Again chance struck. Unfortunately, the signal that reached *Fearless* appears to have stated that the *Tangos* 'were unable to sail'.[136] The amphibious staff on *Fearless* were now certainly aware of a hitch and a delay, but they seem not to have been able to comprehend from the signal that the LCUs were unaccounted for rather than 'unable to sail'. Upon receipt of the signal, *Fearless* waited for at least another three hours and a quarter. It even sent out a search party with helicopters equipped with night vision—the whole Task Force only had four of these—from one of its two accompanying frigates to look for the four landing craft in the dark.

Fearless's delay, in turn, had its own unexpected consequences. When *Fearless* finally accepted that the *Tangos* were a no-show at around 4am, the Task Force's staffs on board had to improvise quickly. As *Fearless*'s two preloaded LCUs (*Foxtrot 1* and *4*) had been packed for weight and not for being able to parry a frontline attack by the Argentines, there was suddenly a problem. The troops that were meant to embark the two arriving *Tangos* were the mortar platoon with its 4.5 miles defensive shell radius and the battalion's three rifle companies with their 1 mile range. Effectively, rations, supplies, ammunition, the Welsh Guards command centre, recce-, machine gun-, and anti-tank-platoon kit and four communication land rovers would be at Bluff Cove with Colonel Rickett but not many troops to speak of to defend the position.

Concerned about exposing his men without a real way of defending the frontline, Rickett went straight to General Moore and appealed to him in person to make the case for aborting the transport, or for an embarkation that made military sense given that the Welsh Guards were holding Britain's frontline with the enemy. He needed at the very least all three rifle companies (around 400 men) to do so, preferably also the mortar platoon.

But time had by now, 4am—some four hours after *Fearless*'s planned return time—run out for repacking the two preloaded *Foxtrots*. There was no room for the mortar platoon and its mortars. *Fearless* had to sail back to San Carlos. With both Moore and Clapp, as well as their staff on board, an air-attack near San Carlos could not be risked—even with *Fearless*'s double frigate escort. Unlike Dingemans on *Intrepid*, *Fearless*'s Captain Larken had gone the extra mile. The final half of the return journey would be after dawn.

Hearing his colonel's appeal, General Moore dismissed the idea of aborting the mission and affirmed his staff's orders, as well as the parameters agreed by the amphibious staff. Moore, however, did partially acknowledge the military risk to which he was exposing Rickett and his men and said, 'don't worry—I'll get the other half to Bluff Cove tomorrow night'. And that was that. The Welsh Guards symbol on the frontline in Moore's divisional operations room was going to be a very thin red line indeed with 150 troops plus just one rifle company to defend them. Leaving the men in his mortar platoon—including Simon Weston—on *Fearless*, its commander embarked with Rickett to stake out the defensive positions of the platoon's mortars at Bluff Cove to save time and move them immediately in position when they arrived the next day.

Improvisation part 1

As the LCU commander had not made the rendezvous, someone else now had to guide *Foxtrot 2* and *4*. Commodore Clapp had stayed up the previous night on *Fearless* for the insertion of the Scots Guards from *Intrepid*. On 7th June, a trusted senior member of the amphibious team, Major Guy Yeoman—who had, in fact, been the first to tell Clapp about the Falklands Task Force on 2nd April[137]—was handling the issues in the amphibious operations room. He ordered Major Tony Todd (woken up by *Fearless*'s captain at short notice) to take over command of the two *Foxtrots* with Welsh Guards and most of their kit.

Yeoman was the General Staff Officer Grade 2 on the team. His 'essential duty as G2 was the loading and offloading of the ships and, under normal circumstances, controlling all landing craft movements', the Inquiry report says about him.[138] In the small amphibious team of twenty only G1 and Clapp's SOO, his second in command, were more senior than Yeoman. Major Todd was Yeoman's assistant. He also had experience with landing craft logistics and was due to replace Yeoman. Moreover, they were specifically tasked to deal with 5 Infantry's amphibious needs.[139] Yeoman is also one of the few people identified by name (like Todd) in the newly released records of the Inquiry Report. He was rated 'experienced', and his taking part in the 1982 amphibious NATO exercise was mentioned.[140]

As a result of the information about the close call with *Cardiff* provided hours earlier by the LCU commander helicoptering in, the two LCUs were accompanied for a few miles by a frigate. But Todd's journey with Rickett and half of his battalion was uneventful. There was a clear moon and Todd dropped off the first half of the Welsh Guards, their weapons, vehicles, supplies and commander before dawn at 7am 7th June, at Bluff Cove's 'Yellow Beach'.[141] Indeed, this is where Todd found the missing LCU commander. The major had been woken that morning by Tim Dobbyns and recalls in his memoirs that, while having morning tea, he was 'disturbed by 2 Welsh Guards provost on motorbikes'. He dashed down to the shore in Mckie's landrover less than a kilometre from the landing beach.[142]

Improvisation part 2

Back in San Carlos, the second improvisation now followed to get the Welsh Guards up to full strength at Bluff Cove. What happened exactly on 7th June has remained a secret for almost forty years. But, the 'General Narrative' of the Board and *Galahad*'s Captain Roberts's eye-opening newly declassified report of 21 pages reveals for the first time what really happened next to fix the latest delay. What he records is entirely different from Falklands orthodoxy so far.

First off, a controversy has raged for forty years whether the *Galahad* was ever to take the Welsh Guards to Bluff Cove (Port Fitzroy) or to Fitzroy (Port Pleasant). That ghost, and all that follows from it, can now finally be laid to rest as a mirage. It is clear beyond any doubt from his report (but not only his)— written ten days after 8th June—that the LSL was to take the Welsh Guards to Bluff Cove all along.

Secondly, on 5th June 8.25am, Fieldhouse's signal to Moore had vetoed the first amphibious plan with the sentence 'catastrophe at sea with large loss of life politically unacceptable'. Subsequently, he ordered the amphibious staff to 'balance risk' in its plans at 4.25pm the same day. Yet, despite this caveat, on 7th June it was accepted 'widely'[143] in the early morning that *Intrepid* and *Galahad* would double up on the same pattern that night. *Intrepid*'s captain Dingemans mentioned again that he was concerned that a 'pattern' was developing. Both the divisional staff and the amphibious staff accepted that, instead of *HMS Intrepid*, *RFA Sir Galahad*, unaccompanied, would sail down the entire safe-from-Exocet corridor to Bluff Cove that Dingemans refused to sail through with a frigate escort.

Phil Roberts records in detail how 7th June progressed. Yeoman, who focused on 5 Infantry, was in charge of the second improvisation in response to the no-show on 6th June, too. Given the lack of OPGEN training of RFA staff such as Roberts, he came on board at 10.30am to instruct the captain in person. *Galahad* was to sail no later than 5pm to arrive at Bluff Cove/Port Fitzroy at 3am in the morning (an eight hour journey), and offload the remainder of the Welsh Guards. This matched like a glove the order to land at Yellow Beach, Port Fitzroy, that was given on *Fearless* the previous night to Major Sayle, the officer in charge of the remaining Welsh Guards. After dropping off the Guards, *Galahad* was to sail back the short distance to Port Pleasant at 5am for arrival at 6:30am to continue offloading whatever else it carried at Fitzroy Settlement. All would take place at night.[144]

Shortly after 1pm, 7th June—by which time the remaining 352 Welsh Guards were all on board for the first drop at 3am at Yellow Beach—Yeoman contacted the *Galahad* again. Via the 'embark/disembark net' (the Navy's short-range voice system) he gave notice to Roberts that the number of field ambulance troops destined for Fitzroy had increased from 30 to 90. The LSL would now also carry 90 Air Defence Team troops and four Rapier units to Fitzroy. The latter would be loaded by Sea King and the helicopter and its crew of 12 would come along on deck. Rapiers arrived down from the hills surrounding San Carlos's harbour by 4pm and after a last-minute piling on at 4.30pm of phosphorous grenades (smoke bombs) for the Welsh Guards that were to cause such chaos a day later, *Galahad* was ready to sail at 5pm.

Earlier during the morning briefing, Roberts had told Yeoman that his ship's capacity had shrunk to 320 men after an unexploded bomb had hurtled through its hull on 24th May and showed him the damaged dormitory and escape routes (on *Galahad*'s forward port side). That problem was also quickly dispatched by 5pm using a hacksaw and a Chinese welder. By now there were 595 troops on board.

The risk of 'large loss of life' that exercised London had by 5pm doubled by embarking on *Galahad* both the 352 Welsh Guards destined for Bluff Cove and the 243 men with their kit destined for Fitzroy. This was all signed off by Clapp's amphibious staff on *Fearless*. Roberts had had to signal the amphibious staff at 3.30pm for approval to carry up to 600 men instead of 500. He received their OK at 4pm, an hour before sailing.

Though not successful as a matter of risk balancing, at least as far as logistics were concerned, the above solved some problems. Having 'waited to rush', the Fitzroy hub on the southern flank was now at last being built up even as a large troop movement was in the final stage. On this sudden urgency, the Board identifies two main reasons: the Royal Marines moving into the 'MOUNT KENT/CHALLENGER region' and the '[a]ppalling weather conditions limiting the

Commandos endurance'.[145] Moore himself would soon be using Fitzroy as his own HQ rather than Teal Inlet –timely functioning Rapier protection was required for that, too. LCUs also moved freely between Port Pleasant and Bluff Cove's Port Fitzroy.

If there was another fly in the ointment, it was the fact that, because of the split, the remaining half of the Welsh Guards had been separated from their commanding officer, Colonel Rickett. His rank mattered. In case of the first two LCU movements to Bluff Cove, the Scots and Welsh Guards colonels on board (Michael Scott and Johnny Rickett respectively) had the seniority to issue new tactical orders. If there was a problem, services officers had to follow their commands even though they were not placed in 5 Infantry's chain of command. For the move on 7-8th June, however, the most senior guardsman was Sayle, a major. His rank was the most junior field rank and did not have this privilege.

It was a well-known issue. Admiral Nelson was very sensitive to its importance and would invariably send a Naval 'officer-in-charge' carrying his personal landing orders. Often this was quite a junior officer in rank, but he would have Nelson's authority to cut Gordian knots and resolve any stand-off between tactical and service officers.

Though Yeoman came on board *Galahad* to avoid the usual Royal Navy to Royal Fleet Auxiliary miscommunication issues, it looks as if the amphibious staff on the Flagship failed to recognise that adding a third organisation, the Army, to this mix was likely to cause similar problems that needed to be addressed. It was this ATP failure that would come home to roost with tragic consequences.

26

The Death Knell

The newly-released Kew records show that the first blow to Yeoman's adaptation ('Plan 3') came in the afternoon on 7th June at 5pm, and not as orthodox Falklands history has it, later in the evening at 10pm.

This may not seem like a great difference, but it changes what happened in an important way and it is worth going into the detail. Although the field ambulance's 90 troops were on board by now for the second stop, their equipment had still not arrived by 5pm. The decision to pack them on *Galahad* as well was made at 1pm but there had been a delay in telling the ambulance to move.[146] Given Yeoman's 5pm deadline, *Galahad* contacted the amphibious staff on *Fearless* via San Carlos harbour's local voice system (the 'embark/disembark net') and asked during the call 'what was the latest acceptable time for SIR GALAHAD to sail San Carlos.' Roberts was now given 8pm as a new deadline.

This was a dramatic change. The three hours delay to Yeoman's schedule meant that, even if *Galahad* sailed from San Carlos immediately at 8pm, she would only be able to sail from Bluff Cove/Fitzroy to the second destination at Fitzroy/Port Pleasant at 8am, or sunrise. While the Welsh Guards' Bluff Cove drop would still take place at night, just, the hour and thirty minutes of the second leg to Fitzroy with the remaining troops would have to take place after first light. Another change, more troops, more risks. Moore's staff on the Flagship seems not to have noticed that this meant additional protection against air raids of some sort was needed or that any further delay after 8pm that night meant that the Welsh Guards move to and disembarkation at the frontline risked being exposed to daylight.

The field ambulance's stores finally arrived at 7.45pm by mexeflote, a quarter of an hour before *Galahad*'s second deadline. Hitherto also unknown is that, instead of being at loggerheads with those ordered to disembark Fitzroy instead of Bluff Cove, the Welsh Guards and the Field Ambulance worked closely as a team. Welsh Guards started helping with loading the medical equipment on board. At 8 pm, Major Sayle and the commanding officer of the field ambulance came to see Roberts on the bridge to say that it would take at least until 10pm to load everything. Shortly after receiving the two officers, Roberts made his decision. At 8.15pm,[147] he flashed (the top priority signal) to the amphibious staff on *Fearless* and to 5 Infantry HQ in Goose Green that he would remain in San Carlos for the night as a consequence of the sailing 'in accordance with previous instructions received embark/disembark net'.[148] Next-day's tragedy would not have happened if the story had stopped here. But Fieldhouse and Moore's strategy to procrastinate and delay had run out of luck.

It was not to be. Roberts's 8.15pm termination signal was received by the duty officer in *Fearless*'s amphibious operations room. (None of the signalling delays of hours that the Board identified seem to have manifested itself that night.) Nor did Roberts's signal ask for new instructions. The duty officer did not file the signal as for superiors to deal with in the morning. Instead, he seemed to have been waiting for it and immediately 'shook' the SOO, Clapp's second-in-command, and told him of *Galahad*'s flash cancelling its sailing that night.[149] Rapidly, at 8.52pm the duty officer flashed new instructions to Roberts—*Galahad* was ordered to sail at 10pm latest.

Things were now going wrong precipitously. At 9:45pm, 15 minutes ahead of the latest schedule, *Galahad* was finally loaded, and, packed to the gunwales, ready to sail by 10pm.

The decision to move *Galahad*'s sailing time to 10pm meant that the Welsh Guards disembarkation at Bluff Cove would now also take place in broad daylight. This was precisely what was not supposed to happen.

This was not the only major *ad hoc* change to 'Plan 3'. In order to get the state of play in the Bluff Cove area, *Fearless* signalled *Tristram* at Fitzroy at the same time whether it was about to return to San Carlos as planned. *Tristram* duly signalled back at 8.30pm that it had failed to discharge all of her cargo and would have to continue to unload.[150] Including what had been achieved that day, 'it would take between 36 and 48 hours [three days with 16 working hours]'.[151] In other words, there was now a nightmare scenario where two LSLs would be offloading in plain sight, one of them decanting half a battalion—in fact, the same total as a battalion if one added the assorted other Army troops on board.

Two LSLs

Had the staffs on board *Fearless* thought this through? The Board thinks so. As to sending *Galahad* instead of *Intrepid*, the amphibious staff 'was well aware of the danger involved especially in the light of the response to the original plan' that Fieldhouse had vetoed because it might expose the Royal Navy's *Intrepid* to daylight for a few hours, the Inquiry concludes.[152] All possible schedules were debated by both Moore's and Clapp's staff on *Fearless* during the day.

But had they? As to air protection, the *Fearless* staffs thought 'air defence could not be achieved until 8 June',[153] though this must count as one of the most economical truths as the detailed Kew report on the matter shows. 'During daylight hours ships remained within San Carlos are under Rapier cover concentrated within that vicinity' and on 3rd June four Rapier 'Fire Units were transported by air to Teal Inlet'.[154] However, what was considered essential to both these hubs, the flagship staff did not the consider essential to the Army's hub at Fitzroy, which was nearest to Port Stanley. In case of Fitzroy, sending four units to protect the hub was merely considered 'desirable' but not a 'prerequisite for LSLs in this area'.[155] Helicoptering them to Fitzroy—like the one to Teal Inlet, equidistant from San Carlos—was considered impossible for 'a lift of this magnitude'.[156]

What about CAP? Moore's staff had asked for additional Harrier cover from 1 to 3pm (two hours before sundown) from *HMS Invincible*. But it appears no one checked whether this was confirmed—*Invincible* said it never received the request.[157] At the same time, Moore's staff had signalled the day before, 6th June, at 4.45pm that Harriers should stay above 10,000 feet over Fitzroy (a precaution to avoid blue-on-blue hits) as if Rapier was already functioning that day.[158]

In fact, the conclusions of the Inquiry that were made public in 2007 on the 25th anniversary didn't tell the full truth about Rapier either.

The newly-released Kew documents reveal that unlike Port Fitzroy, the LSLs in Port Pleasant hadn't been considered. 'No instructions had been issued to include the ships in the protective cover of the Rapier', it concluded.[159] Unlike San Carlos and Teal Inlet, shipping cover had not been ordered and the Rapier missiles that could have been fired at the 1.10pm Skyhawks weren't because the topography screened the harbour.[160] And so, none were. The Royal Fleet Auxiliary LSLs and those on them had truly been left to their own salvation by everyone, including staff on the Flagship, unlike the Royal Navy and Royal Marines' assets in the north.

None of this is easy to understand. Using a Royal Navy LPD in daytime was unacceptable because it might be destroyed despite having a chaperone frigate while sailing home. Dingemans also worried about *Intrepid* travelling at night around Lafonia because of highly unlikely night bombers and a small Argentinian observer outpost on Sea Island, 15 miles off Lafonia's tip. Even then it must have sounded exotic. But not to Moore and Fieldhouse.

In effect, the Flagship assumed on 7th June that, because the weather had been bad so far, 'medium or poor visibility'[161] on 8th June was going to create the robust protection Fitzroy's hub needed against an Argentinian air attack on 8th June. About this, but only this, the experts on the Inquiry were withering. Without mincing words their Report concluded, 'In planning the support activities at FITZROY['s Port Pleasant], weather had not been considered as a governing factor although the presence of [Argentine] OP's (Observation Posts) was strongly suspected.' This blunt statement about the amphibious group's decisions that day is one of the most devastating in the report.

More human errors

And yet. Though Plan 3 as executed by the Flagship staff raised the stakes considerably on 'large loss of life' during *Galahad*'s journey from San Carlos to Bluff Cove, it would still be workable once the LSL arrived at Yellow Beach at first light. The Sea King on board could quickly airlift the Welsh Guards and their mortars, bergens etc onshore. Yellow Beach was equidistant from Fitzroy and the helicopter could even airlift the four Rapier units in position with *Galahad* sailing after 8am to Port Pleasant/Fitzroy. There, the remaining 243 Army troops could have disembarked at Fitzroy's jetty as well as the field ambulance vehicles and other stores.

Though a risk, the Argentinian air force would need between two and three hours to organise and despatch aircraft to East Falkland and daylight visibility really only began at 9am that day. This all added up to a daylight risk of around three to four hours. Nor would the smaller number of troops have looked to the Argentine Observation post as if a major troop move crammed on *Galahad* was taking place.

We will return to the real Achilles heel of Yeoman's plan, but, in the meantime, another human error struck. Amphibious staff communications were never perfect (hence their handholding of RFA staff), but they certainly failed that evening on *Fearless*. Both divisional and amphibious staffs discussed Roberts's flash not to sail at 8pm and agreed together to order to *Galahad* to sail at 10pm to Bluff Cove. As mentioned, the duty officer was duly instructed to signal the order but the result was that 'SIR GALAHAD was instructed to sail to FITZROY'.[162]

Why?

The simple reason was that a shorthand had crept into the duty officer's paperwork. At 12.38pm, a summary of the day ahead ('night intentions') had gone out from *Fearless* to ships in San Carlos. These summaries were roundups sent at the same time each day. Like a Royal Navy gazette, they provided the bigger picture for the staffs of amphibious units as to what was going on. In fact, eight minutes before the summary mentioning 'FITZROY' was sent out, Yeoman had popped back to *Fearless* having ordered Roberts to go to both destinations—Bluff Cove *and* Fitzroy. About half an hour later Yeoman made his voice call from *Fearless*'s staff room, but merely to triple the number of field-ambulance troops on *Galahad* from 30 to 90. Seven hours prior, Yeoman had, of course, already dispatched his assistant Todd to lead the two *Foxtrots* with Welsh Guards to Bluff Cove at 4am.

The 12.38pm intentions signal sent by the duty officer from the same operations room from which Yeoman was shortly to make his call had summarised the LSL's movements as 'SIR GALAHAD TO FITZROY. SAIL AT 21.00 [5pm—Yeoman's first deadline given to *Galahad* in the morning]'. It was correct. *Galahad*'s end destination was indeed 'FITZROY'. But the duty-clerk's telegram style elided the first stop Yeoman had ordered for the Welsh Guards—'Bluff Cove'.

A summary sent at 9.18am, exactly three hours earlier, had used Bluff Cove as shorthand for the two-pronged operation. This earlier 'situation report/intentions' signal read: 'Tonight—GALAHAD transport balance of 2WG [sic] to BLUFF COVE'.[163] To underline its importance, this 9.18am summary had been signalled priority to *Galahad*.

It didn't matter then. As part of RFA handholding by the Flagship, Yeoman had gone on board *Galahad* an hour later to give in-person orders for two hours and to do a full inspection. Furthermore, 5 Infantry who were further afield at Goose Green had also been cc-ed at 9.18am—Wilson's brigade was of course deeply anxious to get its two rifle companies and mortar platoon moved to Rickett on the frontline and to know when it would happen.

When Roberts signalled at 8.15pm that he was postponing departure until next evening, there was however no further handholding in person or via voice calls. Signals were the only means of communication left.

In the signals that followed, three amphibious staff members were to end up at cross purposes. First there was the senior staff member on board *Fearless* who passed the joint order of Flagship staffs for *Galahad* to sail at 10pm on to the amphibious duty officer. This senior officer 'meant BLUFF COVE', the Board found.[164] The duty officer on board who 'drafted and relayed'[165] this order to *Galahad*, however, used the short-hand 'FITZROY'[166] after clearing the text of the signal with Clapp's SOO whom he had shaken.[167] The SOO should have picked up on the ellipsis in the signal the Report concluded.[168]

Despite communication problems being well-known by now, it is unclear whether the Royal Navy staffs on duty on *Fearless* considered that an ambiguous order could prompt the RFA staff on *Galahad* to make a wrong turn with its frontline troops. And so the printer's devil of Royal Navy to RFA communications nestled on *Galahad*.

Lacking Royal Navy communications training, Roberts's staff informally interpreted *Fearless*'s duty officer's signal incorrectly as a formal change to Yeoman's orders to sail to two destinations.[169] In effect, they erroneously invented 'Plan 4' and assumed incorrectly that the Royal Navy had taken Bluff Cove off the list and that they were ordered to sail straight to Port Pleasant only.

Had there been a Royal Navy landing officer on board, he would have under-stood immediately that the signal only changed the sailing time, not the plan itself. If *Fearless* had indeed meant to change Yeoman's destinations, Moore's divisional staff would have had to issue ancillary orders to the Welsh Guards on board telling them what to do after disembarking at Fitzroy. All this is standard ATP, standard Nelson. As it was, *Galahad*'s RFA staff did not make this critical connection between amphibious orders and arms orders. The RFA's job was to be the Task Force's transport of stores to destinations. They were not expected to have or, indeed, obliged to have military tactical training.[170]

QE2 revisited

It seems difficult to imagine, but yet more communications mayhem followed. Roberts had cc-ed his termination signal of 8.15pm to 5 Infantry's HQ at Goose Green. As on *Fearless*'s staffs, this had had the effect of a brick in a pond. The last Wilson's staff had gleaned on this move was the 9.18am priority signal that *Galahad* would sail to Bluff Cove with its Guards— as per orders given to their troops on board. Wilson's brigade immediately tried to contact Moore on *Fearless* to ask what was going on given the half-baked infantry formation on the frontline. Even an Argentinian probing attack would likely lead to dead soldiers.

However, the Kew documents reveal another new fact that has remained hidden for forty years. The Flagship had sailed from San Carlos at 6.35pm for Teal Inlet.[171] Moore wanted to take stock in person with the Royal Marines' brigade staff on location and assess the attack-readiness of the Marines stationed on the northern flank at Mount Kent. The Teal Inlet trip clearly didn't preclude robust signal communications with Roberts's *Galahad* in San Carlos at 8.15pm, but reaching Goose Green was a different matter.

The Inquiry provides granular detail on this problem. The link to Goose Green relied on High Frequency radio (HF). Medium- and short-wave HF was fine during the day but 'unreliable at night'. Moreover, if *Fearless* left San Carlos, on 'some occasions the link broke completely'.[172] This was because, when moving, *Fearless* HF receiving unit for ground wave 'became masked by terrain phenomena'.[173]

The evening of 8th June was clearly one of these 'rare occasions'. Having detailed 5 Infantry's desperate attempts to get hold of their general on HF that night, the Board concludes improbably that these were 'unfamiliar in Naval communications'.[174] Moore's staff on *Fearless* simply did not receive Wilson's staff's appeals about the Welsh Guards after 8pm. Nor was the divisional staff on the Flagship able to accompany its order to *Galahad* to sail at 10pm with verbal instructions to make sure there was no misunderstanding on the Royal

Navy to RFA line. The voice embark/disembark net only worked in San Carlos, not beyond.

The Inquiry characterised Moore's decision to move away on *Fearless* that night as the general being 'confident that [5 Infantry] were aware of the intentions of SIR GALAHAD'.[175] That doesn't quite seem to do justice to the foreseeable impact Moore's decision to move out of reach could have on the final night of the troop move to the frontline.

When the duty officer on *Fearless* flashed the order at 8.52pm to *Galahad* to sail at 10pm to Fitzroy, he could not reach Goose Green if Goose Green could not reach him. Until *Fearless* was back in the morning in San Carlos, Wilson's staff had no way of finding out that *Galahad* had sailed with the Welsh Guards after all. That night, Moore seemed to have created a *QE2* situation of his own making. While his staff rolled the dice on visibility at Fitzroy, Moore himself was rolling the dice on the chances of war by moving out of reach from Goose Green and Fitzroy.

The Inquiry spends a lot of time discussing the signals the amphibious staff on the Flagship ought to have sent and that 5 Infantry had poor communications. But the truth is that, even if *Fearless*'s operations staff had followed the book, they were offline and the signals would have disappeared in the ether. All the Inquiry has to say about Moore's calamitous decision is a bland general observation that 'communications with the Command Ship must not be susceptible to her movements'.[176]

As midnight passed, no one in the Falklands realised that *Galahad*, having invented Plan 4 as a result of *Fearless*'s staff imprecision, was going to skip Bluff Cove and head straight to Port Pleasant with all of its troops. Maintaining radio silence to avoid detection by Argentinian tech, *Galahad* sailed into Fitzroy Port Pleasant with us at 6.50am on 8th June to anchor next to *Tristram*.

Meanwhile, as stipulated by Army protocol, expecting the other half of his battalion to arrive at Bluff Cove following General Moore's personal assurance the previous night, Colonel Rickett had sent two Welsh Guards officers to Yellow Beach, one inlet over. They could not understand where their troops were, or, indeed, what was going on in the first place. Another day, another improper amphibious manoeuvre.

27

Shambles

It was a complete shambles, but the arrival that morning of the *Galahad* with 595 troops and cargo at Fitzroy was still not necessarily a disaster. On *Tristram* were the two amphibious majors who knew the ins-and-outs of the Guards' failed troop movement to the front line over the previous two nights. The *Tangos* LCU commander knew that the Welsh Guards were destined for Bluff Cove from his original orders, and so did Major Todd who had taken his place as improvised commander of the two *Foxtrots* when the four *Tangos* didn't make the rendezvous on 6-7th June. Also, six LCUs—three quarters of the Task Force's amphibious work horses—were available in Port Pleasant on 7th June.

Tristram had arrived just before dawn on 7th June. It had left San Carlos at 11pm, an hour later than *Galahad* would leave the next evening. It had sailed a little after *Fearless* had departed with the battalion of Welsh Guards with the various staffs still counting on meeting up with the four *Tangos* later that night to insert the battalion into Bluff Cove. *Tristram*'s captain had been briefed by Yeoman in the same way as *Galahad*'s captain Roberts would be the next day. In fact, Todd had assisted Yeoman with the loading of *Tristram* in San Carlos on 6th June.

The new Kew reports make clear that, unfortunately, there already was another form of Royal Navy-to-RFA confusion as to Port Pleasant. All the plans that had been discussed mentioned Bluff Cove and *Tristram*'s captain, too, heard—as Roberts was instructed the next day—that Bluff Cove was his destination. 'After some confusion the captain was clear that his instructions were to proceed to FITZROY', the Inquiry says.[177] When I first read this sentence in the trove of documents, it puzzled me. What was there to be confused about for an experienced captain such as *Tristram*'s Robin Green?

But then the map I discovered subsequently illustrated the consternation he must have felt. Port Fitzroy served the settlements on both banks—Fitzroy's hub on the southside and Bluff Cove's front line on the northside. Port Pleasant, however, only gave access to Fitzroy. More importantly from his point of view, Port Fitzroy was much wider and did not have the shape of a narrow tube to create a shooting gallery for air attacks like Port Pleasant. Nor did it have Port Pleasant's very narrow and complicated entry channel where *Tristram*'s hull had only a foot clearance to the bottom and less than 20 feet to rocks on either side. Port Pleasant made little sense. In the Falklands habitual foul weather, it was truly a trap. But since he thought he had been ordered to go to Fitzroy via Port Pleasant that is where he anchored on 7th June. At the same time, the Scots Guards arrived in Port Fitzroy (at the top of the map), however.

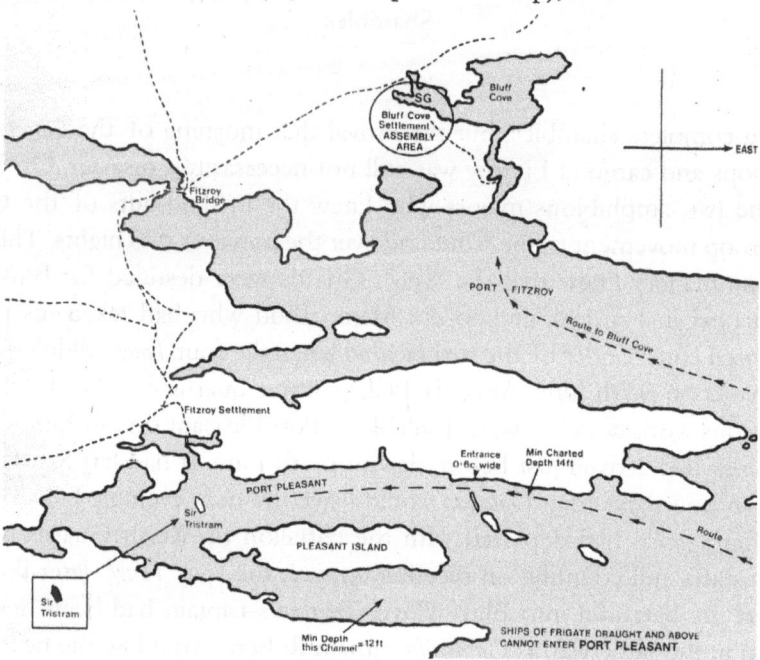

It is interesting, therefore, that one of the themes of the Inquiry is the interchangeable terminology among amphibious officers (but not Moore's divisional staff) between ambi-harborous Fitzroy Settlement and the name of the inlet with access to Bluff Cove—Port Fitzroy. Indeed one of the thirteen annexes is entirely devoted to explaining the confusion between the two on board *Fearless*. Unlike *Galahad*'s captain's report, *Tristram*'s captain Robin Green's report will only be released in 32 years from now and we won't know the detail of his consternation until then. Interesting, too, is the fact that the new Kew documents do reveal that RFA Captain Green (quite rightly, as we know) worried about the absence of air cover at Bluff Cove.

Upon *Tristram*'s arrival on the other side of Fitzroy, the four *Tangos* waiting for *Tristram* at Bluff Cove, Port Fitzroy, also sailed to Port Pleasant along East Island to meet the LSL at 7am, the Report details.[178]

In order to lay the first stone of the Fitzroy hub, *Tristram* carried an Amphibious Beach Unit (ABU). This team belonged to *Intrepid* (it was loaded on to *Tristram* when Dingemans's *Intrepid* developed 'engine problems' on 6th June and *Fearless* took over the transport of Welsh Guards and *Foxtrots* later that evening). On 7th June, at the waterline closest to *Tristram* the ABU troops rolled out their dock equipment to haul stores, petrol, pallets of ammunition, food, etc off landing craft and on to their shore dumps 50 yards behind the beach organised by 5 Infantry's 81 Ordnance troops.[179]

The ABU's commander soon made an unpleasant discovery as his men set out their stall. Though Port Fitzroy had been recced extensively, the reconnaissance of Port Pleasant where *Tristram* anchored had been less thorough. It turned out that the beach where the ABU deployed was not continuously usable.

Although on this inlet's side, the Fitzroy anchorage had a jetty that could be used 24 hours a day for men and light kit, unfortunately, usage of the adjoining shingle beach was restricted by nature. Because it submerged around hightide, it could not be used for heavy equipment or palletised cargo for 8 hours of the day. High tide on 7th June was reached at 6.29am and when the four *Tangos* arrived from Bluff Cove's Port Fitzroy at 7am—it would take until 8.29am before any of *Tristram*'s heavy cargo could get to the beach. That window would close again from around 5.45pm to 9.45pm after which there would again be eight working hours bathed in full-moonlight.

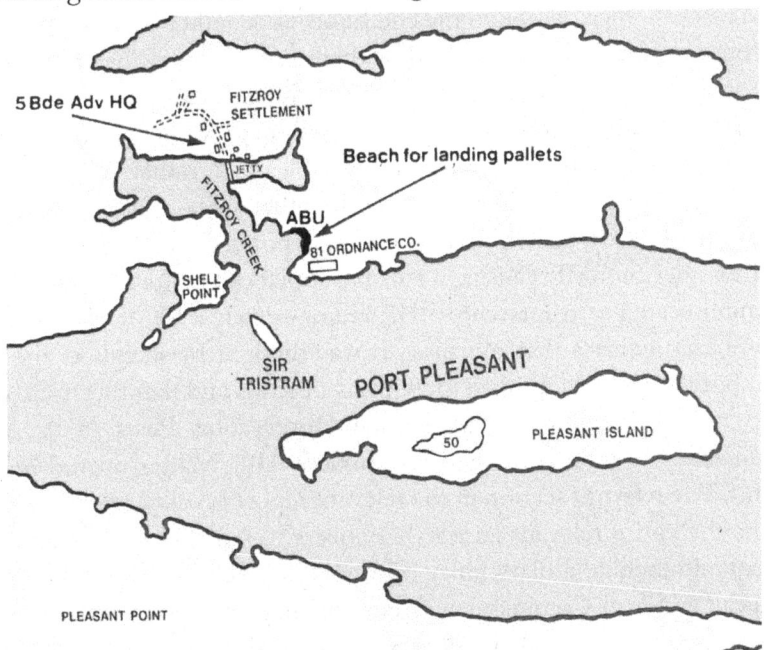

To make matters worse, the pebble beach had an underwater obstruction that restricted how many LCUs could berth at the same time or together with the mexeflote *Tristram* had brought along.[180] The next unfortunate discovery was that the incline of the beach was too steep for access. The new documents reveal that this was addressed by asking for 5 Infantry's help. 2 Para stationed at

Fitzroy supplied troops to smooth down the incline. Until they were done, there was nothing that could be done to unload *Tristram* at the anchorage.

It was also discovered that the 'Michigan tractor' that was supposed to haul stores from the beach to the 81 Ordnance dumps gripped the ABU's trackways in such a way that it chewed up the shingle. Only a smaller piece of hauling equipment, an Eager Beaver, could be used in a complicated zig zag to get pallets off the landing craft on to the beach and onwards. *Tristram* fortunately had its own Eager Beaver and lent it to the ABU which doubled the offloading capacity and lessened the problem a little.[181]

Fortunately, in San Carlos, Yeoman and Todd had loaded in total only 900 tons of stores on to *Tristram*. This was a modest 30 per cent of *Tristram*'s full capacity. Ever since the first LSL voyage to Teal Inlet on 30th May had taken two LCUs an entire day at San Carlos to load a whole ship, LSLs' cargo had been reduced to even out the LCU usage for other tasks in the Transport Area. Since the roundtable-class to which *Tristram* and *Galahad* belonged were designed to offload 90 tons an hour, and Yeoman and Todd knew on 6th June that there would be at least four LCUs at Bluff Cove (two *Tangos* and two *Foxtrots* that had swapped places—there would in the end be six all together because of the failed rendezvous), everything was designed by them in such a way that *Tristram* would be back in San Carlos in the morning of 8th June. Except of course that she couldn't because Port Pleasant—the poor anchorage where *Tristram* ended up on 7th June, a beach south of Fitzroy (Port Pleasant) rather than one east of Fitzroy (Port Fitzroy, with Bluff Cove on the other side)—had not been as well recced as Port Fitzroy, according to the Kew reports.

Here another butterfly causing a storm popped out of its cocoon. The ABU unit communicated over unsecure VHF radios—likely a lot of traffic given the litany of beach failures that morning. It was thought by members the *Intrepid* unit that both the terrain masked these transmissions and that they were too low powered to be picked up by Argentine Observation Posts in the area.[182] Unfortunately, this was wrong and the careless ABU chatter proved helpful to the enemy. The relevant section in the relevant report is still secret under Section 3(4), as is the entire relevant annex that covers it, but the newly released Kew documents do include a diary entry of Captain Aurelio Gaffoglio, Argentina's swashbuckling Naval Commander in Port Stanley. He writes on 7th June, 'By means of radio interceptions it appears that they are disembarking amphibious vehicles on a nearby beach, which could be Fitzroy'.[183]

As Paras helped smooth the beach in the morning of 7th June, it seems therefore that the four *Tangos* had even more time on their hands when the moved to join *Tristram* in Port Pleasant at 7am. They already had had 24 hours of down time at Bluff Cove on 6th June. But with the beach out of order, there was not much they could do. There was plenty of time for an unwritten rule to be observed and have a breakfast competition between the *Tangos*. In rivalry to be the best, the four crews made 'the boss' four breakfasts that morning, their LCU commander recalls in his memoirs.[184]

The existing Fitzroy jetty may not have been much in use either for offloading that day. The *Tangos'* commander 'insisted the crews stopped as much as possible during this natural "break" around high water and got rest, showers and hot meals as best they could from the ship [*Tristram*].'[185] The crew were well looked after. Clapp and the LCU commander write that the latter exercised 'great concern for his men and, in turn, for their efficiency, but his actions did not always meet with everyone's approval.'[186]

As to his own day on 7th June, 'Once orders had been issued I was superfluous to the offload', the major concluded in his own memoir. Going ashore, he went to spend time with local Falklander friends ('Janet Blakely—our elderly babysitter'). This was, he writes, not just about 'coffee-housing' but also about gaining 'much useful information' from Port Stanley refugees. He commiserated with them on the 'harsh realities of war'.[187] Later in the afternoon—dusk seems to have fallen as lights were on—he also went to 'clock in' with 5 Infantry's local embryo HQ—a shed at Fitzroy Settlement. It was 'warm and comfortable'. There he found Major Barney Rolfe-Smith and he introduced himself to the 2 Para officer.[188] This appears to have been after 5pm when darkness fell as the LCU commander recalled being concerned about 'lamps blazing beneath huge skylights pointing to the stars'.

One of the topics the two officers covered was 5 Infantry's poor communications.[189] Virtually all orders at Fitzroy were still issued by Brigadier Wilson flying in by helicopter. Rolfe-Smith had use of 2 Para's portable HF equipment which had the same issues as HF from Goose Green to San Carlos: no signal at night and in any case they could only reach the Scots Guards at Bluff Cove. The Guards themselves could only at times reach 5 Infantry's HQ at Goose Green as the LCU commander had discovered himself on the eventful evening with atrocious weather of 6th June. On top of that the HF equipment was not secure. But Rolfe-Smith was expecting the *Monsunen* later that evening to bring two communication vehicles from Goose Green that would finally establish secure VHF and HF links between Fitzroy and Bluff Cove and by extension Goose Green on a good day.

The two *Foxtrots* at Bluff Cove

Meanwhile, what about the two *Foxtrots* that Major Todd had navigated to Bluff Cove to drop off the first half of Welsh Guards? Sailing through the Z-bend, he joined *Tristram* at Port Pleasant with the LCUs. He had disembarked Colonel Rickett and his half of the Welsh Guards at 3am and made it to *Tristram* at 7am.[190] Clearly, Todd performed his duties very well. He was to be mentioned in despatches, a highly respected decoration just short of a gallantry medal. It names a member of the armed forces in an official report written by a superior officer sent up the chain of command and in which their gallant or meritorious action in the face of the enemy is described. In Todd's case, his superior officer was Clapp. In 1982 the award was signified by a bronze oak leaf worn on the relevant campaign medal.

On 7th June, Todd's *Foxtrots* didn't idle. They also lent the *Tangos* a partial hand with offloading *Tristram*. *Foxtrot 4* initially 'lay up recovering from her overnight trip',[191] but then began helping offload *Tristram* from 4pm to when the hightide window closed at 5.45pm.[192] *Foxtrot 1* did start helping with offloading during the whole beach window once the Paras were done making the anchorage serviceable; but it was in addition sent back to Bluff Cove to transfer troops from one side of the inlet to the other inlet of ambi-harborous Fitzroy.[193] Had *Tristram* anchored at Bluff Cove, this would of course have precluded the need for LCUs to yoyo for an hour each way between the two inlets (and a lot more that was to happen the following day).

What did Yeoman's assistant Major Tony Todd or the Beachmaster of the ABU make of Port Pleasant's poor anchorage? Separately, both came to the conclusion that instead of a single day, *Tristram*'s offload would now really take between 36 and 48 hours—ostensibly five times longer than Todd's superior officer Yeoman had planned. Likewise, the LCUs' commander says that during his visit at dusk to 5 Infantry's Rolfe-Smith, he told the Para major, 'We knew we could not complete the task that night, [7th June] but if we worked fast, I suggested, she might, just might, be ready to sail the following night.'[194] In fact, neither *Tristram* had been given a deadline when to head back for San Carlos originally, nor had the ABU's Beachmaster been given a deadline for *Tristram*'s offload by the amphibious staff on *Fearless* the previous evening.[195] Since the anchorage proved to be a bottle neck, Fitzroy's new dock was going to have unrushed days from 7th June around.

While all this was still to take place in Port Pleasant on 7th June, the Flagship was feverishly concocting Plan 3 with *Galahad*. *Fearless* had at this point still no idea that *Tristram* would not be returning that night, it seems, not until 8.30pm later in the day at any rate. And when it did, amphibious staff did nothing with the information. When *Galahad* sailed directly for Fitzroy at 10pm, *Fearless* was out of the picture heading towards Teal. There were no safeguards left to fix the plan with another patch.

A Sound of Revelry by Night
'The Eve of Waterloo', Lord Byron

In his *Reasons in Writing* (1993), the LCU commander describes his evening on *Sir Tristram* before her destruction on 8th June. As we already know, by this time the Argentine military on the Falklands were aware of likely activity at Fitzroy as a result of the VHF transmissions by some of *Intrepid's* ABU troops setting up Fitzroy's beachhead who didn't realise that their chatter was not secure.

The commander vividly recalls the details that evening: 'Dinner, served by impeccable Chinese stewards, was conducted as though there was no outside world. Having been rebuked by Robin [*Tristram's* Captain Green] for knocking the "weevils" out of my biscuits during the cheese course—an old and harmless affection which did not reflect on the ship's purser—I felt I should repay the officers with a bottle of port. The conversation touched only fleetingly on the business in hand; for the most part the meal was a lovely oasis of civilised behaviour and amusing stories with old friends and colleagues set in an angry and arid desert. I revelled in it more perhaps than I should have done.'[196]

For the avoidance of doubt, the Inquiry did not find wrong-doing or criticise anyone who was on *Tristram* that evening. This was a case of alcohol, and good conversation, shelter, warmth, snow white starched tablecloths, properly cooked food, hot showers and warm beds for the night in Port Pleasant, 3 miles from 1000 Scots and Welsh Guards dug in at Bluff Cove and 6 miles from Argentina's 155mm Howitzer envelope around Port Stanley's garrison of 9000 troops.

It is unusual for a sharp physical reaction to be caused by a book. But, given how many lives were lost and young men injured the next day, reading these 1993 passages for the first time decades later, I felt a deep surge of emotions and had to put the book down.

The Next Morning, 8th June

At 6:30am while it was still dark, Roberts reports that he announced to everyone on the *Galahad*'s Tannoy that she was approaching the harbour in enemy sight and a full blackout needed to be maintained with 'silent routine', no banging on the hull or on deck, no auxiliary machinery, or unsecure broadcasts. Action stations had to remain manned for the whole day with sandwiches brought up to staff. As one of his first planning actions in London, Clapp had ordered Bofors anti-aircraft artillery to be installed on all RFA ships. In addition, the connection with *HMS Exeter*, the CAP scout for air attack red alerts of fifteen minutes, was checked by the radio operators. Recollections vary.

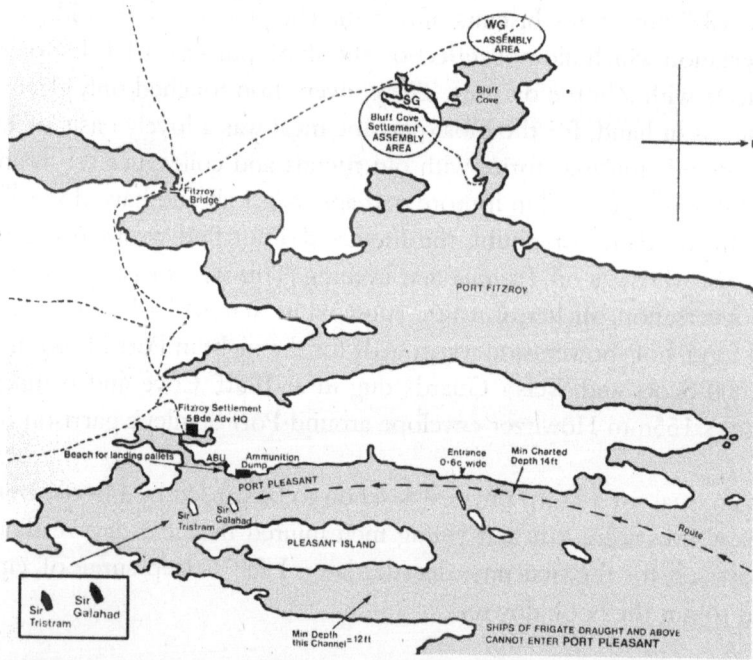

Aided like *Tristram* the day before by a full moon and no clouds, *Galahad* care-fully eased herself through the narrow rocky channel ('you could spit to each side, Captain Roberts recalled) to Fitzroy as she followed the wrong orders. Dawn broke shortly after and the ship dropped its port anchor at 7.15am and was secure 10 minutes later. In an interview with Legasee, Captain Roberts revealed that he was already communicating with *Tristram* staff well before then: 'They must have known we were coming because I was talking to *Tristram* about the depth over the bar, the entrance [see graph]... and he replied... in fact he had been on the original signal for me to go to Fitzroy/Bluff Cove'. The Sea King on deck immediately started offloading the Rapier units to their locations in Fitzroy, leaving the ship by 10am. What follows has not been made public for four decades.

Despite the flurry of activity on *Galahad* it took until 8.15am for an LCU, *Foxtrot 4*, to arrive. Roberts's report confirmed our memory of the morning.

Overnight, *Tristram* had indeed received a signal that *Galahad* was on her way. Roberts himself says in his captain's report, 'our Navtrack and ETA were advised to all concerned' when *Galahad* sailed at 10pm. It could have been that signal which arrived 'overnight' on *Tristram*'s teleprinter as *Fearless* would not return from Teal Inlet until later in the morning. Or, perhaps, *Fearless* sent another signal once back before dawn at San Carlos. (We won't know until all evidence is made public.) In any case, since the Royal Fleet Auxiliary did not have a tactical role, its Operation Corporate procedures were not the same as those of the Royal Navy staff in *Fearless*'s amphibious operations room. The signal remained unread on *Tristram* at night and it wasn't apparently until after 8am that an amphibious officer picked it off the machine to read.[197]

Ready to disembark for Bluff Cove on the tank deck stood 352 Welsh Guards. Mustered by Major Sayle from the moment of anchoring, they had been waiting for more than an hour—ready to disembark at the front line. Sayle had been given strict orders as to what to do and where to go.

This was when the first snag in failing to adhere to ATP doctrine manifested itself as we know. He was met by service officers who had received no orders from the Flagship the previous night apart from permission to carry on offloading *Tristram* for another couple of days. Among them was *Foxtrot 1*'s LCU commander who had been ordered to direct the landing craft to *Galahad*. Welsh Guards Major Bremner said, 'it arrived at the stern ramp; it was full of ammunition. We were offered space for some twenty men' in *Above All, Courage*, Max Arthur's 1985 book on the Falklands.

The disconnect wouldn't have mattered, though, given the five other LCUs that were at Port Pleasant the previous day. Despite the delay, there was still plenty of time. Two LCUs could take all the troops to the frontline at Bluff Cove in an hour. Given the clear, calm weather that morning, they could even enter the inlet through a short-cut through the kelp between Bluff Cove and Port Pleasant at East Island (which is a few hundred yards off Position BC17).

Except for one small thing. The five other LCUs were no longer at Fitzroy, as they had been withdrawn. In the twelve hours prior to *Galahad*'s arrival the chances of war intervened in a brutal way while Argentine generals sniffed an opportunity as a result of the chatter. At 4pm the previous day, their number had gone down by four *Tangos* when they left Port Pleasant at 4pm on 7th June, an hour and forty five minutes before the anchorage's hightide window closed. That left Port Pleasant with only two *Foxtrots*.

The inefficiency of Moore's decision at the end of May to slow down the southern flank, focus on the north flank and disembark 5 Infantry at San Carlos rather than straight into Goose Green on 2nd June, was coming to the fore with a ghastly sting in its tail.

San Carlos had by now lost ten LCU days' worth of loading and unloading. Dingemans was the first to create this problem when he decided mid-voyage to forego the planned drop-off/collection of *Tangos* during the Scots Guards move on 5-6th June. 'The absence of the LCUs was caused by Captain Peter Dingemans', a senior logistics officer agreed in 2022.[198] Had Dingemans stuck to the plan to return with the *Tangos* on 6th June as planned, the Task Force's hub wouldn't have lost its first four LCU days. Yeoman's LCU-swap by *Fearless* in accordance to Plan 2 did preserve San Carlos's prevailing LCU capacity. But when that rendezvous also failed all six LCUs ended up in Bluff Cove and there was not a single one left in San Carlos to aid the mexeflotes and LCVPs on 7th June.

Tristram had been instructed by Flagship staff that the *Tangos* were to rendezvous in the morning of 8th June with Dingemans's *Intrepid* at Lafonia's Low Bay. This location in West Falkland's Adventure Sound was even closer to San Carlos than the location under Lively Island where Dingemans had prematurely cast off the Scots Guards two days earlier. It has been said that this instruction was given before *Tristram* sailed on 6th June, but that would mean *Fearless*'s staff knew then already that the *Tangos* at Bluff Cove weren't going to make their rendezvous an hour later at 12.15am. It would also mean that the four-hour search party by one of the two frigates and night-vision equipped helicopters had been ordered for no reason.

This order to the *Tangos* reveals another extraordinary fact about 'Plan 3'. Dingemans was collecting the LCUs with an empty *Intrepid*. Instead of sailing empty, all that was needed was for him to do was to take the balance of the Welsh Guards forward, for the two *Foxtrots* to be ordered to join the rendezvous, embark the two Welsh Guards rifle companies and the mortar platoon at the meeting point and take them to Bluff Cove. All of the heaviest Welsh Guards equipment had already made it to the front line. The same trip had been made so many times now, with plenty of time to spare for the exchange, that there was little chance of *Intrepid* having to return after dark.[199]

Instead of spreading the risk of a 'large loss of life' over two ships, the Flagship staffs 'widely' agreed, however, to shunt it all on the LSL that had just returned that morning from delivering stores to Teal Inlet in the north: *Sir Galahad*. She was the only source for aviation fuel to the Royal Marines hub there. In an interview with Legasee, Captain Roberts remembered, 'we had all these helicopters off the stern waiting to come in... there must have been forty of them'. The *Tangos'* instruction must have been sent to *Tristram* before Yeoman boarded *Galahad* at 10.30am to execute the Flagship orders he had received and he started loading up this vessel with Welsh Guards instead of *Intrepid*. As the Royal Navy's *Intrepid* sailed empty, RFA *Galahad* would in the end sail at twice its capacity of 300 troops at 10pm.

Tristram and *Fearless* didn't appear to communicate with each other much that day (we won't know this for another 32 years either). Had the team on *Fearless*, for example, known that *Tristram* was still full of cargo before 4pm, it could also have left one *Tango* at Port Pleasant to deal with two ships at its sub-par anchorage the next day. Yeoman's plan at 10:30am on 7th June foresaw that *Galahad* would arrive at Port Pleasant by 6.30am next day.

As it was, we saw that *Fearless*'s amphibious staff appear to have found out about *Tristram*'s massive offload delay four and a half hours after the *Tangos* departure at 8.30pm at night.[200] The amphibious group seemed to share information poorly in any case. The LCU commander of the *Tangos* only found out about their extraction orders from Port Pleasant when he went on board *Tristram*—after talking to Rolfe-Smith at 5 Infantry in the afternoon.[201] Either way, from 4pm he was left in command of the two *Foxtrots* in Port Pleasant only.

The further reduction to a single LCU was indirectly a consequence of that same talk between the two majors about the absence of a secure 5 Infantry communication link between Fitzroy and Goose Green.

5 Infantry's Rolfe-Smith was expecting the captured Argentinian coaster *Monsunen* finally to deliver two communication vehicles later that evening from Darwin. They would (after six days) give him a secure link to the Scots and Welsh Guards HQs at Bluff Cove and, through them, finally to the brigadier at 5 Infantry's Goose Green HQ.[202] But what he really wanted was communication vehicles to talk securely and directly to Brigadier Wilson's staff at Goose Green. He had put in helicopter requests to Moore's staff without success, he told the LCU commander. With six LCUs in the harbour and their LCU commander telling him they were under-utilised, Rolfe-Smith had also asked him whether one of them could be sent to Goose Green. The LCU officer politely turned him down, however.

Another twist turned up, the Kew reports reveal. When the *Monsunen* arrived in the evening as planned, the two vehicles established an HF link by 9pm for Rolfe Smith. However, a host of problems developed. The main issue appears to have been that it was unreliable at night-time—like 5 Infantry's Goose Green HF link to the Flagship in San Carlos due to atmospheric interference.[203] It was to take until 5am for the HF to work in some fashion and until 9am for a secure link to be established with the Scots Guards. Not knowing yet in the evening that this success would be achieved the next morning, Rolfe Smith renewed his request for help to the LCU commander—who, after dinner with the Tristram captain and officers, wrote he had 'turned in fully clothed in case of problems'.

This time he was lucky. The *Monsunen* situation was unusual as we saw. It had 'comms with the R[oyal]N[avy]'.[204] Not only that, there was also a Royal Navy Lieutenant on board to command it and two Royal Navy crew who had to clear itineraries with *Fearless*. As per Clapp's lack of 'trust', the Army's 5 Infantry was not given control over available amphibious assets and Army officers required inter-cession orders from his amphibious staff who made sure that their assets weren't used beyond what was allowed for in Flagship planning.

About what next happened, the *Foxtrots'* commander writes frankly, 'I was later taken to task, quite rightly, for myself sending an LCU on an unauthorized journey as it was in the area specifically to unload *Sir Tristram*'.[205] The Kew documents now reveal that, in 'full agreement',[206] the ABU's Beachmaster and the LCU comman-der decided to help Rolfe-Smith and send *Foxtrot 4* back in the evening with the *Monsunen* to pick up better communications vehicles.[207] It was another fateful deci-sion involving the LCU commander. Ending his memoir with a chapter called 'Reflections', he adds as one of them: 'I wish most of all that I had accompanied Colour Sergeant Johnston in *Foxtrot 4* to Goose Green from Fitzroy'. Earlier he also wrote, 'It was another decision I was to regret and possibly the one I regret most. Whether or not the subsequent loss of *Foxtrot 4* would have occurred if I had been embarked, I cannot of course say.'[208]

It is a hideous irony of the Falklands War that *Foxtrot 4*—as she returned mid-afternoon from Goose Green along Choiseul Sound on 8th June—was attacked and destroyed by the second wave of the Argentine Air Force. Even though there were no Harriers to hunt them down at Fitzroy, with Rapier firing six missiles in the afternoon, there was nothing for the Skyhawks to achieve at the settlement. Air protection on alert is very effective. Even a few minutes after the successful first attack on *Tristram* and *Galahad*, a trailing group of Skyhawks had been driven away from Fitzroy mainly by the concentrated ground fire of all four of 5 Infantry's units and not just the Welsh Guards—Scots Guards, 2 Para and also a company of Gurkhas in the area. Having been chased away, the second wave was scouting for an opportunity target elsewhere.

Foxtrot 4's Royal Marine and Royal Navy crew thus perished as a result of the success at Fitzroy in repelling the enemy's second wave of attacks. 5 Infantry's com-munication vehicles on board *Foxtrot 4* were destroyed, but the signallers manning them managed against the odds to make it to the shore. It is a grim thought that, if *Foxtrot 4* had not been ordered away from Fitzroy/Port Pleasant, her crew would have had a chance to survive the war. *Foxtrot 4* would of course also then have been able to help get the half battalion of Welsh Guards to Bluff Cove on the morning of 8th June. The chances of war are always unpredictable, but Moore's original plan of attack on 9th June would likely have proceeded as planned—even if the first four Skyhawks of the Argentine air force had struck the two LSLs.

The Achilles heel

One of the stringent conclusions in the newly released documents is that Clapp's SOO failed to 'grasp the significance' of what he was told when shaken at 8pm and that the information spelled a 'change of events'.[209] These were so serious that he should have 'called' his superior 'personally' before ordering *Galahad* to sail at 10pm to Bluff Cove.[210]

As we saw, contrary to Yeoman's and Todd's planning, two large ships would be docked at the same time in Port Pleasant's 'restricted' water because *Tristram*—despite its modest 900 tons on board—would not make it back that night. Not only that, one look at the map shows that, because of the narrow long shape of Port Pleasant, they would be helpfully lined up for Argentine bombers as two-for-the-price-of-one targets in a shooting range. Add to that the failure to consider 20/20 weather visibility on 8th June. Furthermore, the bay was visible from a location that was known to have an occasional Argentine observation post. This is what Captain Koops meant when he wrote above on deck, 'if we can see them, they can see us'. The topography only allowed the elevation of one LSL to be hidden by a cliff. *Galahad* 'had to sit outside and was very obvious', Clapp said in 2002 at a discussion held at the Joint Services Command and Staff College, Wiltshire.[211]

The one triumvirate commander who was able to grip the decision before *Galahad* sailed was Moore next door, as *Fearless* headed for Teal Inlet that night. However, Moore's staff seem to have been comfortable with the shooting-range scenario.

Admiral Woodward, however, was not. He did receive the information but only after *Galahad* had sailed by way of confirmation of its route, by which time there was little he could do to countermand the order. While it was accepted that Woodward as Admiral was the senior commander among equals, 'and thus had a large responsibility for all the events in the South Atlantic', he didn't have exclusive access to Commander-in-Chief Fieldhouse in Northwood, London, as Moore and Clapp went directly to Fieldhouse.

In any case, even if he was able to reach *Fearless* at Teal Inlet that night from *HMS Hermes*, *Galahad* had already sailed and would maintain radio silence to avoid detection until her arrival. Woodward had realised the wider problem of visibility as early as 7th June. In his memoirs, he writes about his regret for not speaking up to his two co-commanders: 'I should have just told Commodore Mike Clapp and General Jeremy Moore that I was not having it and the hell with their reactions.' In his contemporaneous diary entry of the next day, 8th June, Woodward added, 'I could strangle that COMAW', though the Board found no fault later during its Inquiry.

Nonetheless, despite the rapid multiplication of errors, matters still didn't enter the danger zone until 12 midnight on 7th June. Despite the lack of communication between Port Pleasant, two LCUs at Port Pleasant would easily have been able to cope with the 595 troops.

Under Clapp's rules, the Royal Navy staff on *Monsunen* had to clear any trips with her amphibious HQ on *Fearless* first. It bears repeating that *Fearless* would have kiboshed the idea to send *Foxtrot 4* away. It would also have ordered *Monsunen* to tell the Beachmaster and LCU commander, as well as Rolfe Smith, to prepare for the fact that *Galahad* would arrive at Port Pleasant in a matter of hours.[212] However, the amphibious staff's inability to receive the *Monsunen*'s captain's query—as they were on *Fearless* out of contact in Teal Inlet—precluded this outcome.

Instead of Colonel Rickett being reunited with his two rifle companies and mortar platoon, Britain's most forward troops on the southern flank were to remain vulnerable for another two days.

At night-time, 10-11th June, suddenly a major helicopter lift was at last allocated to the Army's 5 Infantry. This was despite the added pressures of the Fitzroy emergency casualty evacuation to both the field hospital at San Carlos and the hospital ship *SS Uganda*; the final logistic effort to get artillery ammunition forward; moving Divisional HQ forward to Fitzroy; and all the other strains on the system (a much busier time than 7-8th June, or indeed 6-8th June).

Who was the helicopter lift for?

Those of us Welsh Guards who were not injured were at Fitzroy. We expected to be taken forward after reorganising the troops and re-equipping with the arms stored by 81 Ordnance on Fitzroy beach. We could put together one amalgamated Welsh Guards rifle company from the men on shore to join the other half of the battalion forward at Bluff Cove. We were keen to get going. But the helicopters were not there to move us forward.

Instead, these helicopters air-lifted two of the reserve Royal Marine rifle companies based at San Carlos to the Welsh Guards and Colonel Rickett on the frontline. We were surprised to be sent back to San Carlos instead and very unhappy about it.

It is a curious thing that a helicopter lift of the two Welsh Guards rifle companies (plus its mortar platoon) seems not to have been considered seriously in the morning of 7th June as part of Plan 3, instead of the *Galahad* (or indeed *Intrepid*, so as to quickly return the San Carlos and Port Pleasant LCUs altogether). It would have plugged the hole at Britain's front line in its war with Argentina in less than an hour.

Major Sayle

There is a lot of technical stuff in the Report, naturally. Damage control, radio procedures, the fact that doors can become jammed after a major blast—that sort of thing. The main points where it deals with the Welsh Guards, however, are unequivocal, even the conclusions that were made public in 2007. In particular, it squarely backs our commanding officer's decision not to order the Welsh Guards to disembark.

'AK [Major Sayle] correctly assumed the duties of OC Troops and carried out the duties associated with this well' (point 52). The team of the Navy's military experts also summarise his orders as follows: 'his last orders were a) To land at BLUFF COVE. b) To allow no separation of his men or equipment'(point 52).

The Navy's Board of Inquiry considered specifically the fact that Sayle declined the LCU commander's advice to march to Bluff Cove and leave Welsh Guards kit behind. It judged Sayle's 'actions to have been justified'. It reached this decision because Sayle 'knew his route from Fitzroy by land would entail a 15-mile march.'

Indeed, I was surprised and delighted to read in the newly-released Kew documents an even more ringing endorsement, submitted forty years ago to the Admiralty by the Task Force's Commander in Chief, Admiral Fieldhouse. He takes an even stronger line than the Inquiry itself on Major Sayle's decision: 'As it was likely that the Welsh Guards would have joined the fighting shortly after disembarkation the apparently inflexible decision of OC Troops to follow his orders and not separate his men from their equipment is considered both *justified* and *prudent*. [My italics.]'[213]

Air Defence

It is an inevitable part of warfare that some groups and individuals struggle under pressure. Logistics staff work organising scarce resources require clear thought and considerable energy in demanding circumstances. These things are part of what former US Defence Secretary Donald Rumsfeld called 'the unknown unknowns'. Warfare is not like the assembly of an iPhone where preparation is perfect under perfect conditions to get the perfect result. It is an attempt to dominate the lethal unknown. Orders, unlike in any other area of human activity, are designed to bring order to this chaos—ultimately a barrier and protection for the troops against violent, unpredictable death. Not doing the utmost to obey them is unthinkable to the military mind and spirit.

Things still go wrong as per Rumsfeld's saying. It is for this reason that activities behind (and at) the frontline happen under a protective umbrella. It is very important to remember that none of the above or what follows would have mattered, if it hadn't been the case that all the layers of air defence designed to protect the Task Force from the enemy failed in unison on 8th June. These layers were there precisely to ensure that the enemy would not be able to benefit from accidental errors such as the concatenation of misunderstandings in the amphibious operations room, or other sudden opportunities. If one were to drill down to other moments in the Falklands one might find other imperfections.

It is almost unbelievable with hindsight, but in the final analysis the three air-shield layers failed for a few minutes only. Yet this was long enough to open a big enough window of opportunity for audacious Argentine pilots to strike lucky, hit Britain's military hard and make history by knocking out half a battalion en route to the frontline.

If anything, it puts in stark relief Colonel Rickett's deep unease about being ordered by General Moore to set up half of his battalion at Bluff Cove with his protective envelope reduced by three quarters in the absence of his mortar platoon that was with us on *Galahad*. His concern was not shared by the top officer on the Flagship. An abiding interest in adhering to standard military safeguards appears to have been applied rigorously only to the Royal Navy and Royal Marines hubs in San Carlos and Teal Inlet.

The Failure of Air Protection CAP

The first layer was the protection offered by loitering Harriers. We already saw that the request for extra jets on 8th June apparently got lost. The Combat Air Patrols (CAP) Harriers tasked generally to protect 5 Infantry's logistic operations around the area were drawn away from the area to follow up what turned out to be an Argentine diversionary attack on San Carlos with three Mirages. This was of course excusable—they were split second decisions in air combat where the British did not enjoy air superiority. Furthermore, they had been told from 7th June (a signal that did get through) to stay at 10,000 feet so as not to get in the hair lines of Rapiers in the area (Rapiers that would actually only arrive on 8th June). What was not excusable, however, is the fact that no one was told that the CAPs were in pursuit of the three Mirages and therefore no longer providing any protection to the troops and shipping around Fitzroy and Bluff Cove. Their station was '57' on the map and by drawing them away the first Argentinian wave had a free run to attack Port Pleasant from the sea.

In addition, *HMS Sheathbill*, the Task Force's Harrier landing strip on East Falkland, was out of action that day. It meant Harriers had to fly from the carriers at sea—reducing numbers available and loiter time before they had to turn back to refuel. Again, no one was told.

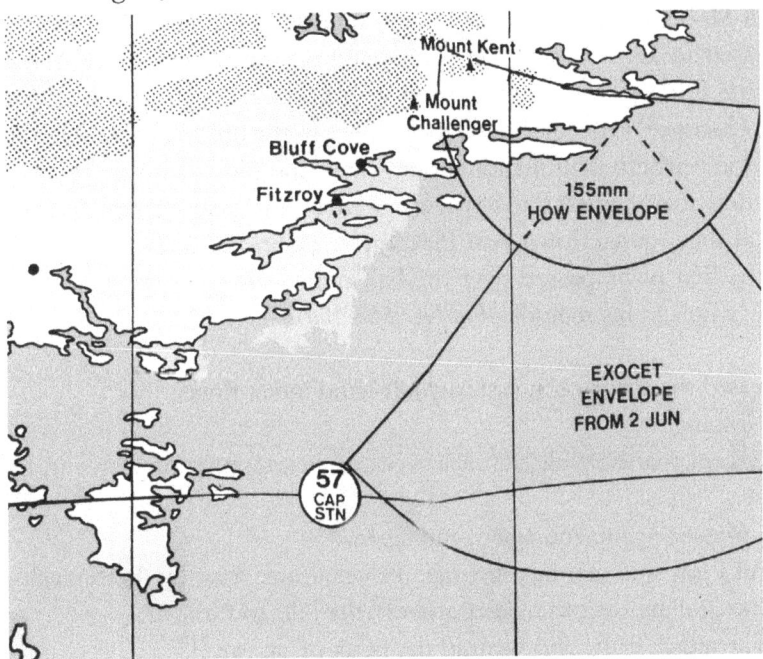

As if that wasn't enough, Woodward's *HMS Hermes*, the flagship of the fleet with the largest number of Harriers on board, cleaned her boilers that day—to do so she sailed a further 100 miles East away from the Falklands. It further reduced the number of aircraft available and their loiter time, leaving the Task Force's airspace undefended with the CAPs chasing after the Mirages. It has since become clear that some of the amphibious staff on the flagship knew about this from 5th June. *Hermes* was the bigger aircraft carrier and supplied four CAP Harriers.[214] Again, no one was told.

The second air-defence layer around Port Pleasant was formed by Fitzroy's battery of four Rapier surface-to-air missile units. By sheer bad luck, the Rapier launcher covering the sea approach of the Port Pleasant shooting-range had call sign 32A.

Previously Rapier 32A had taken part in the defence of San Carlos as the Task Force fought Argentine fighter jets at the end of May. However, it had stopped being operational when its radar/IFF tracking system malfunctioned. Instead of relying on Rapier lining up automatically when it sighted a target such as an approaching Skyhawk, this unit had to change to manual swivelling which cut its 'reaction time down to a matter of seconds'. And that was only the beginning of other faults. A repair was made but the Rapier's tracker head continued to make 'woodpecker sounds' to indicate it was faulty when it was nonetheless loaded on to *Galahad*.[215]

Why 32A was picked for the Fitzroy hub with its known problems is curious. Why did Moore's staff have a faulty one sent out to be fixed in Fitzroy if it was much easier to keep 32A in San Carlos and do the repairs there? Many of the spare parts for Rapier lay at the bottom of the ocean as they had been packed on *Atlantic Conveyor*.[216] As dumb luck would have it, the unit was placed in the corner of the dome where malfunction would cause the most damage. It was through this window that the first five Skyhawks were able to attack Fitzroy without being blasted as they soared down Port Pleasant at the line of boats.

As the first plane passed over the bay at 30 feet, 32A's Rapier Gunner Tony McNally writes in his memoir *Watching Men Burn*:

> I pressed the fire button with my left-hand index-finger.
> Nothing.
> Except that horrible, familiar woodpecker, tapping on a tree in my bone-dome.
> I pressed again, and again, and again.
> All I got was that tap, tap, tap, drowned out, now, by the screech of their engines, rolling over the water and off the hills towards us.
> The attack came and went in the blink of an eye.[217]

The newly-released Kew documents contain more ugly facts about the state of Rapier at 1.10pm, two hours after the four units were in position and tested. 32A was not the only unit that didn't fire: 32D also had system defects. In addition, 31A had 'a temporary fault' when push came to shove and couldn't fire missiles either.[218] 33C was the only one that did work. However, because of where it had been sited the terrain screened the LSLs and fighter jets from its envelope.

Even the six missiles that were fired at the second Argentine attack had their problems. One curved like a boomerang and headed back for Fitzroy.[219] It was well known that, even in ideal conditions, it would take at least an hour for a unit in good condition to be set up for action. Even so, 'high equipment failure rates were experienced up to 24 hours after the move.'[220] The earliest Rapier would be reliable was on 9th June. In other words, shortly before Moore's staff would move their field HQ to Fitzroy.

The third and last-ditch defence layer was the air-raid warning that allowed ships to go to 'action stations' in good time. Both *Galahad* and *Tristram* had gun turrets. In addition to the anti-aircraft Rapier battery ashore, there were plenty of heavily armed troops both on land and on the ships themselves. Yet this third system and its weaponry required at least a few minutes warning to go live. Even this failed.

HMS Exeter, the 'picquet ship', the term for the ship charged with scanning the airspace for enemy aircraft and on station that day as far west as was feasible, did indeed broadcast its warning of the approaching Argentine planes. The new release finally documents the exact time the first alert came through. At 12.47pm Exeter received a report that Skyhawks would arrive in Falklands air space at 12.50pm. It immediately sounded the alarm. In any case, at least 12 minutes before the attack took place it was put on the net. *Exeter's* warning was not far off the benchmark briefed to the troops and upon which the whole Task Force relied.

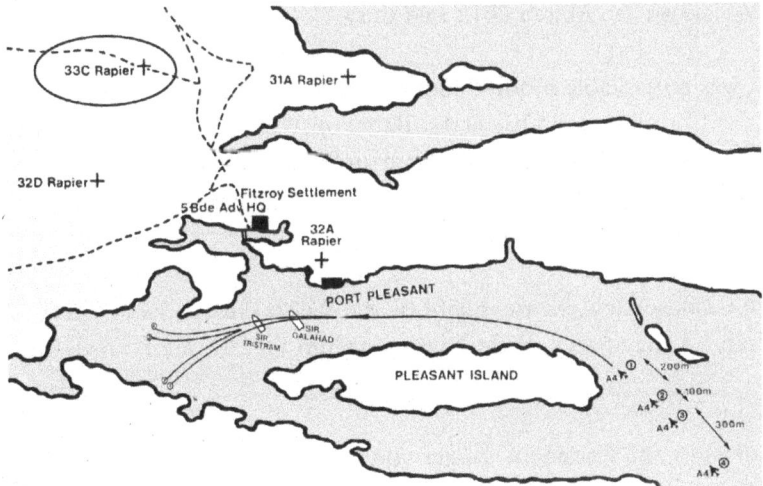

Tragically, the air raid warning was received on *Tristram* but thought only to apply to San Carlos. *Galahad* appears to have been on the wrong radio frequency. Staff on board (all civilians) may not have properly understood or been briefed on the procedures for receiving Air Raid Warnings. It meant that the sound of jet engines at maximum speed as they buzzed down to strafe and bomb was the first warning we had. The report also notes that the two LSLs' Bofors anti-aircraft guns may have been positioned incorrectly. But that was not the only SNAFU, *Invincible* never received *Exeter's* report either and didn't scramble extra Harriers.

The second gasp at 3pm that day of the Argentine Airforce was based on the illusion created by the success of the first attack that the harbour was defenceless. But by the time the second wave of Argentine planes came in mid-afternoon the layers were working more or less as they were supposed to. Had Fitzroy's air defences been properly planned, most of the 8th June disaster wouldn't have happened.

The gallantry of the Royal Fleet Auxiliary sailors

Perhaps one of the most distasteful parts of the section of the Inquiry Report—to me at least—made public in 2007 is its view of the Chinese crew on *Sir Tristram* and *Sir Galahad*. The Report saw 'failures, including the morale of the Chinese crew', and its recommendation was 'to replace the Chinese crews of LSLs with UK seamen.'[221]

The Chinese crewmen I met on *Galahad* came across as cheerful and helpful—most unsurly, if I could put it like that. During the attacks, a Hong Kong Chinese sailor called Chiu Yiu Nam managed to get hold of an asbestos suit and, in horrific circumstances, led at least 10 men to safety. Some of them were Welsh Guardsmen. Chiu was awarded the George Medal in July 1983. His obituary in the *Daily Telegraph* on 7th March 2012 said this:

> Chiu was remarkably modest about what he had done.... It was only later that the Commanding Officer 1st Battalion Welsh Guards, Lt-Col Johnny Rickett... interviewed his guardsmen and heard about an unknown rescuer whose identity had been hidden behind a protective hood. Further inquiries revealed this had been Chiu.

More Chinese crew, please, might be the Welsh Guards view. On the 25th anniversary of the attacks, Lady T wrote to him on House of Lords writing paper:

> Heedless of the imminent danger you were in, you worked to save the lives of others as the flames took hold. Your courage that day ensured that many more families were spared the grief of mourning. And your actions are a reminder to us all of the best and noblest aspects of the human spirit. Britain will never forget your service or your heroism.

Lady T's words could have applied to many on *Galahad*.

The National Army Museum might want to publicise other citations for gallantry on that day, including the Military Medals for CSM Brian Neck, Lance Sergeant Dale Loveridge and my indomitable platoon runner Guardsman Steven Chapman. Or the understated account of how a Welsh Guardsman, Simon Weston, with 46 per cent of his flesh burned and scarcely able to breathe tried to get through a wall of flame to reach another Welsh Guardsman—his chum and fellow rugby player but to no avail. Only then did he try to save his own fast-fading life.[222]

31

Squandering Half a Battalion

The Falklands War was a ringing military victory for Britain. At the same time, it was also the scene of Britain's worst loss since 1945. The Task Force had managed to squander half a battalion. The last time Britain had incurred close to such a major loss in a day was in 1951 at the Battle of Imjin River. But that was when the Glosters were valiantly defending themselves against the Chinese Communist Army eighteen to one. This was an almost casual loss, however, of a kind that had no parallels in Britain's military history.

The one person who experienced most objectively the risks General Moore was taking with his sea-route was the commander of the *Tangos*. He was the Task Force's foremost Falklands marine expert around whose detailed knowledge the admirals had planned Operation Corporate in April. With his expert navigational insight, he saw more than anyone the danger that the battalion of Welsh Guards and the battalion of Scots Guards were being placed in by this move.

He wrote in his memoirs, '[t]he forthcoming operation, to my mind, was as important as anything conducted since [the planning in] Plymouth.' In his log of 6th June, just before taking the Scots Guards in the *Tangos* to Bluff Cove, he adds, 'where would we be if we lost a battalion? Worse off, I would suggest, than if we lost a frigate, or an LPD or even perhaps [aircraft carrier] *Invincible*.' When they were dropped off at 10:30pm at 50 miles distance rather than 5 miles from Bluff Cove in a calm but pea-soup night, small wonder that he told Dingemans, the captain of *Intrepid*, before embarking 'I think the whole fucking thing stinks'.[223]

'We were about to launch six hundred men [the Scots Guards battalion] in four small, very lightly armed, unarmoured and unprotected craft designed to operate in ship-to-shore movements of a few miles under continual visual guidance of a mothership or, in the old days, and LCR (radar). We were going to transit hostile waters, with a thirty-five-mile open-sea approach towards, and then along, enemy-held shores, in the dark. We did not have up-to-date or large scale charts, we had no log for speed and distance through the water, we had no echo sounder, we carried no hand-bearing compass and the only steering compass had at least a 30 degree error, we would pass through a known area of magnetic anomalies, we would not be able to use the radar except in limited and very short bursts and we would be launched from an uncertain position', he summarised in his memoirs.[224]

The initially hostile encounter with frigate *HMS Cardiff* when they reached the location where *Intrepid* was supposed to have launched them, led Admiral Woodward to remark later, correctly, that 'the landing craft were late and in the wrong place'. They should have been at BC17, less than a mile from Bluff Cove, rather than fifty miles.

One can understand why the LCU commander was livid when he reached his destination on 6th June and wanted to impress hard on the amphibious staff on *Fearless* how close the Task Force had come to 'perfunctorily' wiping a whole battalion as a result of its own doing—and himself in the process. A repeat of the same casualness the next day would expose another entire battalion—us, the Welsh Guards, him at the helm of the LCUs—to being killed by our own side or the enemy (he appears at this time to have been under the impression that the shore was enemy-held).

With victory in the bag, the Task Force's top officers could be certain to receive the rewards for the success. At the same time, at least one them would have to take the fall for the epic and unprecedentedly casual failure of 8th June. Lord Carrington, the Foreign Secretary, had set a high bar in April. He resigned a few days after Argentina invaded the Falklands on 2nd April. Wrong-footed by the Argentines through complacency, poor communication and lack of foresight, the Foreign Office had not seen it coming. Even though his own involvement had been slight, Carrington accepted that he was personally responsible for his department.

When General Mario Menéndez surrendered Port Stanley at 9pm on 14th June, the question became which officer was going to suffer the consequences for the loss of the Welsh Guards? Even if it was thought this was just a rare case of the chances of war, Admiral Fieldhouse's head was on the block. As the civil servant who processed the Inquiry's Report at the Admiralty presciently noted on 13th December 1982, '[t]here is bound to be continuing speculation about this incident fuelled by media "events" such as the forthcoming [ITV] World in Action programme; by books and stories; and perhaps the debate on the Falklands White Paper [there wasn't apart from Callaghan's comment]. There may be a disposition to hunt for scape-goats, political or military.' Someone had to become the scape-goat in the public eye to take the heat for the disaster that had happened in the Falklands.

32

Admiral Fieldhouse

As mentioned above, only as I came to the end of the editorial stage of this book, I discovered that there were newly released documents at Kew—DEFE 69/926 ANNEX G—with the location of wounded shown on a plan of *Sir Galahad* and where the bodies were found. Quite how anyone who wasn't there knows, I wondered? I knew it was going to be a tough session in the National Archives at Kew—reliving the whole ghastly day, again. Just out of personal curiosity to see all original documents, I received the entire set of newly released documents, too.

As I read further through the sombre, yellowing documents, I came across one amongst them with a 'Secret' stamp. My interest perked up once again. It was Admiral Fieldhouse's 'case explained' of 8th June. Fieldhouse was a full admiral at the time and the top commander of the Falklands Task Force that summer. The Board of Inquiry into the loss of *Sir Tristram* and *Sir Galahad*— whose newly-released documents are liberally cited above—was convened by him personally. He had appointed its six members, and he was the last person to see its report with enclosures before he attached his own analysis, and sent it to his superiors at the Admiralty Board. No one else but him and the Sea Lords and his political master at the time had read this secret document for some four decades.

I was intrigued and soon incredulous. What Fieldhouse wrote in secret must count as some of the most disgraceful pages in the history of the British military. It was instantly clear to me that he was attaching the full weight of his position to a lie in order to preserve his own career. These may seem like strong words, but that is what the documents show us.

In a section innocuously coded 'Departures from Doctrine', Admiral Fieldhouse points his finger directly at Tony Wilson, the brigadier of the only Army formation on the Falklands, 5 Infantry. In an unusual departure from normal practice, Fieldhouse claims that Wilson personally and not the Royal Navy was in charge of the Fitzroy landing craft that day and that, by implication, any difficulties or failures belonged to him: 'Tactical control of the ship-to-shore movement assets was delegated to the Commander Fifth Infantry Brigade.'[225] Amplifying this non-existent arrangement, he called this doctrinal departure 'sensible in view of the rolling programme envisaged for the movement assets (LSLs)'—that is, a standard troops movement could be sensibly dealt with in a non-standard way. If that indeed were 'sensible' any 'doctrine' to which such an exception applies is of course meaningless.

In effect, what the Admiral told his superiors is that, in contravention of the rules and regulations under which the Royal Navy operates, at Fitzroy, but only at Fitzroy, there was an 'unusual arrangement' (his words) whereby Army orders were paramount and that all commanders of amphibious assets—such as LCUs, the mexeflote, the Sea King helicopter had to submit to instructions from 5 Infantry officers that day.

That the Admiral's secret sentence to the Sea Lords was a fiction is clear from the encounter between Welsh Guards Major Sayle and the commanding officer of the landing craft that met *Sir Galahad* in Fitzroy harbour. If what Admiral Fieldhouse said was true, the famous altercation between Royal Navy and Army officers (witnessed by Captain Koops) would never have happened. Sayle's orders as arms officer to take the guards and their kit to Bluff Cove that moment would have been the law to every service officer present. In addition, Fieldhouse's sentence stood in violent contradiction to how the Falklands triumvirate commander differentiated between the Task Force's two brigades, 5 Infantry in the south and 3 Commando in the north. (As we saw, in his 1993 memoirs *Amphibious Assault* Commodore Clapp neatly summarises Task Force policy: 'I had agreed with Jeremy that all landing craft would remain under my operational control but that I would give tactical control to Julian [Thompson of 3 Commando] for those in Salvador Waters. Despite requests, I was not prepared to give tactical control of the landing craft to 5 Infantry for I was never to trust their command to employ them sensibly.')[226]

Fieldhouse's words did the job. His deceit remained unchallenged and Wilson was the only senior officer not to receive honours after the Falklands War. Fieldhouse's own career was safe. Having been able to take credit for the Falklands War victory, and having lied to make Wilson personally responsible for Britain's worst military failure in forty years, his career continued its glittering upward trajectory.

He was promoted to First Sea Lord, Chief of Naval Staff, Admiral of the Fleet and Chief of the Defence Staff—Britain's most senior military position below the monarch, reporting directly to the Minister of Defence—and elevation to a peerage and a seat in the House of Lords followed after his retirement.

33

Fieldhouse's Fingerprints

I carried on with the Kew documents, going through them with a toothcomb. When all its facts are parsed it is clear that there were two military problems as a result of the Argentine attacks that were categorically different. There was the large loss of military equipment and, separately, the historical waste of half a battalion before fighting. As to the latter, the meticulous chronology in Captain Roberts's 21-page report of 18th June is invaluable. He records every movement around his ship, including *Foxtrot 1* that sailed up to it from *Tristram* after dawn. It was here that Fieldhouse's most intractable problem was located if he wanted to blame Wilson.

Over the past decades, the idea has formed that LCUs weren't allowed to travel to Bluff Cove in daytime. The other idea that has formed is that an alternative route was proposed by amphibious officers—a bridge. The bridge that linked Fitzroy and Bluff Cove cutting the distance by two thirds of boggy terrain had been blown up. As part of its medley of troops, *Galahad* had in fact on board a troop of Army engineers tasked with reconstructing it. Fitzroy troops may or may not made some temporary repairs that permitted foot passage but specialists were needed to secure its proper functioning.

The new Kew documents make clear that neither idea has any foundation. As mentioned above, on 7th June, the same crew of *Foxtrot 1* 'also was sent to BLUFF COVE to transfer some troops from one side of the COVE to the other.'[227] Clearly the bridge wasn't very useful and there was free passage between the two inlets as far as amphibious staff were concerned. Furthermore, a march would take at least eight hours if the bridge was passable, possibly twenty-four hours if not through the boggy fields. Rickett's express orders to Sayle not to be separated from his kit reflected battle realities. The suggested alternative route rearranged those priorities—without a superior officer backing up those changes.[228]

Foxtrot 1

One of the things Roberts's meticulous report establishes beyond any doubt are the exact times when *Foxtrot 1*—Fitzroy's single LCU on 8th June—met with *Sir Galahad*. It is clear there were only three instances that day.

Foxtrot 1's first arrival alongside *Galahad* clocks in at 8.15am and lasted 15 minutes. It then took two and a half hours for the LCU to return, since Roberts times its second arrival at 11am. The third arrival followed much more quickly. Roberts times this one at 12.10pm.

Crucially, Roberts's report finally uncovers the planned destinations for the LCU on all of these arrivals. As to the first he writes, the 'LCU left at approximately 1230 [8.30am] to discharge their ammunition ashore [at Fitzroy]'. As to the second at 11am, he writes 'the LCU returned to pick up the Welsh Guards to take them round to Bluff Cove as previously arranged'. Further to the third arrival shortly thereafter, he says, 'The LCU returned at approximately 1610 [12.10pm] again with the intention of taking the Welsh Guards to Bluff Cove'. Only the first arrival at 8.15am, therefore, was not destined for Bluff Cove.

The awkward (and deeply sad) truth is that its crew laboured under no further confusion on subsequent arrivals at *Galahad*'s stern. In addition, from that time stamp, there were four hours (less five minutes) until *Foxtrot 1* arrived to take the Welsh Guards to Bluff cove at 12.15pm, more than five and a half hours if you start from *Galahad*'s anchoring.

In all there were six hours and twenty-five minutes from the time *Galahad* entered Port Pleasant, 6.50am, to the time she was attacked, 1.15pm. In that fallow period, a second LCU would have made all the difference—even if the amphibious staff may or may not have been expecting *Galahad* to arrive, even if *Galahad* should have gone to Bluff Cove first, even if the ABU of 5 Infantry's had been set up on the wrong side of Fitzroy because *Tristram* took a false turn into Port Pleasant that *Galahad* was to repeat the following day.

Regret at the despatch of the second LCU away from Fitzroy a few hours before is one thing. We had no idea at the time that there had been a second LCU there.

But what really shocked us on the day and for forty years afterwards is that we could have been moved promptly and safely to Bluff Cove in just the single remaining LCU—*Foxtrot 1*. A round trip from Fitzroy to Bluff Cove's Yellow Beach including unloading, took at most two hours, possibly less.

Two round trips in a single LCU carrying the balance of the Welsh Guards who should have been delivered to Bluff Cove in a convoy of four LCUs on 6-7th June could have accomplished the mission set by General Moore of reuniting the two halves of the battalion on the front line—by noon or shortly after. If the whole process had kicked off at the time *Galahad* anchored (07.15) we could have been complete in Bluff Cove by eleven or shortly after. And the first group could have made part of the journey under cover of darkness—sunrise at 7.52am.[229] It would have secured the Welsh Guards' position at Grid Square 2167 on the battle map on the wall in *Fearless*'s divisional operations room, ready to go into battle. The 243 other troops destined for Fitzroy, including the field ambulance, would meanwhile have used the mexeflote to the jetty and have been safe ashore. Our officer intuitions on *Galahad*'s tank deck in 1982 were all depressingly true. Roberts's report captures frame by frame the ugly facts that stared Fieldhouse in the face. It was not just a case of the chances of war.

The alternatives

Roberts's thorough narration of 8th June shows what the real alternatives were that day. The only instance of confusion when *Foxtrot 1* wasn't destined to go to Bluff Cove was on its first arrival at 8.15am as it left to discharge its 'ammunition ashore [at Fitzroy]'.[230] Instead of leaving, the other option would have been to move its load on to *Galahad* with the aid of the 352 Welsh Guards and the 90 Field Ambulance troops returning the favour of the previous night in San Carlos where necessary. Or, *Foxtrot 1* could also have ditched the ammunition in the water in fifteen minutes flat. There can't have been more than 30 tons of stores on board the LCU. From 8.30am, even one empty LCU would have been able to avert the accidental loss of half a battalion in Moore's land force/Fieldhouse's Task Force.

All that the LCU needed to do was repeat its journey of the previous day and take everyone to Yellow Beach, Bluff Cove. Mission accomplished. As the new Kew documents show, *Tristram* was under no particular orders to be offloaded against a specific deadline.[231] Carrying on with the *Tristram* ammunition was a hugely unattractive option in any case in view of Port Pleasant's sub-par anchorage. That day the beach would only be serviceable from 9.07am (hightide plus 2 hours)—another 40 minutes from when *Foxtrot 1* left *Galahad* at 8.30am. But there was no landing (ATP/Nelson) officer who could grip the situation.

Nor was Sayle told by the amphibious officers that they were challenging his orders to take the Welsh Guards to Bluff Cove in *Foxtrot 1*. The Royal Navy Board confirms that Sayle was given to believe shortly after 8am that 'the landing craft would return *relatively quickly* [my italics]'.[232] The LCU commander confirms that he himself went ashore almost immediately to seek help. As we now know from Roberts's report, it was to take *Foxtrot 1* however almost three hours to return to the *Galahad*—what caused this fateful *long* delay is not easy to understand.

Onshore, the long delay was getting noticed, too. In a Falklands article published on 25th May 2022, 3 Commando's services Colonel Ivar Hellberg recalls helicoptering to Fitzroy in the morning of 8th June with one of his own logistics officers as well as a logistics officer from Moore's divisional staff, a fuel expert. The Task Force's three top logisticians had arrived to check out the use of Fitzroy as an even larger supply base, intending it to take over some of the functions of San Carlos. It seems Teal Inlet as a location was faltering further. They arrived before 11am, while Rapier was still being assembled on shore.[233] The trio went on board to talk to Roberts on *Galahad* about the Welsh Guards' stalemate as Hellberg thought both LSLs were needed in San Carlos (another Royal Navy-Royal Fleet Auxiliary disconnect, as *Tristram*'s captain hadn't been told by the amphibious group to hurry up at 8.30pm the previous evening—or it had been clear to him there was no rush).

Hellberg was particularly exercised, he writes, by the fact that the Field Ambulance hadn't been set up yet in Fitzroy (all medical supplies were also still on board *Galahad* as only *Tristram* was being tended to and would be destroyed in the Argentinian attacks). Sayle told Hellberg that he couldn't reach his commanding officer Colonel Rickett at Bluff Cove over his Regimental Command Net (before we left for the Falklands our dependable 1960s radios had been replaced with this new kit). On the Quartermaster's Divisional Command Net, Hellberg then spoke directly to Colonel Baxter, Moore's deputy Chief of Staff in charge of logistics, to complain about Sayle and 'to request permission for LSLs *Sir Galahad* and *Sir Tristram* to offload and immediately return to Ajax Bay [San Carlos] with or without the Welsh Guards.'[234]

This is an extraordinary piece of new information about 8th June. In the newly-released Kew documents, the Inquiry spends many words painting a picture of 5 Infantry being out of reach that morning, and censuring the brigade's communications. But it doesn't mention that a divisional helicopter landed before 11am with three of Moore's senior staff. It turns out, there was after all a direct and secure line to the divisional staff on the Flagship that day— something that the Kew documents that are currently public go at some considerable length to obfuscate.

According to Hellberg's 2022 account, Baxter said he would get back to him, and his party continued their inspection of the Fitzroy hub logistics. Instead of the divisional staff backing up Hellberg's request, however—which oddly prioritised cargo logistics at San Carlos over the Welsh Guards' prompt destination as front-line bayonets—it seems that his message about the delays at Fitzroy finally unjogged the system. On *Fearless*, Moore was having a conference with Wilson and Thompson about the final thrust toward Port Stanley. The message made clear the Welsh Guards were not yet *in situ* on the front line. As Koops remembered, all of a sudden, the pace changed. At last, *Foxtrot 1* returned to *Galahad* at 11am.

Hellberg's tripwire alert had come too late, unfortunately, to make a difference. A few hours later the attacks started. Hellberg was still in Fitzroy at 5 Infantry's Advance HQ and witnessed them. Again, he raised Baxter on the divisional net 'to what had happened, and he initially refused to believe it, realising the consequences of such a disaster.'[235] It turned out that it was extremely fortunate that their divisional helicopter was there in addition to the Rapier Sea King. It, too, was already bravely hovering over *Galahad* to winch people off the bow away from the flames and later used its rotor blades downdraft to push the lifeboats towards shore.

This was the abyss into which Fieldhouse stared before the Inquiry was set up. Had *Foxtrot 1* indeed returned 'relatively quickly', no Welsh Guards would have been left on *Galahad* or indeed any of the other troops—forget Yeoman's instructions to load *Galahad* rather than *Intrepid* or the sending away of *Foxtrot 4*. Had there been no troops left on *Galahad*, the three bombs that struck would likely have had the same consequences as the three bombs that struck *Tristram* in the same place: two Chinese crew members. (A number that indicates, perhaps, the reason why supply-carrying LSLs were considered 'expendable'.)

In fact it was even worse. Until I read Roberts's precise timeline of events, I had always suspected that *Foxtrot 1*'s leaving us at 8.30am had sealed the fate of the troops left on board at 1.15pm when the Skyhawks attacked. Roberts's tabulation uncovers something else that is new—hidden so far.

Foxtrot 1's arrival with Fitzroy's amphibious staff on board was preceded by the Fitzroy mexeflote (the 66-foot motorised harbour jetty) a quarter of an hour earlier 'at the stern ramp'.[236] It left at the same time at 8.30am as the LCU. Yet it never returned from the beach that morning to *Galahad*. It is not an exaggeration to say that had it done so, this would have made a monumental difference. The field ambulance's materiel had come on board in San Carlos on a mexeflote (on 7th June only this type of landing craft was available as a result of the failed rendezvous with the *Tangos*—San Carlos had no LCUs at all that day). All that needed to be done, therefore, was for the Fitzroy mexeflote to be ordered to do the reverse. Also, Roberts notes that 'it was considered by the Chief Officer that there was ample room on the mexe.' All 263 non-tactical troops could have been ferried immediately at 8.15am to the Fitzroy jetty—which was serviceable for 24 hours a day—to get to their destination with all their medical supplies etc. Instead it left empty. The mexeflote only came back to *Galahad* after the 1.15pm attacks bravely to rescue casualties from the burning and explosion-ridden *Galahad*, returning again with great courage to take off the final small group of Welsh Guards officers and NCOs, which was when Koops and I scrambled on board.

In other words, the lack of an (ATP/Nelson) landing officer meant that some five hours of moving *Tristram*'s pallets of ammunition on shore was prioritised *de facto* over the quick offload of 595 troops on board. It was a second event that was to seal what was to happen when the Argentine airforce unexpectedly swooped. The mexeflote could have taken all of the non-Welsh Guards to shore at 8.30am.

It was not just that the amphibious moves as they panned out that day prioritised non-urgent *Tristram*'s ammunition over troops but also that they held the
front-line destination of the Welsh Guards in suspended animation, despite the
fact that the dubious anchorage was known by some, as was the urgency of the
situation 3 miles away—Colonel Rickett was on the front-line with only one rifle
company of 150 and no mortar platoon.

As the two relevant annexes that cover this moment in detail will remain clas-
sified for another 11 years, we don't know which officers were involved and what
was said on board the LCU and mexeflote. But, the possibility of imminent air
attacks on Fitzroy that sunny day appears not to have been a great concern to
Fitzroy on the basis of the information available in the Report, presumably
relying on the three air-protection layers to work.

After all, what if the air attack had happened before 11am? The four Rapier
units were still being assembled by their Sea King helicopter until 11am and were
clearly not operational at all. It was well-known to the Argentine airforce that
Rapier's gyrosystems required at least 24 hours' settling to become operational.
This raises another question. Did the Argentine Observation Post see the Rapiers
being lifted in location? Did the Argentine airforce thus realise they had 24 hours
before the dome was live and also have a fix on the absence of *HMS Hermes*'s
Harriers? Whatever anti-air-raid arrangements there were at Fitzroy, they seem
also to have been considered sufficient for its expansion into the Task Force's
logistical base. That plan only folded after the 8th June attacks.

In fact, from Roberts's report it emerges that 8.15-11am 8th June had all the
hallmarks of a cascade of crass blunders. The first return of *Foxtrot 1* took
almost three long hours. Yet the second return (taking the field ambulance's vehicles and stores ashore) took only one hour and 10 minutes Even allowing 40
minutes of high tide for the beach to become usable it means that it took at least
twice as long for the LCU to come back. And then, of course, there was another
very unfortunate coincidence that, when it finally was ready to take the first batch
of Guards to Bluff Cove at 12.10pm, 'the ramp on the LCU was inoperable
making astern discharge into it impossible'.[237] It took 20 minutes for a plan B 'to
discharge into the LCU via the after ramp hatch', requiring ammunition to be
moved 'from the after end of the Tank Deck to no 2 hatch'.[238] It was a fateful
separation of the troops from their kit, which had to be lowered into the LCU
before they themselves could follow their bergens.

It took its own extra time and effort and, as we know, when the Guards finally
climbed down on netting in their gear, the Argentinian Skyhawks appeared on
the horizon from their unanticipated angle to do their job as enemy and wreak
havoc.

Shifting responsibility

In a single-page letter (dated 22nd December 1982) that is also part of the new release at Kew, the Admiralty Board's Vice Chief of the Naval Staff (VCNS) Peter Stanford summarised a plain conclusion for its handful of members. He identified 'staff and communications failures in a fast moving situation' as one key problem. No disagreement there. Although one should point out that *Tristram* only picked up the *Galahad* arrival info off its signal printer at 8.15am on 8th June—one hour and twenty-five minutes after *Galahad* entered Port Pleasant under a full moon—and that *Galahad* was communicating with *Tristram* shortly after entering Port Pleasant at 6.50am. It's a long time interval. The removal of its Fitzroy's second LCU was the consequence of *Fearless* being out of reach on its way to Teal Inlet. 'These were not decisive in themselves', the VCNS continues. That is not quite true as to the loss of half a battalion of bayonets. From 8pm the previous evening safe exits were stripped away one by one.

As to all the losses of the whole day, all those present assumed air cover would be tight. After all, Fitzroy was the advance HQ and hub of 5 Infantry (and would soon be General Moore's HQ from 11th June). Here lay the primary cause, the VCNS concluded. 'Given adequate air defence assets in the form of either A[ir]D[efence] Frigates or Carrier borne aircraft [the amphibious group] would not have been placed in the unenviable position of deliberately placing these LSLs at risk in this calculated way to provide vital support to the land battle'.[239] Stanford is almost correct on this point. A Rapier with properly functioning units (all four of them and not just three) from 3rd June would have precluded the entire debacle of 8th June. Surely another blunder lurked here.

What the VCNS should also have added to his short letter was that, given the poor communication as a result of LSLs sub-Royal Navy standard, the second half of the Welsh Guards battalion were by extension 'placed' at the same increased risk as the LSLs when they were ordered to embark *Galahad* (as were the other 243 troops on board). The Royal Fleet Auxiliary (RFA), for all their virtues, was not the same as the Royal Navy. In training exercises, the RFA was not expected to go to anti-aircraft action stations in the same way as the Royal Navy, nor was it trained in the same procedures such as air raid signals. During such exercises, RFA staff (civilians on considerably lower pay) were there to support the Navy with transport, food, starched white table linen, port and so on. The Inquiry Report, in fact, exhaustively details the differences between the RFA and the Royal Navy, demanding further review. Moreover, the route to position BC17 at East Island's Z-bend was safe from Exocet to and fro at night for LPDs and there was no requirement whatsoever to replace their security with the 'expendability' of LSLs. Frigates could even accompany *Intrepid* or

Fearless to about the same distance. There was of course also the fact that Royal Navy troop-carrier *Intrepid* did make the same journey as *Galahad* on 7-8th June for part of the way to gather its four *Tangos*. Empty. At night time. Protected by a frigate. It didn't even run the same risk as *Tristram* when the LSL came under attack in daytime on 8th June in Port Pleasant. While neither of these two vessels, in fact, ran the risk of a 'large loss of life', the *Galahad* did.

While it may have been a political decision that had prompted a 'calculated' wager on the troops' lives on 7th June, politicians may not have fully realised that restricting LPDs to night-time use only would be used as a reason to restrict their use even further. However, Admiral Fieldhouse as a navy man would have been intimately aware of it. And this was Fieldhouse's direct link to the disaster. He was the one who had personally authorised the wager as commander chief of the Task Force when Clapp asked him whether he could use 'expendable' LSLs like *Galahad* and *Tristram* instead of LPDs *Fearless* and *Intrepid*. 'Fieldhouse replied that this would not be vetoed by politicians' writes the amphibious commander in his memoirs, about the authorisation he received from the commander in chief.[240] But by authorising a 'few bayonets' (the term for frontline troops) in his signal to the amphibious group (Clapp as COMAW) and the landing group (Moore as CLFFI), Fieldhouse had also put his own career in the firing line after it led to half the Welsh Guards disappearing off his military map.[241]

Nor does the VCNS mention the other point that links Fieldhouse directly to the debacle. His omission to declare NATO's ATP as the Task Force's doctrine created confusion at all levels, but particularly at the interface between Army and Royal Navy. The former read up on ATP only to discover that the amphibious group followed its own beam. It directly dovetailed into the other blunders of 8th June. Had Fieldhouse given the termination system as per doctrine on 23rd May, the amphibious group would have been subsumed under Moore's chain of command. Moore's staff themselves were not once confused about geographical locations. The amphibious staff would have used these same orders instead of interpreted them into their own chain of command.

I myself was an accidental witness that day to the accuracy of information generally available on *Fearless* and Moore's operation room in particular on 7th June. Before leaving for RFA *Galahad* with my platoon, I made sure I updated my battle map—it was the sort of thing Major Sayle, my commanding officer, was meticulous about. I had to wait for someone to come out of the operations room shared between Commodore Clapp's amphibious staff and General Moore's divisional staff—and then ask to go in.

It was a Royal Naval lieutenant-commander, as it happened—everyone on *Fearless* was friendly and helpful.

'Of course. I'll take you in but be quick', he said. From the large-scale map covering an entire bulkhead (wall), I added to my own map with a chinagraph (a waterproof crayon much favoured by the military) 5 Infantry's boundaries, battalion positions, and the approximate enemy front-line.

It doesn't take long if you are familiar with the symbols which had been drummed into us at Sandhurst and the School of Infantry. The military symbol for an infantry battalion since Napoleonic times is a backpack with a diagonal strap across it. On the map there we were with a minus sign (to warn of an incomplete unit) at Bluff Cove. '1WG(-)' was displayed next to it. It clearly indicated our front-line destination. Hard to miss for anyone.

In fact, it was exactly as Yeoman had himself clocked *Tristram*'s arrival in Port Pleasant and described sending off Colonel Rickett in the two *Foxtrots* early in the morning in the amphibious group's log in their part of the operations room. 'Overnight Sir Tristram to *Fitzroy*. Also Fearless attempted to land 1WG at *Bluff Cove* but LCU's [sic] failed the R[endez]/V[ous] [my italics]', it stated.[242]

As I left, I said thank you to the lieutenant commander. He wished me the best of luck and then grinned as he noticed I was wearing a tie, 'Do you always wear a tie in combats?' Fifteen hours later, that tie had become a tourniquet.

Admiral Fieldhouse himself didn't have to worry too much, however, that the VCNS's summary would generate probing or even awkward questions at the Admiralty about the obfuscation and simultaneous scapegoating of Wilson. Fieldhouse's covering letter, the report, annexes, witness statements and whatnots were scrutinised by a select committee rather than the full Admiralty Board. The letter was addressed to five functionaries only: the Chief of Staff Fleet, the Chief of Naval Staff, the First Sea Lord, the Second Sea Lord and the Minister of State for the Armed Forces. In fact, this meant there were only four people who saw the materials as the First Sea Lord doubles as the Chief of Naval Staff.

The First Sea Lord happened to be newly appointed on 1st December 1982. It was also John Fieldhouse himself. The Admiral had, in effect, written his covering letter of 23rd September for himself to receive in his new job some two months later. The Second Sea Lord was also newly appointed—in November 1982—and Peter Blaker was the Minister of State for the Armed Forces who had been instrumental in persuading Margaret Thatcher to fight Argentina with a Task Force in April 1982. A scandal was the last thing he wanted.

The VCNS who wrote the one-pager was himself also newly minted—he was appointed in October 1982 and from December a direct subordinate of the First Sea Lord. The fifth and final functionary addressed by Stanford was the Chief of Staff Fleet. He reported to the Commander-in-Chief Fleet, who was, until he moved over as First Sea Lord, also known as—John Fieldhouse.

34

General Jeremy Moore

I assumed Fieldhouse's cover letter to the Inquiry Report would be the low point of the day, until I turned to another folder and I discovered yet another document.

There has been great controversy over the years about why *Galahad* went to Fitzroy rather than nearby Bluff Cove at the front line, closer to Port Stanley, where the other half of our battalion was already along with the Scots Guards. It seems to have gathered particular momentum in April 1987 when the *Mirror* newspaper ran an article about 8th June 1982. As we saw, the two places are only three and a half miles apart as the crow flies, six and a half miles by sea but 15-20 miles by land. Over the decades the debate has raged whether the Welsh Guards were meant to go to Fitzroy all along and whether Major Sayle should or should not have disregarded the orders he received from his superior, Colonel Rickett. Both the Report and Fieldhouse agreed whole-heartedly with Sayle. Nonetheless, because their assessments were conveniently kept secret for decades, the issue began to fester.

However, it has always been clear and undisputed that General Moore, Commander Land Forces Falkland Islands, and his divisional staff had ordered the Welsh Guards to 'land at Yellow Beach (Bluff Cove, western bank), move through 2SG's position on foot to Grid Square 2167.[243] Dig a defensive position astride the track to/from Port Stanley. Await further orders there'. General Moore had reassured Rickett when the battalion was split in half and he had to sail without his mortar platoon and two other rifle companies: 'Don't worry—I'll get the other half to Bluff Cove tomorrow night.' Whatever the controversies, it is accepted that General Moore's staff, and he personally, ordered us to Bluff Cove. Which was why when we unexpectedly sailed on the morning 8th June into Fitzroy our company commanders—having received their direct orders in turn from Rickett upon speaking to Moore personally—insisted that the single remaining landing craft take us and all our heavy equipment immediately to Bluff Cove.

Parts of the Navy have always maintained Fitzroy was our intended destination—and that the first half of our battalion (only half a battalion because 2 landing craft missed the rendezvous at sea to pick us up) was dropped at Bluff Cove in error.

And then I turned to Annex E8—Destination for Off Load Sir Galahad. On the first page it states, 'General MOORE understood the point of disembarkation to be FITZROY'.[244] All the statements under this heading have codes (317.0 Amphibious Group, 317.1 Landing Group, that is Moore divisional staff, etc), but this statement is his personally. Whereas Fieldhouse backs Sayle in his 'Case Explained', General Moore, Sayle's land commander pulls the rug from underneath his subordinates and what he told them to their faces on 7th June and before.

There can be only two explanations for this. Either Moore's evidence to the inquiry (not publicly available until 2065) has been doctored. As one of the witnesses in the Inquiry, he would not have seen Annex E8 before Fieldhouse sent it to the Admiralty Board. Or, he lied.

I think I prefer the first. The second—after 38 members of our battalion were blown apart or burnt alive and more than 80 wounded on the way to execute the general's battle plan—that Moore intentionally did not answer truthfully and tried to shift the blame for carrying out his express words onto his subordinate 5 Infantry's Tony Wilson, and thereby us, is just too much—even now, forty years on.

35

A Swiss Cheese

It was not until I subsequently scrutinised every single of page of the new releases at Kew that I fully understood how the Inquiry's Report itself was implicated and created the building blocks for Fieldhouse's deceitful manipulation of the facts. In my Ministry of Defence intelligence work, the first assessment is whether a report is meant to illuminate or confuse. The Inquiry clearly fell into the second category. Since Fieldhouse had, at the stroke of a pen, made 5 Infantry's Brigadier Wilson the scapegoat looking at any mention of '5 Infantry' became the clue to look for deception. If the report's final 'Conclusions' did not tally with the facts these were potentially the places where the scapegoating was dressed up by superimposing Fieldhouse's fiction on to what the witnesses reported to the Board in their statements.[245]

It soon became clear how the Board's Conclusions report helped stitch Wilson up. The First mention comes in a section on page four called 'The Landing Beach and Assets at Fitzroy' on page 4. As we know, as per the divisional policy sanctioned by Moore on 1st June, 5 Infantry, had no (operational or tactical) control over what went on in Fitzroy harbour. Only a Royal Navy/Royal Marine officer or an officer on Commodore Clapp's staff could issue orders. If the brigade needed amphibious support, they first had to ask Moore's divisional staff.

And so it kicks off, in rapid succession. The Report concludes that the discovery of limited beach usage on 7th June as *Tristram* was being offloaded and its reporting up the chain of command 'was in fact the responsibility of 5 Inf Bde Advanced HQ to do so, but this did not occur' (conclusion 40). Hardly surprising as no landing craft responsibility had been handed to Wilson. In any case, tides and their effects must surely have been part of the initial beach recces by engineers, divers and special forces on 5th June.

On this point, the Report obligingly creates a smokescreen for Fieldhouse where it says that the problems with the anchorage 'did not become a major matter of importance however until the W[elsh] G[uards] were to be disembarked from SIR GALAHAD' (conclusion 41). In fact, it is not possible to draw this conclusion in good faith. Had *Tristram* been offloaded as planned by Yeoman or had the Flagship known of its difficulties, none of the next day's problems would have arisen.

Four conclusions on, this fiction is deployed again however to shift the blame to Wilson. The Report concludes that 'If Bde Advanced HQ had known that SIR GALAHAD was to arrive on 8th June they may well have reconsidered their decision to send F4 to GOOSE GREEN and kept her to assist in the assist in the offload of both ships' (conclusion 45).

Adding insult to injury, the subsequent conclusion reads: 'More than 1 LCU and Mexeflote were needed to ensure the rapid disembarkation of personnel, stores and equipment from both SIR GALAHAD and SIR TRISTRAM. That this was not so is due to the fact the 5 Inf Bde did not know she was coming' (conclusion 46). If 5 Infantry had been in control, it would have simply sent one of the four *Tangos* idling at Bluff Cove on 6th June at night to Goose Green and back to pick up the vehicles. These would have provided the Advanced HQ a direct line to Wilson to monitor what was happening with the balance of the battalion of Welsh Guards instead of desperately and unsuccessfully trying to get hold of Moore in Teal Inlet to find out what on earth was going on.

Even more insidiously the Report adds to 5 Infantry's failure—'nor what she was carrying'. In a mere five words, the Report stealthily introduced the lie that what happened the next day to the Welsh Guards was somehow a consequence of 5 Infantry's incompetence. It set in motion, as well as sanctioned, the vicious idea that that 5 Infantry were somehow the architects of Moore and Fieldhouse's lack of care for the Army units. It is difficult to imagine something more dishonourable from a military report.

Where it is protecting Admiral Fieldhouse and General Moore, the report appears to have holes as large as a Swiss cheese.

Conclusions are angled away from the evidence that was before the Board. We know now from Roberts's report that, on the morning of 8th June, it took some three hours for *Foxtrot 1* to return to *Galahad* for its second visit at 11am. 'The limited assets and the conditions of the beach rather than a lack of urgency caused the relatively slow offload',[246] says the Board. No one on *Tristram* was working under a deadline and the offload of the Field Ambulance's stores only took an hour before the LCU returned to *Galahad*. But the point to be investigated is really not that one. It is the 'relatively quickly' Major Sayle was told that is the carefully avoided elephant in the room.

Another example of the Board's style of drawing conclusions is where it addresses the grasp the Task Force's staffs had of NATO's amphibious doctrine in ATP. Royal Navy and Marine 'units regularly employed on Amphibious Operations are reasonably well traineed [sic] in these publications but Army personnel were not', it says in one location.[247] This observation was not supported by its detailed analysis in a different Annex of the actual 'units' who made up the Task Force's amphibious group. 'The Board were somewhat surprised at the lack of previous amphibious training by the Staff',[248] the Report said. As to the Army's 5 Infantry's component of the Task Force, it concluded that its 'HQ Staff did study the [ATP] books and then were amazed to find that Amphib Ops were not being conducted very much like the book.'[249] That is distinctly different from saying that 'nevertheless they made some attempt to get to grips with it',[250] which leaves in the middle that there was not much point in studying ATP because it had not been made a shared point of reference and it didn't even apply informally.

Some factual statements in the Report's Annexes are wrong at such an elementary level that it is hard to see how its validity to remain standing can be preserved. As to the accidental bifurcation in terminology on *Fearless* between 'Fitzroy' and 'Bluff Cove' that would prove to have such lethal consequences on 8th June, the Board claims 'All signals originated by CTG 317.0 [amphibious staff] refer to Fitzroy, signals originated by CTG317.1 [divisional staff] refer to BLUFF COVE'.[251] That this is factually untrue, we have already seen from the priority signal that the amphibious staff (CTG 317.0) sent out in the morning of 7th June at 9.18am (before Yeoman boarded *Galahad*). They signalled: 'Rapier.... to BLUFF COVE... 2WG [sic] to BLUFF COVE.'[252] On 23rd September 1982, the Board replicates the confusion of 8th June among the amphibious chain of command, but it is difficult to see how they could have done so innocently on the central question of 8th June.

In other instances the 1982 Report presents a different record as remembered years later. In his 1993 memoir, Commodore Clapp revisits the 7th June communications between *Fearless* and Roberts on *Sir Galahad*: 'Phil Roberts asked me for a twenty-four-hour delay to his sailing of *Sir Galahad*, or, at least, firm clarification of his route. As I knew she could make Fitzroy by dawn and, as I had no reason not to believe that the visibility had not remained suitably poor, I told her to sail immediately for the settlement', he wrote. However, the Board states that the commander 'personally was not called and did not see the relevant signals until next morning'.[253] Further down the Board repeats as to the 8.52pm signal sent to *Galahad* that '[t]he officer responsible for the deficiency above is considered to be S[taff]O[perations]O[fficer]/CTG317.0; he was the most senior officer to whom the matter was referred.'[254]

The 40th anniversary of the Falklands War in 2022 has brought further insights into what happened. In March, the 8th-June LCU commander wrote a letter to the *Daily Telegraph* in response to both an unpublished war account by Colonel Ricketts that the National Archives had just released as well as Army General Sir Michael Rose's view cited above that the Inquiry Board was a 'complete whitewash'. In his letter, the Royal Marine major attacked Rose, the one-time Falklands SAS Commander, ('should not comment' and 'muddled') and criticised 5 Infantry ('overstretched').

The Royal Marine also warned that 'history must not be tampered with' and he revealed that he was an observer at the Board of Inquiry. This is in itself an extraordinary fact. Given that there were no Army observers, let alone Welsh Guards, present, and no copy of the unredacted report, enclosures and statements ever reached the Welsh Guards, it seems that a witness to the events was also a proceedings' observer.

Notwithstanding the strong opinions angled at General Rose, it seems the LCU major himself rejects the conclusions of the report with as much vehemence as General Rose does. As described in the previous chapter, the Royal Navy Board of experts unequivocally found that Army Major Sayle acted 'correctly'—even 'prudently' in the opinion of Task Force Commander-in-Chief Admiral Fieldhouse. But in his letter, the major disagrees strongly.

> On my arrival on board, I noticed that *Sir Galahad* was not the only full of vital munitions but was also carrying two companies of the Welsh Guards. I immediately found two guards officers and offered them and their men a lift ashore—a mere cable away. This was declined, as they wanted to go to Bluff Cove—where *Sir Galahad*, a 6000-ton ship drawing 13ft, simply could not sail. They also refused to embark their men in a landing craft half-laden with ammunition. I argued that *Sir Galahad* was laden with considerably more explosives and that I would take them to Bluff Cove/Port Fitzroy that night, after the bulk of the logistics had been offloaded. I emphasised the danger both ships were in and suggested the guardsmen must get ashore for their own safety. Then they could either wait till dusk for their nautical lift to Bluff Cove/Port Fitzroy or walk. They refused to move.[255]

The letter proceeds with an even stronger tone describing Sayle with terms such as 'unprofessional' and 'appalled and disgusted'.

> Astonished at this unprofessional attitude, I gave a firm order to disembark, but they would not accept such an instruction from a Royal Marines major (then the equivalent rank to an Army lieutenant-colonel). Appalled and disgusted, I went ashore to find a more senior army officer. In the meantime, the ammunition and field hospital were disembarked.[256]

The fact that a main actor on the day, and an observer of the Board's work, publicly attacks its findings does underline the fact that a full Court Martial is urgently required to establish the truth while many of the participants of that day are still alive to give their differing views. Given the billowing clouds of confusion, the victims and the public deserve to know what happened on 8th June.[257]

Army Doctrine

Carl von Clausewitz, the Prussian general and warfare theorist, famously coined the idea of 'friction'. As he pointed out, not counting the enemy, even the simplest things in ordinary life often become difficult in war: the weather, fatigue, fear, routine cock-ups, minor inefficiencies, misunderstandings, the list goes on and on. All conspire to ambush military forces with often lethal consequences. They happen in every war no matter how well-trained or equipped the troops are, no matter how good the plan is, no matter how talented the generals and senior officers. As we have seen, despite being a victory there was too much friction on the British side during the campaign against a frankly poorly commanded enemy. Better planning and tougher, more inspired military leadership could have significantly enhanced our military capability and reduced our casualties.

Friction is perennial in war—reduceable, manageable sometimes; nevertheless, always lurking. But Clausewitz would have been surprised by one particular aspect of the British Falklands friction to which I have already alluded above, particularly as every member of Her Majesty's armed forces who sailed South was a volunteer professional. As mentioned, the arrival of the Army's 5 Infantry was at best tepidly received by the Royal Navy's 3 Commando at San Carlos. The natural, virtuous and legitimate martial pride that every battalion or regiment has in its own outfit was allowed (or encouraged?) to morph into something very different and internally destructive. Once the penny dropped that General Moore intended, as doctrine laid down, for 5 Infantry to play a full part in the attacks on Port Stanley; and that, on his orders, a Royal Marine unit would not be moved forward to the frontline but instead continue to provide the Task Force's reserve far to the rear, a wounded vanity was allowed to rear its head.

When 2 Scots Guards left for the front on 5th June some of the Royal Marines from 40 Commando still at San Carlos and in reserve were livid. After retaking San Carlos from the Argentines, they had expected—and indeed had been told before the on-land Falklands command passed to General Moore—that they would be taken forward in preference to either of the two guards battalions. When we, the Welsh Guards, departed for the front a day later some simply could not believe it—even though the orders came from one of their own, a Royal Marine general. Discipline over this matter broke down, and grit in the wheels of Britain's Task Force started to benefit the enemy.

Ultimately, the lack of leadership and poor planning that led to the losses on the *Sir Galahad* can be traced back to a lingering fantasy (also in military thinking a heresy) that Port Stanley could be taken by the Royal Marines without the help of Wilson's 5 Infantry. The clearest illustration of this problem presented itself at General Moore's command level. Even though 5 Infantry had a fraction of the behind-the-front-line support in comparison to the Marines' ample if not luxurious support (despite having to pare down their kit from what they were used to), Moore never ensured that both parts walked in tandem. Instead, where the Royal Marines were equipped for the climate, moved with speed supported by helicopters, tracked vehicles and efficiently organised naval shipping—all the mod cons of expeditionary warfare, 5 Infantry was left largely to fend for itself without Moore or Fieldhouse caring about safeguards—less well fed even, as I have pointed out.

The results were staring Moore in the face. He, as described previously, decided to land 5 Infantry about as far from Port Stanley as was possible with no arrangements in place to get us forward. The day the Welsh Guards attempted to move out of San Carlos on foot no help was allocated to us by helicopter or land vehicles other than the illusion of two Snowcats. Because of poor Naval staff work, the sea move of the Scots Guards narrowly escaped being a disaster that would have dwarfed *Galahad*. Landing craft earmarked to take us to Bluff Cove on the night 6-7th June failed to materialise; decanted from specialist landing ship HMS *Fearless* onto a civilian ship when, at the same time that very night, the other Royal Navy specialist troop landing ship HMS *Intrepid* was making a similar journey forward to recover her LCUs, but not carrying any troops. *Intrepid* could easily have been tasked to take us forward and recover some or even all of her LCUs at the same time—under the cover of darkness, but the Royal Navy was 'Not in Service' for 5 Infantry. The Welsh Guards had to wait a further seven hours for other units to load, including a field ambulance that could easily have moved forward at any time in the following few days; no night cover on arrival; delivery to Fitzroy, not Bluff Cove, neither location aware in advance of our arrival because the land commander was out of reach on the other side of the Falklands. Too few landing craft, because one was sent away without authorisation and *Fearless* was at sea. It goes on.

The Falklands War could have been fought very differently and at a cost of fewer British lives—probably Argentine conscript lives as well. As touched on above, General Moore only had experience commanding one Royal Marine brigade—an exceptionally well-resourced brigade with few changes in personnel compared to the large majority of brigades in the British armed forces. He lacked experience in suppressing the tribal pride of brigades, or rather welding them together, and sufficient insight into the logistics that support a war with more than one brigade. As it was, in my view, the Royal Marines helped themselves to more than their fair share of the scarce resources available and did less than their fair share of the fighting. Some of them know this perfectly well which explains why so many of their military memoirs have a sour undertone.

The fact that Moore was out of his depth was ultimately not his mistake (quite apart from his role in the postmortem under Fieldhouse's Inquiry). He didn't appoint himself and which general would have declined the role for fear of lack of experience? But both Admirals Lewin and Fieldhouse, who staffed the Task Force as Britain's two top military officers, knew from the start that there would be more soldiers than marines in the Falklands when the time came to attack Port Stanley. It was these two Royal Navy officers who decided to put a Royal Navy officer who lacked relevant experience in charge.

How would an Army general have handled the Task Force differently?

On his arrival on the Falklands to take over, an Army general would have given short shrift to Brigadier Thompson's idea that the war should be fought 'in digestible bites'[258]—the Pedigree Chum style of fighting is just not the way the Army does things. In a land war with a sizeable enemy the principle of concentration of force applies—landing knockout blows. Fast and furious to save lives. Some instruction on how a brigade fits in with a division would have been useful. Basic signal drafting also—for instance, a subordinate formation must not earmark units from another brigade for a task. Yet there was an attempt by Brigadier Thompson to replace Royal Marine 40 Commando as the Force's reserve. Long before arrival, instead of merely assuming command, an Army general would have studied the troops under his command, their personalities, resources, and above all how to shape them to his orders.

An Army general would not have allowed COMAW staff to remain independent and would have leant in if they produced lopsided results over and over again: there were the three sea moves forward for the Army's 5 Infantry, none of which worked well. Royal Marine 3 Commando battalions were five days too early to the front line. But 5 Infantry's battalions were a day or more late on top of the two-day delay caused by the attacks on *Sir Galahad*. Competent, co-operative commanders and staff officers could have got both brigades forward, allowing each three days to patrol aggressively against their allocated objectives. Imagine the effect of that on Argentine morale. We know that the unit the Argentines were most afraid of was 5 Infantry's Gurkhas. They were, bizarrely, never used.

And, as early the night (probably) of 8th June, both brigades should have attacked all along the Argentine defensive line. 7 major units could have been brought to bear with 1 or 2 in reserve. The most General Moore managed during the entire Falklands War at any one time, however, was 3 units—quite a difference. There would also have been enough artillery ammunition to go round if scarce land-based artillery had been more judiciously used. Quite why 'massive' artillery bombardments were needed against conscripts is a mystery. Have it on call as 2 Scots Guards did at the Battle of Mount Tumbledown.

In practical terms, it means that an Army general could have won the war a week earlier and with fewer casualties. The *Sir Galahad* debacle would likely never have happened and even the tragedy of the civilian casualties in Port Stanley would have been avoided.

Ironically, I suspect an experienced Army general might have given the soldiers of 2 Para the vital job of divisional reserve in the assault on Port Stanley—letting them regroup and recover for a few days after their exhausting victory at Goose Green. They could have protected the entire land force from the alarms and excursions threatened by intelligence in the final days of the campaign. These proved unfounded in the end but were an extreme worry at the time. An Army general would have been happy to throw Royal Marine 40, 42 and 45 Commandos more vigorously into the battle for Port Stanley.

One of the researchers on one of the documentaries I have mentioned in a previous chapter told me that the overriding impression they took away from interviewing Royal Marine officers was one of tremendous frustration—that a military campaign on paper designed by the gods specifically for the Royal Marines, controlled throughout by Royal Marines, involved them in so little fighting. Indeed, most of the fighting was carried out by the Army: 2 Para, 3 Para and Scots Guards were the units that brought about the Argentine defeat on land. It was after the Scots Guards fought their way to the top of Mount Tumbledown that the Argentines folded. Only 48 hours earlier the Royal Marines had declined to attack this objective.

As to Tumbledown, a Royal Marine commander remarked: 'Meanwhile, we were quite happy to leave it to someone else to crack. Besides, while Tumbledown was also defended by conscripts [not quite true—the officers and senior NCOs were professionals], they were Marines, and it would have been a pity if we had had to fight men with whom, under other circumstances, we would naturally have expressed fraternal solidarity.'[259] If the Army had such sentiments, practically every battle would have raised such branch-of-military pity.

The researcher also remarked that there was acute embarrassment about the performance of the original Royal Marine garrison in Port Stanley. The Battle of Port Stanley is not part of this book, but what might have been one of the epics of military history: a Thermopylae, Rorke's Drift or the celebrated action by the French Foreign Legion at Camarone—was instead a rarely mentioned humiliation of the marines. The researcher added there was a taboo on discussing casualties. There were more Royal Marines killed in the 'Battle of Two Sisters' by other Royal Marines (4) in a tragic friendly fire incident than by the enemy (3 plus an Army sapper). There were also the extraordinarily light fatal casualties during the 'Battle for Mount Harriet' (2).

45 Commando lost 4 men to the Argentine Air Force. 40 Commando lost 1. The Welsh Guards lost 38 to enemy bombing. The heavy casualties suffered by the Army highlighted the extraordinary luck of the Royal Marines with their own butcher's bill.

37

The Darkest Day
Wednesday 14th July 1982

After the end of the war The Prince of Wales's Company (1 Welsh Guards) spent some days on *Canberra* returning prisoners of war to Argentina—including many rugby players and a group of Welsh speakers from the historic Argentine Welsh community at Trelew in Patagonia. There were no problems. We felt sorry for the young conscripts who had clearly had a rough time and did what we could to get them cleaned up and given medical attention, mainly for trench foot. The officers, held separately as required by the Geneva Convention, were insufferable. Not once did any of them make any inquiries about their men.

On 14th July we said a sad farewell to Captain Koops who had been such an example to us all in the heat of the attack, and moved into Port Stanley Town Hall. At least there would be no more long runs if we irritated him. There was plenty to do, the Argentines having left the town in a disgraceful state. Mail began to pour in and books and magazines. Penguin books appeared in quantity—I bagged what P.G. Wodehouse I could, which helped. Fiction took me away from reality. I felt sorry for those who don't read much but instead rely on television (there wasn't any). Or those who wanted some of the other pleasures of life (not in service for 5 Infantry, or available at Port Stanley). Wodehouse has always been for me the perfect antidote. Fear of death, despair, awful food, damp and cold: read about Jeeves and Wooster's experience at the Prize Giving at Market Snodsbury Grammar School.

Watching the live rather than printed penguins on the outskirts of the town on austral evening strolls (while being careful to avoid minefields) was a joy. Occasionally small groups of us would be asked onto ships in the harbour to get cleaned up and have a decent meal.

On 14th July I took half my platoon onto a huge freighter. The day began well. We handed over our grotty, smoke (and worse) scented clothes—whisked away to the ship's laundry; and were taken to our respective messes.

I was on my own in the wardroom watching a video, quite a new thing then; and drinking gin and tonics quickly. The captain of the ship had been charming—straight out of central casting: chunky polo neck under his uniform, pipe in his mouth and a soft West Country burr. He handed me my first gin and tonic but then returned to the bridge saying he would like a longer chat over lunch which would kick off once my clothes came back very soon after.

A few minutes later a ship's officer came in and said that the captain wanted to see me on the bridge immediately. This officer seemed concerned, almost embarrassed. I was still in a big, off white, fluffy dressing gown with DMS boots on my feet, but that seemed to be OK so I followed him up to the bridge, wondering what on earth was going on.

I tried to 'put my feet in' (stamping your feet together as a drill movement) as I got to the bridge being aware that compliments should be paid to merchant navy captains on their bridges. But my boots weren't laced up. To avoid looking foolish I wobbled to attention. The captain smiled but I could tell something was very wrong straight away. Then his face creased and he became deadly serious:

'I don't know how to tell you this, lad. But something awful has happened at the airport. There are Welsh voices on the radio and I'm afraid I think it's your people. Let's listen.'

Most of us had spent many days at RAF Stanley helping to clear the runway, a truly balls-aching task. The runway had to be wiped clean: every stone, pebble, empty ammunition casing, piece of shrapnel removed. Cold, wet, and still filthy, I felt miserable but concealed it from my men. The extraordinary, unstoppable, dry-dark humour of the guardsmen kept us all going. I usually manned a huge bass broom trying to feign enthusiasm—much to the amusement of the troops.

The party on the dreadful day in question had been provided by Support Company of the Welsh Guards and included unwounded survivors from RFA *Sir Galahad*—most of whom, frankly, were very lucky to be alive. An RAF Harrier taking off on a Combat Air Patrol—General Menendez had surrendered the Argentine forces on the Falklands, but nothing else—had skidded on the icy runway detaching a Sidewinder missile. The missile didn't launch but bounced onto the runway shattering into chunks at more than 150 mph that cut through one of our clearance parties. Eleven Welsh Guardsmen were injured, some losing limbs. At the time we didn't know that they would all survive. It was the darkest day of all for me.

Colonel Rickett, our commanding officer, says this in the memoir he wrote in 2020 during the first lockdown:

It seemed cruel that after the *Galahad* we should endure yet another catastrophe and I secretly wondered if this would ever end.[260]

38

EYEWITNESS: CAPTAIN KOOPS

Walk on Wales

Over time I have come to understand the term 'lived trauma' and I count myself incredibly fortunate to not only have survived the bombing, but also to have lived a full and positive life without suffering any debilitating consequences of what is today called Post Traumatic Stress Disorder (PTSD). The stress has been, nevertheless, and always will be, a part of my makeup. There are triggers that set off a variety of different powerful emotions, ranging from anger, disorientation through to a deep sense of resentment at the way the voyage of the *Galahad* was handled and the tasteless, frankly ludicrous comments of some individuals who should know better. Blocking these emotions is not the solution as one's behaviour then tends to become irrational as a feeling of frustration pushes its way to the surface in an often more destructive way. With support, guidance and understanding one can feel these triggers tighten and then step back, take a deep breath and move one's mind to a safe place.

Not always easy to do.

Whilst one can readily identify with others who face similar challenges, there is nothing quite the same as being with those who were there with you in the moment of your experience. You are completely on the same page with an unspoken understanding of the implications of the shared trauma. Tension falls away and for the time you are in their company a peaceful, balanced, and supportive feeling softens the jarring of the painful memories.

In 2013, thirty-one years after the conflict, a group of friends and I put together a charitable walk around the Welsh Coastal Pathway, naming it 'Walk on Wales'. Walking in the memory of those we had lost on the *Sir Galahad*, we raised just under half a million pounds for our two nominated charities—The Welsh Guards Afghanistan Appeal and Combat Stress. Prior to the Walk we commissioned a beautiful silver baton on which were engraved the names of the 51 Welsh Guardsmen who have lost their lives in active service since the Second World War. Each day of the walk was dedicated to one of those we had lost and their families were invited to join us and carry the baton for the day. At some point during the day the family would have a quiet moment to themselves when they would place a small wooden cross in remembrance of their loved one.

The people of Wales responded to our Walk in a truly humbling way. Each morning local radio stations reported on our activities. Communities opened their doors to us as we passed through, lining the streets and setting out food and drink on tables. Pubs held quiz nights to raise funds for our charities. Free accommodation was made available, ranging from village halls, private homes to 5 Star hotels. If there was a way of supporting us, the people of Wales found it; any opportunity for auctions for the charity at many dinners held in golf clubs, grand houses, pubs, clubs and hotels was taken. Two songs were written and released to support our efforts.

Central to the energy the Walk created was the sharing of each day. As we walked along the stunningly beautiful coastline, conversation began to freely flow between all those present. Slowly and gently many difficult and painful memories tumbled out in a way that is not always possible in everyday life. Alongside those willing and able to listen, we walked in a safe space where everyone cared for and supported each other in a wholesome and life-affirming way. As we walked to the steps of the Senedd in Cardiff Bay on the final day of our 870-mile journey, I looked back along the line of just under 3000 walkers and witnessed that we had all shared in a life changing experience.

39

Return South

In March 2002 I had been lucky enough to be despatched to the South Atlantic by my regiment. Its most senior serving member at the time, who should have gone, was the general in London. But he was unable to leave the capital for an unpredictable length of time because of Her Majesty Queen Elizabeth the Queen Mother's failing health. The Falkland's RAF Mount Pleasant airport can be shut to passenger aircraft because of high winds—before anyone gets any ideas the RAF's Interceptors fly in all weathers.

I flew South with the regimental adjutant armed with several wreaths. It's a long, dry flight via Ascension—where you can buy a beer at a small booth on the side of the airfield. The seats were uncomfortable, as ever, and facing a different way from civilian flights. As we approached Falklands airspace, bouncing around the bazaar because of the high winds, a pair of RAF Typhoons rose in perfect unison to escort us in. One on each side. Marvellous. As we landed, after burners kicked in and they soared over Wickham Heights.

I've always been a bit of a sentimental blubber. Moving films can set me off, especially *The Sound of Music,* some of Shakespeare's speeches, photographs of badly treated animals especially dogs and donkeys; music, mainly Mozart—not because of its melancholy (most of it isn't) but its perfection. Watching the Red Arrows one summer at the Dartmouth Regatta—swooping low over the river in perfect formation got me going through a combination of patriotism and perfection. But the tears never came for the Falklands—not even a nice, private blub.

During my visit there on the St David's Day just before the 20th anniversary of the war I laid a wreath at the Welsh Guards Memorial that sits starkly on a grassy outcrop overlooking Port Pleasant. A Celtic cross of a type that would have been familiar to St David himself commemorates the 42 Welsh Guardsmen and attached cap badges (Royal Electrical and Mechanical Engineers and Army Catering Corps) who died in the conflict; including three SAS men lost in the Sea King crash of 24th May and Lance-Corporal Thomas 03 killed by artillery fire outside Port Stanley on 13th June. It's made of Welsh Granite—harsh, unforgiving, reassuringly permanent. The Army engineers who sited it had both a sense of ground (all engineers do), also a sense of occasion.

The cross is in exactly the right place in relation to the surrounding land and the water in the bay.

The previous day we had climbed Tumbledown Mountain. God knows what it must have been like for the 2nd Battalion Scots Guards on the night 13–14th June 1982 with 5th Argentine Marine Battalion (manned by professional officers and NCOs) trying to blow you to bits. Even my unopposed, daylight, 'administrative' ascent twenty years later was hard physical work.

At the summit by the Scots Guards Memorial, a young Scots Guards piper stepped forward to play the *Crags of Tumbledown* and that most haunting of all laments *Flowers of the Forest,* commemorating the heavy casualties suffered by King James IV's Army at the Battle of Flodden—a curious, affective melody that at the same time sets the teeth on edge and the heart racing. I didn't cry although I could see that some of the military and civilians in attendance were deeply moved.

I had chatted to the young piper on the RAF trooping flight South—since joining up it had been his greatest ambition to play the *Crags of Tumbledown* on its summit. He was on great piping form and I congratulated him. He offered to play the lament at the Welsh Guards Memorial at Fitzroy the following day— very thoughtful, but I declined as we would have an Army bugler on hand to play Last Post and Reveille and the bagpipes (I thought) were not really a Welsh thing.

The next day he was already in the van that was to take us to Fitzroy and Bluff Cove/Port Fitzroy when the rest of the group, including the governor, piled in. I noticed he didn't have his pipes and was rather regretting not agreeing to his offer to play for us.

A moving service was held by the RAF padre, and the governor and I laid wreaths. The bugler played his calls either side of the two minutes' silence—not that there is ever complete silence in the Falklands as the strong westerlies produce a constant moaning sound as the air rushes by. The moment was made even more poignant by the presence of Mrs Ann Reid, mother of Guardsman Paul Green (Missing, presumed dead: *RFA Sir Galahad,* 8th June 1982). An extraordinary lady whom we had called on at her house in Port Stanley the night before.

After a family trip down South in the mid-1980s to see where her son had been killed, she had decided to settle in the Falklands. On meeting her I was, of course, on my best behaviour and nervous about what I should say. She was charming and had put me immediately at my ease. I mumbled something about being close to your son or something on those lines which seemed sensible enough—I knew from my reading about the Great War that families found some solace from visiting the great cemeteries and memorials near where their fathers, brothers, sons, and sweethearts had fallen—even where there was no body but just a name on a memorial, as was the sad case with our dead on *Sir Galahad*. She smiled and said it wasn't really that at all—but the welcome she had received on her visit, the generosity and friendliness of the Falklanders that made her realise the islands would be a good place for her to live her life.

After just a few days back on the islands I could see her point. We had had our first daughter by then and another on the way. I was beginning to understand in my early 40s just how strong love for a child could be. Maybe a mother just wants to be close to her child—somehow.

My parents said they would have opted for burial on the Falklands if I hadn't made it, but the problem with the *Galahad* was that there were no bodies. Just a position on a chart off East Falkland where the burned-out hulk was torpedoed by a Royal Navy submarine. Too unstable and dangerous to attempt the recovery of bodies (the Royal Navy tried—and they deserve our thanks), it couldn't be left as a ghoulish hazard to shipping. I can't think of a more melancholy task for a submarine crew.

The young piper caught my eye, moving his fingers as if on a chanter. I nodded. His pipes were stashed behind the van, bless him. The notes of *Flowers of the Forest* poured out, lingering only briefly by the memorial before being swept away by the wind. The Welsh Guards group moved closer and joined hands. We stood together heads bowed—half in prayer, half against the wind.

I returned to Blighty, my job in the Cabinet Office and to my wife Caroline, seven months pregnant with our second child. The trip South had certainly helped to lay a few demons to rest.

But, seeing the ground again, particularly the minimal distance as the crow flies between Fitzroy and Bluff Cove; and the huge distance between the Divisional Administrative Area at San Carlos and Port Stanley jogged the deep unease that I had experienced during the war and which was to grow over the subsequent decades. What happened to us simply didn't make military sense. The genesis of this short book really began not in June 1982 or June 2021, but on St David's Day 2002.

Our second daughter was born at Queen Charlotte's in Hammersmith at the end of May. All had seemed under control in the very early stages of labour as I took a short stroll around Wormwood Scrubs awaiting upon events. By the time I got back things had moved on rapidly. Caroline was close to giving birth. Splendidly, our younger daughter arrived without drama or difficulty. I forget what she weighed but was irritated as always by her weight being given in kilogrammes. British (with a bit of Welsh and a large dash of Australian) babies are born in pounds. Whatever the figure was, when I picked her up for the first time, she weighed about the same as a full ammunition pouch.

I noticed she had extremely long fingers, elegant as if belonging to a girl much older. A great sense of well-being enveloped us both. I wrote about touch at the beginning of this book. Hugging your wife as she is holding a newly born child must be one of the most intense touch experiences possible. And then I knew I was going to burst into tears.

I was a 42-year-old man visiting a maternity hospital in Hammersmith. But suddenly I was a 22-year-old young officer in the Falklands again, trying to keep going somehow in the face of imminent death. Seeing this lovely child, I realised that none of this would have been possible if I had been posted as missing, presumed dead in 1982, burned alive or blown apart on *Galahad*.

The successful attacks at Fitzroy had always seemed odd to me—even at the time. But now, comfortably ensconced with Caroline and our new daughter in Queen Charlotte's my suspicions began to crystalise.

I should maybe have felt anger at the time—an emotion that, if properly channelled, can lead to action and the urge to do something about the anger. Instead, I felt sad, immeasurably sad for all those killed and wounded on that fateful day. Sad also for my friend Hilarion, wounded that day and lucky to escape alive: he died in a car accident three years later—his body badly damaged, only identifiable in the morgue by his burned hands.

I didn't want to worry Caroline at this happy moment and, pretending I had an urgent call from the Cabinet Office, walked out onto Wormwood Scrubs, found a bench, and finally cried about that horrific, ill-fated day—8th June, 1982.

Postscript

We would not have considered writing this memoir if the findings in the Board of Inquiry's Report had fairly continued to stand the test of time. War is not for the faint of heart. However, the Board's narrative gave license for the memory of the fallen of 5 Infantry to be tainted posthumously—who is there to defend them but us? For reasons unknown, five very senior Royal Marine and Royal Navy officers sought to stop publication of this book upon the appearance of a pre-publication newspaper extract, causing further delay for an additional expert read through. We leave it for the reader to decide whether the justice of a fair Inquiry has yet been served and whether all documents of 1982 should be released to preclude further speculation and provide clarity.

> The dead go on before us, they
> Are sitting in God's house in comfort,
> We shall see them face to face—
>
> Plain as lettering in the chapels
> It was said, and for a second
> Wives saw men of the explosion
>
> Larger than in life they managed –
> Gold as on a coin, or walking
> Somehow from the sun towards them

PHILIP LARKIN, THE EXPLOSION, 1974

[1] Colonel Jacot does everything he can to stay awake through the night. He wants to sleep physically but is afraid of dreaming. For him dosing and timing are everything. He tries to consume enough alcohol to soften the pain in his burned hands and body but not so much that he crashes out while it's still dark; and enough cocaine to stay awake until dawn—but not too much in case he overshoots. Once it is light and the day starts around him in his Paris flat above a boulangerie in the *rue Bonaparte* on the Left Bank, he knows he can fall into a drunken, drug-fuelled stupor—safe from his unconscious and the past.

[2] I am grateful to my comrades for all the help and encouragement they have given.

[3] *The Blob* is a 1958 film about a sticky, aggressive, red jelly-like blob whose invasion by meteorite of small-town Pennsylvania seems unstoppable until Steve McQueen takes it in hand. In modern usage, usually a group with obvious vested interests who over rate their talents, insist that all pay homage to their views and opinions and have a massive sense of entitlement. Often aggressive, always solipsistic, most blobs eagerly exalt their own narrow interests over those of lesser human beings whom they regard as outsiders. Blobs occur in all parts of our national life but thrive best where the taxpayer foots the bill.

[4] I also served for a further twenty years in uniform mainly in Northern Ireland and the British Army of the Rhine.

[5] Usually.

[6] LS143/2 E2.

[7] LS143/2 E2 - 5.

[8] LS143/2 E2 - 7.

[9] LS143/2 E2 - 9.

[10] LS143/2 E2 - 9.

[11] LS143/2 E2 - 8.

[12] LS143/2 E2 - 24.

[13] LS144/2 E12 - 3.

[14] Seminar 'The Falklands Campaign 1982', 21 June 2018, Canberra, Australia: Michael Clapp and Julian Thompson, https://researchcentre.army.gov.au/library/seminar-series/amphibious-operations-and-falklands-war: pdf 01, p6.

[15] Seminar 'The Falklands Campaign 1982', 21 June 2018, Canberra, Australia: Michael Clapp and Julian Thompson, https://researchcentre.army.gov.au/library/seminar-series/amphibious-operations-and-falklands-war: pdf 01, p6.

[16] LS143/2 E2 - 6.

[17] Kenneth L. Privratsky, *Logistics in the Falklands War*, Kindle edition, page 129.

[18] Michael Clapp and Ewen Southby-Tailyour, *Amphibious Assault Falklands*, page 183.

[19] Julian Thompson, *No Picnic*, page 90.

[20] Julian Thompson, *No Picnic*, page 90.

[21] This is an easily transportable gun and slightly smaller in calibre to the Royal Navy's 4.5-inch gun (114mm).

[22] Julian Thompson, *No Picnic*, page 94.

[23] Julian Thompson, *No Picnic*, page 106.

[24] Julian Thompson, *No Picnic*, page 105.

[25] Julian Thompson, *No Picnic*, page 94.

[26] LS143/3 E3 - 1.

[27] LS143/2 E2 - 2.

[28] LS143/3 E3 - 5.

[29] LS143/3 E3.

[30] https://www.defenceviewpoints.co.uk/military-operations/op-coporate-retrieving-the-falklands-island-1982

[31] LS143/2 E2 - 29.

[32] LS143/2 E2 - 29.

[33] See, for example, 'the actual allocation of helicopters was in the hands of CLFFI's [General Moore's] staff', Ewen Southby-Tailyour, *Reasons in Writing*, kindle.

[34] LS143/3 - 7.

[35] Ewen Southby-Tailyour, *Amphibious Assault Falklands*, kindle.

[36] LS143/3 E3 / LS143/4 E4-5 041637.

[37] LS143/3 E3 / LS143/4 E4-5 050029.

[38] LS143/3 E3 / LS143/4 E4-5 050233.

[39] Julian Thompson, *No Picnic*, page 90

[40] Michael Clapp, Ewen Southby-Tailyour, *Amphibious Assault Falklands*, page 238.

[41] LCUs *Foxtrot 2* and *3*.

[42] 3 Commando Brigade normally deploy with more than 1000 vehicles. They restricted themselves to 177 vehicles. Kenneth L. Privatsky *Logistics in the Falklands War* (2017), page 34.

[43] Johnny Rickett, *Not Just a Conflict*, page 29.

[44] Ian Gardiner, *With the Yompers*, kindle edition, page 155.

[45] Seminar 'The Falklands Campaign 1982', 21 June 2018, Canberra, Australia: Michael Clapp and Julian Thompson, https://researchcentre.army.gov.au/library/seminar-series/amphibious-operations-and-falklands-war: pdf 02, p21.

[46] Report to Commander-in-Chief, Fleet of the Board of Inquiry into the loss of RAFs Sir Tristram & Sir Galahad in June 1982, Appendix 1 to Annex B page 2.

[47] Professor Lawrence Freedman, *Foreign Affairs*, Vol 61, No 1 (Fall 1982) *The War of the Falkland Islands, 1982*, pages 206-7.

[48] Johnny Rickett, *Not Just a Conflict*, page 32.

[49] Admiral Sandy Woodward with Patrick Robinson, *One Hundred Days*, page 444.

[50] Seminar 'The Falklands Campaign 1982', 21 June 2018, Canberra, Australia: Michael Clapp and Julian Thompson pdf 01, p3.

[51] Report of the Board of Inquiry into loss of an Army Air Corps Helicopter over the Falkland Islands on 6th June 1982. 6 Nov 1986.

[52] Admiral Sandy Woodward with Patrick Robinson, *One Hundred Days*, page 444.

[53] Ibid, page 444.

[54] Michael Clapp, Ewen Southby-Tailyour, *Amphibious Assault Falklands*, page 238.

[55] An amphibious officer present wrote in addition, 'No mention was made to the Welsh Guards of the possibility of landing at Fitzroy' Ewen Southby-Tailyour, *Reasons in Writing*, page 280.

[56] Colonel Rickett called everyone 'boy'. Still does, even though most of his young officers are now in their 60s. It's rather charming.

[57] The crew of *Fearless* from their formidable Captain Jeremy Larken down to the most junior sailor had been marvellous.

[58] LS143/1 E1 - 6.

[59] For example, 'unknown to me was the fact that the shores were not enemy-held, at least not unless we approached Bluff Cove from the east, and nobody in the Flagship expected us to do that—did they?' Ewen Southby-Tailyour, *Reasons in Writing*, kindle.

[60] LS143/4 E4 p6 051654.

[61] LS143/6 E5 - 11.

[62] In 2013 when I was walking with Phil Roberts (a thoroughly charming and affable person) on a stretch of Walk on Wales (a charitable walk around Wales I and others organised in memory of the regiment's post Second World War casualties—more of which towards the end of the book). I asked him directly, whether with the benefit of hindsight he could have lowered the stern gate and rammed the ship ashore at some point that morning. He said that 'this was totally impossible because of the shallow rocks'. He added, 'there was absolutely nothing you could have done differently as it was all out of your hands.' We've known this from the start.

[63] Sandy Woodward with Patrick Robinson, *One Hundred Days*, page 456.

[64] '9 knots' or 10mph, Michael Clapp, Ewen Southby-Tailyour, *Amphibious Assault*, kindle.

[65] Martin Middlebrook, *The Argentine Fight for The Falklands*, Kindle edition, page 321.

[66] Sandy Woodward, *One Hundred Days*, page 455.

[67] He was an ensign (a second-lieutenant in a Foot Guards regiment).

[68] I've used it in one of my Colonel Jacot books.

[69] Even the inglorious commander of the original garrison in Port Stanley piles on.

[70] In March 2022, Southby-Tailyour takes Col. Rickett, the commander of the Welsh Guards, to task for having 'no first-hand knowledge of events that fateful morning'.

[71] Ewen Southby-Tailyour, *Reasons in Writing*, page 285.

[72] *Abandon Ship: The Real Story of the Sinkings in the Falklands War*, Paul Brown, 2021.

[73] DEFE 69/920 'Operation Corporate (Falklands Conflict) Report of the Board of Inquiry into the Loss of the RFA Sir Tristram and Sir Galahad'.

[74] Royal Navy Captain (President), Royal Navy Commander, Royal Navy Surgeon Lieutenant Commander, Senior Executive Officer (Navy) Directorate of Supplies and Transport (Secretary), Royal Fleet Auxiliary Captain, Royal Fleet Auxiliary Technical Superintendent.

[75] Johnny Rickett, *Not Just a Conflict, page 49*.

[76] Where senior officers are involved in a court martial, the custom in all the armed services is that the president of the court must be of a higher rank than the most senior accused.

[77] Still all the data and sources of the Inquiry Board have not been published.

[78] 2018 Seminar, Michael Clapp, Julian Thompson pdf 01 p4. Michael Clapp, Ewen Southby-Tailyour, *Amphibious Assault*, kindle.

[79] 2018 Seminar, Michael Clapp, Julian Thompson pdf 03 p16.

[80] 2018 Seminar, Michael Clapp, Julian Thompson pdf 03 p16.

[81] LS144/3 E13 - 6.

[82] LS144/3 E13 - 2.

[83] LS144/3 E13 - 2.

[84] LS144/3 E13 - 6.

[85] 44 Royal Navy, 25 Royal Fleet Auxiliary and 43 Merchant Navy, 2018 Seminar, Michael Clapp, Julian Thompson pdf 01 p5-6.

[86] LS144/3 E13 - 7, 11.

[87] Michael Clapp, Ewen Southby-Tailyour, *Amphibious Assault Falklands*, kindle.

[88] LS144/3 E13 - 14.

[89] 2018 Seminar, Michael Clapp, Julian Thompson pdf 01 p4.

[90] LS143/2 E2 - 27.

[91] LS143/2 E2 - 28.

[92] 2018 Seminar, Michael Clapp, Julian Thompson pdf 03 p3.

[93] 2018 Seminar, Michael Clapp, Julian Thompson pdf 03 p3

[94] Michael Clapp, Ewen Southby-Tailyour, *Amphibious Assault Falklands*, 1996.

[95] Michael Clapp, Ewen Southby-Tailyour, *Amphibious Assault Falklands*, kindle.

[96] LS143/4 E4 - p5 032110.

[97] LS144/4 E7 - 2.

[98] LS144/4 E7 - 1.

[99] LS144/4 E7 - 2.

[100] Kew, 'Loss of Sir Tristram and Sir Galahad – Narrative' - 4a.

[101] LS143/4 E4 - p6.

[102] Ewen Southby-Tailyour, *Reasons in Writing*, kindle.

[103] Ewen Southby-Tailyour, *Reasons in Writing*, kindle.

[104] Michael Clapp and Ewen Southby-Tailyour, *Amphibious Assault Falklands*, kindle.

[105] Michael Clapp and Ewen Southby-Tailyour, *Amphibious Assault Falklands*, kindle.

[106] Michael Clapp and Ewen Southby-Tailyour, *Amphibious Assault Falklands*, kindle.

[107] Michael Clapp and Ewen Southby-Tailyour, Amphibious Assault, kindle.

[108] Michael Clapp and Ewen Southby-Tailyour, Amphibious Assault, kindle.

[109] Ewen Southby-Tailyour, *Reasons in Writing*, kindle.

[110] 'I quickly took her away after a discussion with Jeremy', Michael Clapp and Ewen Southby-Tailyour, Amphibious Assault Falklands, kindle.

[111] Michael Clapp and Ewen Southby-Tailyour, *Amphibious Assault Falklands*, kindle.

[112] Admiral Woodward was also concerned.

[113] 2018 Seminar, Michael Clapp, Julian Thompson pdf 03 p10.

[114] 2018 Seminar, Michael Clapp, Julian Thompson pdf 03 p10.

[115] 2018 Seminar, Michael Clapp, Julian Thompson pdf 03 p10.

[116] 2018 Seminar, Michael Clapp, Julian Thompson pdf 03 p10.

[117] 2018 Seminar, Michael Clapp, Julian Thompson pdf 03 p10.

[118] 2018 Seminar, Michael Clapp, Julian Thompson pdf 01 p4.

[119] 2018 Seminar, Michael Clapp, Julian Thompson pdf 01 p4.

[120] 2018 Seminar, Michael Clapp, Julian Thompson pdf 01 p4.

[121] 2018 Seminar, Michael Clapp, Julian Thompson pdf 02 p20.

[122] 'I was relieved when he [Moore] decided that those left behind in San Carlos should be Royal Marines who were used to helicopter and landing craft drills as well as being experts in amphibious warfare.... I don't think that Malcolm Hunt (40 Commando's Commanding Officer0 would ever quite forgive me if he knew that I supported Jeremy Moore's decision.' Michael

Clapp and Ewen Southby-Tailyour, *Amphibious Assault*, kindle.

123 2018 Seminar, Michael Clapp, Julian Thompson pdf 01 p14.

124 2018 Seminar, Michael Clapp, Julian Thompson pdf 01 p4.

125 2018 Seminar, Michael Clapp, Julian Thompson pdf 01 p4.

126 2018 Seminar, Michael Clapp, Julian Thompson pdf 02 p18.

127 'I had listened sympathetically to their account as their Second in Command wrung out and dried his sleeping bag in my cabin. As a result I tried to explain to Sandy [Admiral Woodward] that marching was out of the question.' Michael Clapp and Ewen Southby-Tailyour, *Amphibious Assault*, kindle.

128 After the plussing and minusing of strategy, as well as mutations of logistics and views from London, on 5th June at 8:30pm, the Scots Guards finally left San Carlos in Dingemans's *Intrepid* protected by a convoy of three frigates. Troops were launched in four LCUs (Tangos 1-4) at 11pm and arrived at 5:30am, 6th June with their weaponry, landrovers and supplies at Yellow Beach, Bluff Cove across the bay from Fitzroy. The four had been preloaded in San Carlos with troops and kit so it had taken Dingemans no time at all before he rushed *Intrepid* back. His behaviour was in stark contrast to 31st May when he made an emergency run in the north to get the first 250 tons of stores with *Intrepid*'s LCUs to Teal Inlet for the Royal Marines' hub. It couldn't exactly be called a tight plan, however. On 5th June, six of Operation Corporate's LCUs, the workhorse landing craft, were in San Carlos (*Tangos 1-4* and *Foxtrot 1* and *4*). The other two Foxtrots were in Teal Inlet, as per Clapp's instructions in the hands of the Royal Marines for their BMA offloading since 30th May. The next day, however, on 6th June the four Tangos— half of the Task Force's workhorses—were stationed at Bluff Cove's Yellow Beach idle for the entire day instead of offloading. They were meant to leave for the meeting point at 9.30pm that evening to rendezvous with Fearless which had the entire battalion of Welsh Guards on board. There was one difference as to the Welsh Guards move in four LCUs.

129 'I had learnt this before joining Intrepid', *Reasons in Writing*, Ewen Southby-Tailyour, kindle.

130 'I had learnt this before joining Intrepid', *Reasons in Writing*, Ewen Southby-Tailyour, kindle.

131 *Reasons in Writing*, Ewen Southby-Tailyour, kindle.

132 *Reasons in Writing*, Ewen Southby-Tailyour, kindle.

133 *Reasons in Writing*, Ewen Southby-Tailyour, kindle.

134 LS144/4 E7 - 10.

135 *Reasons in Writing*, Ewen Southby-Tailyour, kindle.

136 Michael Clapp and Ewen Southby-Tailyour, *Amphibious Assault*, kindle.

137 2018 Seminar, Michael Clapp, Julian Thompson pdf 01 p2.

138 Michael Clapp and Ewen Southby-Tailyour, *Amphibious Assault Falklands*, kindle.

139 'I had agreed with Jeremy… To task the landing craft my two Staff Officers' Michael Clapp and Ewen Southby-Tailyour, *Amphibious Assault Falklands*, kindle.

140 LS144/3 E13 - 3.

141 LS143/6 E5 - 13.

142 *Reasons in Writing*, Ewen Southby-Tailyour, kindle.

143 LS143/4 E4 - 14.

144 DST(FMV) 74B270 Confidential Roberts report p1.

145 LS143/3 E3 - 9.

146 LS143/6 E5 - 17b.

147 DST(FMV) 74B270 Confidential Roberts report p3.

148 DST(FMV) 74B270 Confidential Roberts report p3.

149 LS143/2 E2 - 21.

150 'At about 2030 that evening' Michael Clapp and Ewen Southby-Tailyour, Amphibious Assault, kindle.

151 LS143/6 E5 - 14.

152 LS143/4 E4 - 13.

153 LS143/4 E4 - 13.

154 LS143/7 E6 - 8.

155 LS143/4 E4 - 14.

156 LS143/7 E6 - 10.

157 LS143/7 E6 - 15.

158 LS143/7 E6 - 21.

159 LS143/7 E6 - 17.

160 LS143/7 E6 - 19.

161 LS143/4 E4 - 13.

162 LS143/6 E5 - 17.

163 LS143/2 E2 - 17.

164 LS143/6 E5 17.

165 LS143/2 E2 - 21.

166 LS143/6 E5 - 17.

167 LS143/6 E5 - 21. LS143/2.

168 LS143/2 E2 - 33, 34q.

169 At the passing of the 5pm deadline *Galahad*'s staff had asked by voice call—the embark-disembark net—what 'the latest acceptable time for SIR GALAHAD' was. 'The reply was "2359" [7.59pm] at the latest, preferably 2300 [7pm]".' This was four hours earlier than *Tristram*'s sailing time the night before and the four-hour window allowed for Bluff Cove as the first destination and Fitzroy as the second—both under night cover. (In his confidential report, Roberts claims that the signal from *Fearless* in Teal Inlet said 'proceed at best speed for Fitzroy Settlement'. But it is not clear whether that is what his staff understood or what the signal said.)

170 DST(FMV) 74B270 Confidential Roberts report p3.

171 LS144/2 E2 - 5.

172 LS144/2 E2 - 5.

173 LS144/2 E2 - 5.

174 LS144/2 E2 - 17.

175 LS144/2 E2 - 5.

176 LS144/2 E2 - 22c.

177 LS143/6 E5 - 8.

178 LS144/4 E7 - 9.

179 LS144/2 E12 16 and LS144/4 and LS143/2 E2 13-4.

180 LS144/4 E7 - 4.

181 LS144/4 E7 - 4.

182 LS143/2 E12 - 13.

183 LS143/2 E12 - 16.

184 *Reasons in Writing*, Ewen Southby-Tailyour, kindle.

185 *Reasons in Writing*, Ewen Southby-Tailyour, kindle.

186 Michael Clapp and Ewen Southhy-Tailyour, *Amphibious Assault Falklands*, kindle, also 'Ewen has done most of the writing'.

187 *Reasons in Writing*, Ewen Southby-Tailyour, kindle.

188 *Reasons in Writing*, Ewen Southby-Tailyour, kindle.

189 *Reasons in Writing*, Ewen Southby-Tailyour, kindle.

190 LS143/6 E5 - 13.

191 LS144/4 E7 - 10.

192 LS144/4 E7 - 10.

193 LS144/4 E7 - 10.

194 *Reasons in Writing*, Ewen Southby-Tailyour, kindle.

195 LS144/4 E7 - 10.

196 Ewen Southby-Tailyour, *Reasons in Writing*, page 292.

197 *The Times*, 'A clear day and a sitting target' 8 June 1983, Jenny Rathbone.

198 Ivar Hellberg (2022) Falklands Logistics: A Reflection on an Ultimate Challenge. 40 Years On, The RUSI Journal, 167:1, 10-30, DOI: https://www.tandfonline.com/action/showCitFormats?doi=10.1080/03071847.2022.2066942.

199 The Board states it 'would have required a long delay', but not how it would have taken longer than the night before.

200 'At about 2030 that evening' Michael Clapp and Ewen Southby-Tailyour, Amphibious Assault, kindle.

201 '"Went on board *Sir Tristram* to find that before sailing *Intrepid*'s LCUs had been instructed to rendezvous in Low Bay... I hope they make it. Offered a shower, dinner and a cabin. Accepted."',*Reasons in Writing*, Ewen Southby-Tailyour, kindle.

202 LS144/2 E12 - 8.

203 LS144/2 E12 - 8.

204 *Reasons in Writing*, Ewen Southby-Tailyour, kindle.

205 *Reasons in Writing*, Ewen Southby-Tailyour, kindle.

206 LS144/2 E12 - 11.

207 LS144/2 E12 - 11.

208 *Reasons in Writing*, Ewen Southby-Tailyour, kindle.

209 LS143/2 E2 - 33.

210 LS143/2 Command and Control point 21.

211 Michael Clapp, in 'The Falklands War', seminar held 5 June 2002 (Centre for Contemporary British History, 2005, http://www.icbh.ac.uk/witness/falklands/), p.62.

212 Instead of castigating Moore, it criticises members in the amphibious group for its failure to communicate more comprehensively on 7-8th June.

213 'Secret' Annex B to 520/242.L 26 October 1982 B-1 point 4 'Further difficulties'.

214 LS143/7 E6 - 5.

215 *Watching Men Burn*, Tony McNally, kindle.

216 https://www.defenceviewpoints.co.uk/military-operations/op-coporate-retrieving-the-falklands-island-1982

217 *Watching Men Burn*, Tony McNally, kindle.

218 LS143/7 E6 - 5.

219 https://www.defenceviewpoints.co.uk/military-operations/op-coporate-retrieving-the-falklands-island-1982.

220 LS143/7 E6 - 11.

221 'My arguments were accepted with good grace.' Ewen Southby-Tailyour, *Reasons in Writing*, kindle.

222 Simon Weston CBE, *Walking Tall*, page 148.

223 Ewen Southby-Tailyour, *Reasons in Writing*, kindle.

224 Ewen Southby-Tailyour, *Reasons in Writing*, kindle.

225 'Secret' Annex B to 520/242.L 26 October 1982..

226 Michael Clapp and Ewen Southby-Tailyour, *Amphibious Assault*, kindle.

227 LS144/4 E7 10.

228 Report to Commander-in-Chief, Fleet of the Board of Inquiry into the Loss of RFAs Sir Tristram & Sir Galahad in June 1982, 23 September 1982, B1-1-5 point 53.

229 A convoy of four LCUs was planned for 6-7th June of which only two had so far made it to Bluff Cove.

230 DST(FMV)74B 270 18 June 1982, page 4.

231 LS144/4 E7 - 4.

232 Report to Commander-in-Chief, Fleet of the Board of Inquiry into the Loss of RFAs Sir Tristram & Sir Galahad in June 1982, 23 September 1982, B1-1-5 point 53.

233 https://www.defenceviewpoints.co.uk/military-operations/op-coporate-retrieving-the-falklands-island-1982

234 Ivar Hellberg (2022) Falklands Logistics: A Reflection on an Ultimate Challenge. 40 Years On, The RUSI Journal, 167:1, 10-30, DOI: https://www.tandfonline.com/action/showCitFormats?doi=10.1080/03071847.2022.2066942.

235 Ivar Hellberg (2022) Falklands Logistics: A Reflection on an Ultimate Challenge. 40 Years On, The RUSI Journal, 167:1, 10-30, DOI: https://www.tandfonline.com/action/showCitFormats?doi=10.1080/03071847.2022.2066942.

236 LS144/4 E7 - 4.

237 LS144/4 E7 - 4.

238 LS144/4 E7 - 4.

239 M3 VCNS 22 December 1982.

240 Michael Clapp and Ewen Southby-Tailyour, *Amphibious Assault Falklands*, kindle.

241 LS143/4 E4 p6 051654.

242 Michael Clapp and Ewen Southby-Tailyour, *Amphibious Assault*, kindle.

243 See, for example, Ewen Southby-Tailyour, *Reasons in Writing*, page 313.

244 LS144/4 Destination for the Off Load Sir Galahad point 3.

245 Appendix 1 to Annex B.

[246] Inquiry Report Annex B1 point 61. In a different Annex, the Board addresses the level of offloading 'urgency' that was applied by the LCU teams the previous day. 'Every attempt was made for a quick offload but this urgency was not backed, nor could it have been, during 7 June with the knowledge that *Sir Galahad* would arrive next morning', it concludes. Irrespective of what the level of urgency was that day, Roberts's report makes clear that when Yeoman boarded *Galahad* at 10.30am the clock started ticking for the 4.30am arrival of the LSL at Port Pleasant (after the first, 3am Bluff-Cove stop). Staff on *Fearless* may not have shared this information with *Tristram*—as mentioned, we won't know for another 32 years—but there was nothing blocking the amphibious staff from letting *Tristram* known on 7th June (we know that arrival information came through overnight and was picked off of the ship's signal printer early in the morning of 8th June).

[247] LS143/2 E2 - 6.

[248] LS144/3 Staff Composition, Performance and Training point 8.

[249] LS143/2 E2 - 27.

[250] LS144/3 Staff Composition, Performance and Training point 8.

[251] Inquiry Report Annex E8 23 September 82 point 6.

[252] Inquiry Report Annex E2 23 September 82 point 17 a and b.

[253] LS143/2 E2 - 21.

[254] LS143/2 E2 - 34q.

[255] Letter nine: https://www.telegraph.co.uk/opinion/2022/04/04/letters-another-week-sponsored-ukrainian-refugee-family-still/

[256] Ibid.

[257] Major Bremner, the 2 Welsh Guards company commander on board, puts it thus in *Above All, Courage*, Max Arthur's 1985 book on the Falklands: 'Eventually a landing craft returning to shore from Sir Tristram arrived at the stern ramp; it was full of ammunition. We were offered space for some twenty men but we turned this down. It had been bad enough being split from the battalion, let alone now splitting our companies.'

[258] Julian Thompson, *No Picnic*, page 137.

[259] Page 246

[260] Johnny Rickett, *Not Just a Conflict*, page 73.

Milton Keynes UK
Ingram Content Group UK Ltd.
UKHW040420111123
432320UK00002B/10